WORKSHOPS IN COMPUTING

Series edited by C. J. van Rijsbergen

Also in this series

Logic Program Synthesis and Transformation
Proceedings of LOPSTR 91, International Workshop on Logic Program Synthesis and Transformation, University of Manchester, 4–5 July 1991
T.P. Clement and K.-K. Lau (Eds.)

Declarative Programming, Sasbachwalden 1991
PHOENIX Seminar and Workshop on Declarative Programming, Sasbachwalden, Black Forest, Germany, 18–22 November 1991
John Darlington and Roland Dietrich (Eds.)

Building Interactive Systems: Architectures and Tools
Philip Gray and Roger Took (Eds.)

Functional Programming, Glasgow 1991
Proceedings of the 1991 Glasgow Workshop on Functional Programming, Portree, Isle of Skye, 12–14 August 1991
Rogardt Heldal, Carsten Kehler Holst and Philip Wadler (Eds.)

Object Orientation in Z
Susan Stepney, Rosalind Barden and David Cooper (Eds.)

Code Generation – Concepts, Tools, Techniques
Proceedings of the International Workshop on Code Generation, Dagstuhl, Germany, 20–24 May 1991
Robert Giegerich and Susan L. Graham (Eds.)

Z User Workshop, York 1991, Proceedings of the Sixth Annual Z User Meeting, York, 16–17 December 1991
J.E. Nicholls (Ed.)

Formal Aspects of Measurement
Proceedings of the BCS-FACS Workshop on Formal Aspects of Measurement, South Bank University, London, 5 May 1991
Tim Denvir, Ros Herman and R.W. Whitty (Eds.)

AI and Cognitive Science '91
University College, Cork, 19–20 September 1991
Humphrey Sorensen (Ed.)

5th Refinement Workshop, Proceedings of the 5th Refinement Workshop, organised by BCS-FACS, London, 8–10 January 1992
Cliff B. Jones, Roger C. Shaw and Tim Denvir (Eds.)

Algebraic Methodology and Software Technology (AMAST'91)
Proceedings of the Second International Conference on Algebraic Methodology and Software Technology, Iowa City, USA, 22–25 May 1991
M. Nivat, C. Rattray, T. Rus and G. Scollo (Eds.)

ALPUK92, Proceedings of the 4th UK Conference on Logic Programming, London, 30 March – 1 April 1992
Krysia Broda (Ed.)

Logic Program Synthesis and Transformation
Proceedings of LOPSTR 92, International Workshop on Logic Program Synthesis and Transformation, University of Manchester, 2–3 July 1992
Kung-Kiu Lau and Tim Clement (Eds.)

NAPAW 92, Proceedings of the First North American Process Algebra Workshop, Stony Brook, New York, USA, 28 August 1992
S. Purushothaman and Amy Zwarico (Eds.)

First International Workshop on Larch
Proceedings of the First International Workshop on Larch, Dedham, Massachusetts, USA, 13–15 July1992
Ursula Martin and Jeannette M. Wing (Eds.)

Persistent Object Systems
Proceedings of the Fifth International Workshop on Persistent Object Systems, San Miniato (Pisa), Italy, 1–4 September 1992
Antonio Albano and Ron Morrison (Eds.)

Formal Methods in Databases and Software Engineering, Proceedings of the Workshop on Formal Methods in Databases and Software Engineering, Montreal, Canada, 15–16 May 1992
V.S. Alagar, Laks V.S. Lakshmanan and F. Sadri (Eds.)

Modelling Database Dynamics
Selected Papers from the Fourth International Workshop on Foundations of Models and Languages for Data and Objects, Volkse, Germany 19–22 October 1992
Udo W. Lipeck and Bernhard Thalheim (Eds.)

continued on back page...

Tony McEnery and Chris Paice (Eds.)

14th Information Retrieval Colloquium

Proceedings of the BCS 14th Information Retrieval Colloquium, University of Lancaster, 13–14 April 1992

Published in collaboration with the British Computer Society

BCS

Springer-Verlag
London Berlin Heidelberg New York
Paris Tokyo Hong Kong
Barcelona Budapest

Tony McEnery, BA (Hons), MSc
Department of Linguistics and
Modern English Language
Lancaster University
Lancaster, LA1 4YT, UK

Chris Paice, BSc.Tech, PhD
Department of Computing
School of Engineering,
Computing and Mathematical Sciences
Lancaster University
Lancaster, LA1 4YR, UK

ISBN-13: 978-3-540-19808-6 e-ISBN-13: 978-1-4471-3211-0
DOI: 10.1007/978-1-4471-3211-0

British Library Cataloguing in Publication Data
Information Retrieval Colloquium:
Proceedings of the BCS 14th Information
Retrieval Colloquium, University of Lancaster,
13-14 April 1992. – (Workshops in Computing)
I. McEnery, Anthony M. II. Paice, C. D.
III. Series
025.04

Library of Congress Cataloging-in-Publication Data
A catalog record for this book is available from the Library of Congress

Typesetting: Camera ready by contributors
Printed by Antony Rowe Ltd., Chippenham, Wiltshire
34/3830-543210

Preface

We hope that all readers will find the papers included in this volume of interest. All were presented at the 14th BCS IRSG Research Colloquium held at Lancaster University on 13th–14th April 1992.

The papers display very well the scope and breadth of information retrieval, as indeed did the workshop itself. They also present a good cross-section of current IR research, and as such provide a useful signpost for trends in information retrieval.

Before we finish we must thank the following colleagues: Simon Botley, Paul Rayson and Paul Jones for their help in the organization of the conference. We would also like to extend a special message of thanks to Professor G.N. Leech of the Department of Linguistics at Lancaster and Roger Garside of the Department of Computing at Lancaster for their support during the conference period. Tony McEnery would also like to express his thanks and gratitude to Paul Baker for his help during the production of this book.

September 1992

Tony McEnery
Chris Paice

Contents

A Logical Model of Information Retrieval Based on Situation Theory

Mounia Lalmas[1] and Keith van Rijsbergen
Computing Science Department
The University, Glasgow G12 8QQ
mounia@dcs.glasgow.ac.uk

Abstract

We use Logics to model relevance in Information Retrieval: a document is relevant to a query if a formula q representing the query can be inferred from a formula d representing the document. Thus to infer is to retrieve, but because of the nature of 'aboutness' often the inference is uncertain. Using a framework based on Situation Theory, the representation of documents and queries, inference, semantic and pragmatic aspects of information can be modelled formally.

1 Introduction

There are different types of Information Retrieval Systems (IRSs) based, for example, on Boolean, Vector Space or Probabilistic models [6, 26]. Most of these models present either a lack of, or only a primitive treatment of semantics and no treatment of pragmatics at all. It should be possible for a user seeking information about 'cold' countries to obtain documents on countries 'having a maximum temperature of 15 degrees celsius' because the concepts of 'cold' and 'maximum temperature of 15...' have a very close semantic relationship. Also, documents on 'Scandinavian' countries should satisfy the request of a user situated in Algiers according to pragmatics and so be retrieved. These relationships are not considered in most conventional systems and where they are, it is in most cases in an *ad hoc* way without any theoretical foundations, thus leading very often to inconsistency. The point of this paper is to determine how an IRS's effectiveness can be improved if semantics and pragmatics are taken into account, based on a formal model.

Different formal Logics have been developed which model semantic and pragmatic aspects of information [3, 12, 13, 19, 20, 21]. In our case, we are particularly interested in a logic that represents the complexity of natural language; then, two objectives in current research in IR can be addressed in one go. On the one hand, the construction of a formal model of an IRS gives a consistent representation of all the different processes involved in IR. On the other, semantic and pragmatic reasoning are formally represented. By this, we mean that the relevance of a document to a query will depend on how the sentence representing the user's request is deduced from the sentences of the document, the inference being modelled by this logic.

In this rather theoretical paper, a model of an IRS is proposed following two phases. First, a formalization of uncertain inference is developed, independent of the logic. This formalisation does not say what it means for a formula to follow from another, but

1 Author to whom correspondence should be addressed

considers the existence of such a logical inference mechanism. Secondly, a specific interpretation of the logical inference is given. It is based on Situation Theory [2]. We will explain later why we chose this particular theory.

The remainder of this paper is divided into three sections. In the *first* section, the definitions and the components of an IRS are briefly recalled. In the *second* section, uncertain inference is presented which leads to the construction of a model based on a formal interpretation of the inference using Situation Theory [2, 8, 22] in the *third* section. At the end some conclusions are drawn, but some open questions remain.

2 Information Retrieval Systems

An IRS is a tool which stores information to be retrieved for future use. We consider only written information: articles, newspapers, medical diagnosis, etc... We use the word 'document' for an information object of this type.

In general, the retrieval process of an IRS does not deal with entire documents due to efficiency criteria, but handles shortened representations of documents. Therefore, an internal representation is used which tries to model the content of documents as faithfully as possible. The translation of an original document into an internal representation is often called *indexing*. In conventional IRSs, indexing yields a set of terms, and sometimes, in more elaborated systems, a set of weighted terms, the weight being proportional to the occurrence frequency of the term in the document [6, 26].

Users access stored information, documents in fact, by submitting queries to the IRS. These queries are evaluated and transformed into internal representations that are comparable with the *representatives* of documents. An IRS compares the internal representations of the query with the representations of each document of the collection and retrieves the documents that are considered to contain, to some extent, the information requested by a user, or in other words documents that *correspond* to the query.

There is a big difference between an IRS and a database system. In the latter, a result, if it exists, answers precisely the request, whilst, in IR, it can do so with a degree of uncertainty. There are two main reasons for this. First, indexing and query translation imply a loss of information. Therefore, internal representations introduce uncertainty. Also the correspondence between document and query is uncertain and depends strongly on several factors like semantics. Hence, the correspondence between the internal representations of the document and the query is even more uncertain.

In Information Retrieval (IR), the documents that the system judges as being *relevant* to the query are retrieved. Many systems determine this relevance quantitatively, and retrieved documents are ranked according to their degree of relevance which expresses the extent to which a retrieved document contains the sought information.

Many IRSs use some kind of *relevance feedback*: If the document retrieved by the system does not satisfy the user's need, the query is modified, either by the user or automatically by the system, then resubmitted to the system. The general structure of an IRS is summarised in Fig.1.

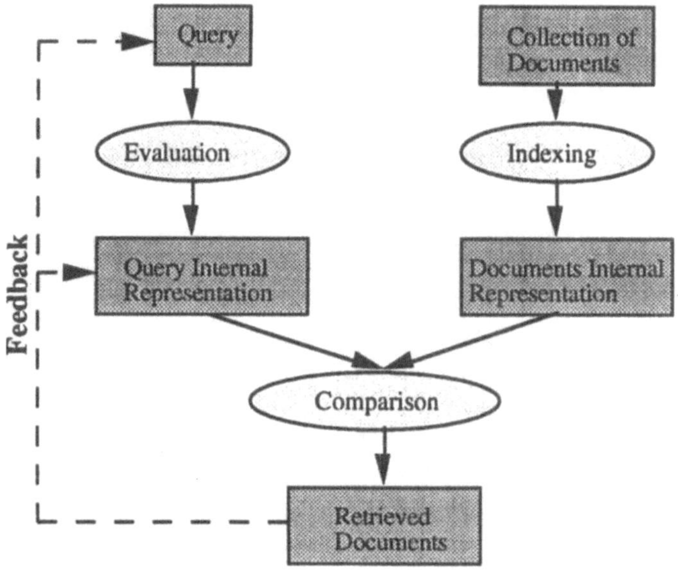

Fig.1- *General components of an information retrieval system*

3 An IRS Based on Logic: Uncertain Inference

Several suggestions have been made to base a model of IRS on logic [24, 25, 27, 28]. Suppose that a logic L is defined with its axioms and rules. Also, suppose that the contents of a document and a query are expressed respectively by the formulas d and q in this logic L. The retrieval process consists of determining if q can be inferred from d using the inference rules from the logic. In many cases, this inference cannot be made directly. Nevertheless, in IR, it should not then be concluded that a document is irrelevant to the query. It may be that q cannot be directly inferred from d because d does not contain all the necessary information, but the assumption of additional formulae makes the inference possible, but uncertain. This idea is captured by van Rijsbergen's Logical Uncertainty Principle [27, 28] where the inference is represented by the symbol →.

Logical Uncertainty Principle (LUP):
"Given two sentences x and y; a measure of uncertainty of y→x relative to a given data set, is determined by the minimal extent to which we have to add information to the data set, to establish the truth of y →x".

The principle does not make precise what is meant by y→x. The interpretation of the inference is undefined, and a part of our work is to provide such a formal interpretation based on a logic.

Let us clarify this principle by considering the following example. Suppose that a document and a query are respectively indexed by d={system} and q = {expert system}. The evaluation of $d \rightarrow q$ depends on the uncertainty introduced by adding the word "expert" to d such that $d \rightarrow q$ becomes certain. Therefore the evaluation of $d \rightarrow q$ is no longer binary, but a value in the range [0,1].

A function C: LxL→[0,1] is introduced to represent the certainty of the inference. From LUP, this value depends on the minimum amount of information which needs to be added for the inference to be performed. For example, in IR, replacing a term by a synonym does not introduce uncertainty, whilst using a more specific/general term does. The goal is to determine $C(d \rightarrow q)$.

Adding information introduces uncertainty. This is formally represented by a second function $\delta: L \times L \rightarrow [0,1]$. δ measures the certainty of transforming one formula to another. Discussing transformation instead of added information is more general. For example, it might be useful to discard information in order to enhance the precision parameter. A certain transformation is represented by $\delta(d,d')=1$ whilst an impossible transformation from d to d' is by $\delta(d,d')=0$.

The function δ has the following properties:

$$\forall d \in L, \ \delta(d,d) = 1$$
$$\forall d,d',d'' \in L, \ \ \delta(d,d') > 0 \wedge \delta(d',d'') > 0 \Rightarrow \delta(d,d'') > 0$$

It seems natural to base the value of $\delta(d,d'')$ on a combination of $\delta(d,d')$ and $\delta(d',d'')$ as illustrated in Fig.2.

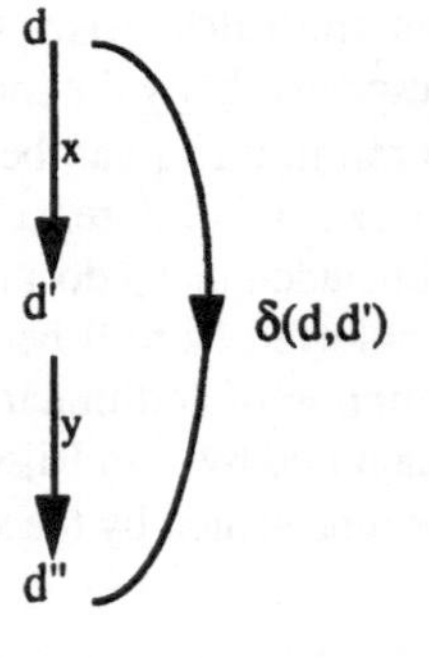

Fig.2- *Combination of Certainty Values*

This combination of certainty is represented by a third function $\theta:[0,1] \times [0,1] \rightarrow [0,1]$. q combines two certainty values into a single value [15, 17]:

$$\delta(d,d'') = \theta[\delta(d,d'), \delta(d',d'')]$$

q has the following properties:

$$\forall x \in [0,1], \ \ \theta(x,1) = \theta(1,x) = x$$

$\forall x \in [0,1],\quad \theta(x,0) = \theta(0,x) = 0$
$\forall x,y \in [0,1],\quad \theta(x,y) \le x$ and $\theta(x,y) \le y$.

This definition is extended for any length of sequential transformations (Cf. Fig.3).

The formula becomes:

$$\delta(d,d') = \theta[\delta(d_0,d_1),\theta[\delta(d_1,d_2),\cdots\theta[\delta(d_{n-2},d_{n-1}),\delta(d_{n-1},d_n)]\cdots]] \quad \text{for } n \ge 2$$

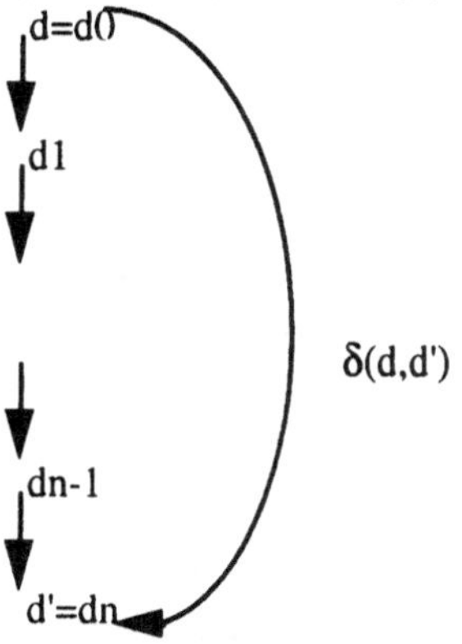

Fig.3- *Sequential transformations*

However, there might be several possible transformations between two formulae d and d' as illustrated in Fig.4.

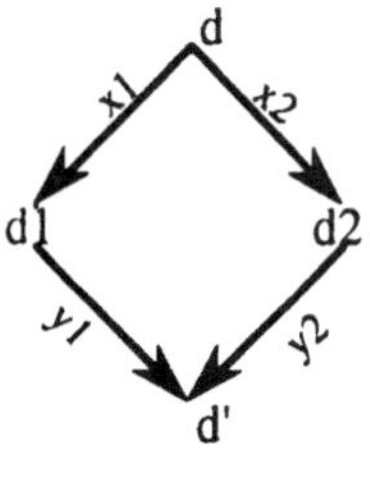

Fig.4- *Two possible sequential transformations*

There are two possible values of $\delta(d,d')$, either $\theta(x_1,y_1)$ or $\theta(x_2,y_2)$. LUP chooses the value leading to the maximum certainty.

$$\delta(d,d') = \mathrm{Max}[\theta(x_1,y_1),\theta(x_2,y_2)]$$

As before, the definition can be extended to the general case.

To summarise, the certainty of the inference C(dÆq) is measured by the transformation necessary to make the inference realisable. Thus C(dÆq) depends on the value of $\delta(d,d')$ where C(d'Æq) =1 and is defined as follows:

C(dÆq) = $\delta(d,d')$ where C(d'Æq) =1

Notice that, if dÆq is certain, then C(dÆq) = δ(d,d) = 1 which respects the formula.

Meanwhile, there might be several d' such that C(d'Æq) =1. As before, LUP resolves this non-determinism by retaining the maximum certainty value.

$$C(d\rightarrow q) = \mathrm{Max}_{\left\{d' \,.\, C(d'\rightarrow q)=1\right\}}\ \delta(d,d')$$

So far, a framework exists which models uncertain inference. What is left is to interpret the implication in some logic. This is developed in the next section.

4 An IRS Based on Logic: The Implication

The model described so far does not make explicit when one formula implies another, nor when it does not. Only the uncertainty of the inference is represented. Therefore, the model requires a formal interpretation of the implication. The study of several logics [3, 7, 13, 19, 20, 21] has lead to the choice of Situation Theory which addresses most of this requirement.

Situation Theory [1, 2] is a recent approach to language and information. It provides a framework to model information as it appears in the real world. The concept of truth becomes secondary. The judgement as to what is made true or false is on the basis of the available information. One does not ask when a proposition *is* either true or false, but what *makes* it true or false. Situation Theory is concerned with what information conveys, not with its truth, just as in IR: a document is not concerned with truth or falsehood of information but instead with the existence of information. In fact, a document might contain conflicting information. This notion of 'conveyed information' corresponds to the flow of information [14]. In addition, the theory allows the formal representation of:

- the incompleteness of information: when information is not present, it does not mean that the information is false, but that nothing is known at this stage (Cf. the closed world assumption of database systems),
- the inference process,
- a formal analysis of natural language [9, 10, 16].

All these are described below.

4.1 Situation Theory

Information tells us that relations either hold or do not hold between objects. Situation theory [2, 12] considers information as a basic component, modelled by *infons.*

Definition:
An infon is a structure «R,a_1,...,a_n;i» which represents the information that the relation R holds (if i=1) or does not hold (if i=0) between the objects a_1... a_n.

The objects a_1,..,a_n are compatible with the relation R. In many cases, two types of object are distinguished to represent temporal and spatial locations. For example, the infon «eat, Mounia, apple,12am,flat;1» represent the information that a person called

'Mounia' was eating an apple at 12am in her flat.

Information is extracted from observations of the world by cognitive agents. In most cases, only partial views of the world are possible. Cognitive agents are restricted by their perception capability and/or the focus of their attention. At any time, an agent deals only with subparts of the world: *situations* [1, 2, 11, 12, 14]. A situation makes information explicitly true or false. In this case, the situation is said to support the information and is formally defined using the definition of infons.

<u>Definition:</u>
Let S denote the set of situations and I the sets of infons. A situation s Œ S supports an infon s Œ I, denoted s |= s, if s is made true by s.

Now, suppose that the three situations s_1,s_2,s_3 in S support their respective infons:

s_1 |= «run, Mounia,11am,KelvinHall;1»
s_2 |= «run, Mounia,9am,BotanicGardens;1»
s_3 |= «run, Mounia,2pm,KelvinGrovePark;1»

These situations have a common feature: a person called Mounia is running. The difference comes from the time and the site where the action takes place. Situation theory abstracts from situations and introduces *types of situation* to classify situations by some common characteristics. In the example above, s_1, s_2 and s_3 correspond to the type of situation A:

A = [$\dot{s}$ | $\dot{s}$ |= «run,Mounia, $\dot{t}$, $\dot{p}$;1»]

where $\dot{s}$, $\dot{t}$ and $\dot{p}$ are parameters. The type A corresponds to any situation where a person called Mounia is running, at a time $\dot{t}$ and a place $\dot{p}$. In A, the parameters $\dot{t}$ and $\dot{p}$ are free and are *anchored* by concrete situations. The parameter $\dot{s}$, called *the situation abstraction parameter*, is bounded. Stating that a situation s is of type A is formally denoted s:A.

Abstracting among situations introduces a level of freedom that allows the modelling of the flow of information. Flow can be viewed as what is implicitly conveyed by a situation. In other words, a situation supports information but carries additional information which is not explicitly supported. Therefore, a situation implies the presence of another (or the same) situation. Situation theory uses *constraints* to reflect this implication.

<u>Definition:</u>
A constraint is defined by a relation ⇒ (read means) on types of situation. A⇒A', where A and A' are types of situations, represents the fact that an occurrence of a situation s of type A (s:A) implies the existence of a situation s' of type A' (s':A').

This definition is extended to take into account uncertainty, where the constraint depends on some conditions to be fulfilled. This is denoted A⇒A'|B where B is called the background of the constraint and represents the conditions. For example, B can itself be a type of situation [12].

Constraints have been used to provide a semantic framework for natural language processing called Situation Semantics [1, 9] which attaches primary importance to the conveyance of information, with truth being a secondary concept. It is with utterance of sentences that the theory is principally concerned.

An utterance of a declarative sentence is referred to as a statement. Situation semantics determines what is the propositional content of a given statement (what claim does it make?) and what is the meaning of the sentence uttered. These concepts may described through an example. Suppose that Keith uttered the following sentence:

Φ = MOUNIA IS RUNNING

This sentence can be uttered many times, by many speakers, each of them referring to a variety of MOUNIA. Then, the meaning of Φ should be such that, given a particular utterance of Φ, the meaning plus this particular utterance together yield the content. This involves two different situations:

- the *utterance situation* u where Keith makes this utterance,
- the *described situation* e which supports the fact that the person referred to as MOUNIA is effectively running.

The propositional content of Keith's utterance u provides one instance of how information concerning the situation must be conveyed. What Keith is claiming is that there is a situation e such that:

$$e \models \text{«run}, \dot{m}, \dot{t}, \dot{p}; 1\text{»}$$

where $\dot{t}$ refers to the present, $\dot{m}$ to a person called "MOUNIA", $\dot{p}$ to the place of action and "run" to the action. In other words, Keith provides the information that the situation e (to which his utterance refers) is of type:

$$E = [\, \dot{e} \mid \dot{e} \models \text{«run}, \dot{m}, \dot{t}, \dot{p}; 1\text{»}]$$

The propositional content of Keith's utterance is to claim that:

$$e : E$$

The meaning of the sentence Φ, denoted $\|\Phi\|$, is defined to be the abstract linkage between the two types of situation U and E where:

$$U = [\, \dot{u} \mid \dot{u} \models \{ \text{«speak}, \dot{x}, \dot{t}, \dot{p}; 1\text{»}, \text{«say}, \dot{x}, F, \dot{t}, \dot{p}; 1\text{»}, \text{«refer-to}, \dot{x}, \dot{m}, \dot{t}, \dot{p}; 1\text{»}, \text{«address}, \dot{x}, \dot{y}, \dot{t}, \dot{p}; 1\text{»} \}]$$

where $\dot{x}$, $\dot{y}$, $\dot{m}$, $\dot{p}$ and $\dot{t}$ are parameters which represent respectively the speaker, the addressee, the person referred to, the spatial and the temporal locations of the utterance of Φ.

An uttered sentence involves two situations u and e. The relation between these two situations corresponds to the *meaning* of the sentence itself, noted :

$u \,\|\, \Phi \,\|\, e$

What has been presented so far is the meaning of a complete sentence. But in fact, the meaning of a sentence depends of the meaning of its subparts. From this remark, a (more or less) complete theory of the treatment of natural language has been expressed using situation semantics. Some semantic rules are established to represent concatenation of words, phrases, sentences. Situation semantics allows the linkage $\|\Phi\|$ of sentences Φ (uttered or written) through the related meaning of expressions $\|\alpha\|$ that are subparts of Φ. See [1, 2, 9] for more details.

4.2 The Model Based on Situation Theory

The logical part of the model presented in section 3 is based on situation theory. The content of a document D is represented by two situations u and d. The situation u could correspond to the utterance situation and d to the described situation in situation semantics. In IR, u corresponds to some external information about documents (for example authors, date of publication, content, some information about the authors, etc). The meaning or representation of a document D is given by:

$u \,\|\, D \,\|\, d$

A query is modelled by infons. For now, we only consider single infon query. Let s be this infon query. What we want to evaluate is with what certainty the situation d supports the infon σ. At this stage, an extension of the support relation is necessary to represent the case where a situation 'may support' an infon which is represented through the concept of subsituations [2] in the original theory. An uncertain support, denoted $|^{a}$, is introduced. Therefore, the goal is the evaluation of $C(d \;|^{a}\; s)$ where, if $d \models s$ then $C(d \;|^{a}\; s)=1$.

The transformations which represent semantics and/or pragmatics described in the previous chapter are modelled by constraints. A network, or thesaurus is defined by the triplet $N=<T, \Rightarrow, \delta>$ where T is the set of types of situation, $\Rightarrow$ models the flow of information and d is the function that weights certainty. $\Rightarrow$ and δ are connected as follows:

$$\forall A, A' \in T,\quad \begin{cases} \delta(A,A') = 1 & \text{if } A \Rightarrow A' \\ \delta(A,A') > 0 & \text{if } A \Rightarrow A' | B \\ \delta(A,A') = 0 & \text{otherwise} \end{cases}$$

where:

$\forall A \in T,\ A \Rightarrow A$

$\forall A, A', A'' \in T,\quad \text{if } A \Rightarrow A'|B \text{ and } A' \Rightarrow A''|B' \text{ then } A \Rightarrow A''|B''$

if the two backgrounds B and B' are compatible. The background B'' depends on the extent to which B and B' are compatible.Transitivity is totally dependent on these backgrounds. In situation theory, the combination of background information is still problematic [12]. The proposed model overcomes this by expressing uncertainty numerically. Nothing so far has been said of how to translate this background information into some numerical values. This is still an open problem. For the moment, we assume that such a translation is possible.

The formula obtained in the previous section becomes:

$$C(d \models \sigma) = 1 \quad \text{if } d \models s$$
$$= \mathrm{Max}_{\{A' \,.\, A \Rightarrow A'|B \,\wedge\, \exists d':A',\, d' \models \sigma\}} \delta(A,A') \quad \text{where } d:A \quad \text{otherwise}$$

But in this case, there might be several starting points in the network. It is possible to have different types of situation A, where d:A, which leads to an evaluation of C(d |* s). Following the LUP:

$$C(d \models \sigma) = 1 \quad \text{if } d \models s$$
$$= \mathrm{Max}_{\{A \,.\, d:A\}}\left[\mathrm{Max}_{\{A' \,.\, A \Rightarrow A'|B \,\wedge\, \exists d':A' \,.\, d' \models \sigma\}} \delta(A,A')\right] \quad \text{otherwise}$$

4.3 The Model

The model is summarised here. A logical model of an IRS is a tuple M=<I,S,|*,N,C> where:

- I is the set of infons,

- S is the set of situations,

- N=<T,⇒, δ> is the thesaurus where:
  - T is the set of types of situation,
  - ⇒ ⊆ TxT is the set of constraints (thesaurus)
  - δ: TxTÆ[0,1] measures the uncertainty of a constraint where the combination of certainty is modelled by a function θ: [0,1]x[0,1]Æ[0,1].

- C:SxIÆ[0,1] evaluates the inference:

$$C(d \models \sigma) = 1 \quad \text{where } d \models s$$
$$= \mathrm{Max}_{\{A \,.\, d:A\}}\left[\mathrm{Max}_{\{A' \,.\, A \Rightarrow A'|B \,\wedge\, \exists d':A' \,.\, d' \models \sigma\}} \delta(A,A')\right] \quad \text{otherwise}$$

5 Conclusion

In this paper, a model of an IRS based on logic has been developed. This has involved two things. First, a general framework, independent of any particular logic, models the uncertainty principle. It provides a measure of the effect of adding (or transforming) information through the function d. Secondly, a logic based on situation theory gives a formal interpretation of formulae and the implication. This logic is based on this theory because it provides a uniform treatment of:

- the representation of document and query through situation semantics,
- the formalisation of the inference via the support relation, which has been extended to deal with uncertain support,
- the representation of semantics and pragmatics through constraints. The uncertainty of those constraints, based on the notion of background in situation theory, is treated quantitatively in the proposed model.

More work is still required in order to check the consistency of the logical model. This depends principally on the properties of the certainty measures. For example, we could force some of the certainty measures to respect the additive properties of probability measures. Therefore many simplifications and/or deductions are possible because Probability Theory is well known and developed. More surveys on measures of uncertainty are carried out [7, 17, 18, 23, 29, 30]. In addition, research is carried out to find, if possible, an automatic method to weight constraints based on Numerical Taxonomy and then to provide a quantitative representation of background information. There are not any results so far.

In addition, now that a formal model has been developed, what is left to do is the implementation of an IRS on this model. An important task is the translation of natural language into infons and situations for the purpose of IR [4, 5, 8, 10, 16]. Then it will be necessary to construct a thesaurus manually or by automatic means perhaps using relevance feedback together with on-line thesauri and dictionaries. It will then be possible to answer the following question: *does taking into account semantics and pragmatics of information improve the quality of the retrieval process without any dramatic decrease in the efficiency of the system?*

An implementation will be developed to test these ideas using the functional language ML on a collection of abstracts from the Financial Times. The implementation, in order to avoid combinatoric explosion, will be based on the backward chaining mechanism used in expert systems.

References

1. Barwise, J., and Perry, J., 1983. *Situations and Attitudes*. Bradford Books, MIT Press.

2. Barwise, J., 1988. *The Situation in Logic*. CSLI Lecture Notes, Number 17.

3. van Benthem, J., 1985. *A Manual of Intensional Logic.* Chicago, University Press.

4. Black, A.W., 1991. A specification of a Situation Theoretic Language for use in a Parsing
System. Unpublished Paper.

5. Black, A.W., 1991. Example semantic descriptions in ASTL, Unpublished paper.

6. Blair, D.C., 1990. *Language and Representation in Information Retrieval.* Elsevier, Amsterdam.

7. Calabrese, P.G., 1991. Deduction and Inference using Conditional Logic and probability. In *Conditional Logic in experts System* I.R. Gooman, M.M. Gupta, H.T. Nguyen and G.S. Rogers (editors). Elsevier Science Publishers B.V. (North Holland).

8.Cooper, R., 1983. *Quantification and Syntactic Theory.* D. Reidel Publishing Company. Vol 2.

9. Cooper, R. 1988. *Introduction to Situation Semantics.* Unpublished.

10. Cooper, R., 1991. *Situation Theoretic Grammar.* The Third European Summer School in Language, Logic and Information. Universitat des Saarlandes. Saarbrucken.

11. Cummins, R., 1989. *Meaning and Mental Representation.* Bradford Books, The MIT, Cambridge.

12. Devlin, K., 1991. *Logic and Information.* Cambridge University Press.

13. Dowty, D.R., Wall, R.E., and Peters, S., 1981. *Introduction to Montague Semantics.* D. Reidel, Publishing Company. Studies in Linguistics and Philosophy, Vol 11.

14. Dretske, F., 1981. *Knowledge and the Flow of Information.* Bradford Books, MIT Press.

15. Dubois, D., and Prade, H., 1987. Combinaison d'Information Incertaines. Rapport L.S.I, Num. 263, Equipe Intelligence Artificielle et Robotique, Communication, Decision, Raisonnement.

16. Fenstad, J. E., Halvorsen, P.K., Lankholm, T., and van Benthem, J., 1987. *Situations, Language and Logic.* Dordrecht, Reidel.

17. Garvey, T.D., Lowrance, and J.D., Fischler, M.A., 1981. An Inference Technique for Integrating Knowledge from Disparate Sources. SRI International, Menlo Park, California.

18. Harper, W.L., Stalnaker, R., and Pearce, G., 1981. *Ifs.*

19. Hughes, G., and Cresswill, M., 1968. *An Introduction to Modal Logic.* London, Methuen.

20. Landman, F., 1986. *Towards a Theory of Information.The Status of Partial Objects in Semantics*. Dordrecht, Foris.

21. Montague, R., 1970. English as as Formal Language. In *Formal Philosophy: Selected Papers of Richard Montague*, pp. 108-221. H. Thomason (ed), New Haven: Yale University Press.

22. Moss, L., 1991. *Foundations of Situation Theory*. The Third European Summer School in Language, Logic and Information. Universitat des Saarlandes. Saarbrucken.

23. Nguyen, H.T, and Rogers, G.S., 1991. Conditioning Operators in a Logic of Conditionals. In *Conditional Logic in experts System* I.R. Gooman, M.M. Gupta, H.T. Nguyen and G.S. Rogers (editors). Elsevier Science Publishers B.V. (North Holland).

24.NIE, J., 1990. Un Modele de Logique General pour les Systemes de Recherche d'Informations. Application au Prototype RIME. These. University Joseph Fourier, Grenoble I. Laboratoire de Genie Informatique. IMAG.

25. Sembok, T.M.T, and van Rijsbergen, C.J., 1990. SILOL: A Simple Logical-Linguistic Document Retrieval System. In *Information Processing & Management*, Vol 26 (1), pp 111-134.

26.van Rijsbergen, C.J., 1979. *Information Retrieval*. Butterworths, London, 2nd edition.

27.van Rijsbergen, C.J., 1986. A Non-Classical Logic for Information Retrieval. In *Computer Journal*, Vol 29 (1), pp 481-485.

28.van Rijsbergen, C.J., 1989. Towards an Information Logic. 12th ACM-SIGIR conference, Cambridge, Ma., pp 77-86.

29. Shafer,G., 1976. *A Mathematical Theory of Evidence*. Princeton University Press.

30. Wong, S.K.M., and Yao, Y.Y, 1991. A Probabilistic Inference Model for Information Retrieval. In *Information systems* Vol. 16 (3), pp. 301-321.

Multilingual MenUSE - A Japanese front-end for searching English Language databases and vice versa

C S Li, A S Pollitt
M P Smith

The Polytechnic of Huddersfield, UK

Abstract

The exchange of information between Japan and the rest of the world has been hampered because of the language barrier and the small number of Japanese databases translated into English and other languages. Multilingual MenUSE (Menu-based User Search Engine), a generic interface and intermediary system for end-user searching and browsing of bibliographic databases, enables Japanese users to search non-Japanese databases, specifying their search requirements in their own language. Similarly MenUSE can provide an English Language front-end to a Japanese Language database. The principle of automatic search statement generation, following concept and term selection during the navigation of an enhanced thesaurus, makes MenUSE very appropriate for multilingual searching and browsing of bibliographic databases. This paper describes the construction of a demonstration version of MenUSE to search the INSPEC Computer and Control database in both Japanese and English using HyperCard 2.0 on an Apple Macintosh. There are also significant advantages in using the MenUSE interface to search Japanese databases in Japanese given the considerable keyboarding effort required to specify queries in Japanese.

1 Introduction

The exchange of information between Japan and the rest of the world has been hampered because of the language barrier and the small number of Japanese databases translated into English and other languages. The cost of translating the source of databases is high and difficult to justify, given the low hit rate of records retrieved. A recent report [Database Promotion Center 1991b] makes it clear that current developments in machine translation are still limited to special applications or experiments both inside and outside Japan, and the need for a multilingual retrieval system, as an alternative approach to direct translation of the source, has been established. This paper describes work recently undertaken at the Polytechnic of Huddersfield on a multilingual version of MenUSE (Menu-based User Search Engine) [Pollitt 88] and in particular a version for Japanese users of English language databases [Li, Pollitt & Smith 1992].

The general need for access to databases using the language of the user where this is different to the language of the database has been recognised in the IMPACT programmes of the European Commission. The demonstration of a Japanese version of MenUSE is intended to indicate the potential of this approach across all languages.

1.2 Background

1.2.1 The Growth in Numbers of Databases Available in Japan

Japan is the most information intensive society in the world, with 21,000 periodicals being published regularly, of which over 10,000 are scientific and technical [King & Sassoon 1989]. Database services started in Japan at the beginning of the 1970s, and achieved remarkable growth in the 1980s. Even so, the database industry in Japan is still in a premature state when compared to other divisions of Japanese industry. Until recently it was commonly accepted in Japan that the Japanese database industry lagged behind that in the West by a number of years. However, things are changing rapidly and there is a great impetus from many sectors of Japanese society to promote and improve the database industry and in particular to internationalise its activities. The database industry is regarded as a vital column to support the highly advanced information society, and the production of databases is currently being promoted in various subject fields.

In October 1991, the number of databases available in Japan totalled 2,354, although only 808 of them were produced by Japanese institutions [Database Promotion Center 1991a]. This growth is illustrated in the table below. Foreign databases, mainly from the US, still numerically dominate the Japanese market. The growth in Japanese databases is shown alongside the growth in databases offered by foreign companies.

number of databases offered	1982	1983	1984	1985	1986	1987	1988	1989	1990
(i) by Japanese companies	122	157	199	281	296	425	528	662	808
(% increase)		(28)	(27)	(41)	(5)	(44)	(24)	(25)	(22)
(ii) by foreign companies	344	522	725	1008	1187	1370	1436	1466	1546
(% increase)		(51)	(39)	(39)	(18)	(15)	(5)	(2)	(5)

Table 1 Growth in Number of Databases Available in Japan

The 808 databases mentioned above, allow the user access to Japanese-language journals, newspapers, documents, statistics, patents and corporate information. Several of the Japanese database producers have produced English-language versions of parts of their services, but 88% of the Japanese databases are still only available in Japanese. Because of the language barrier, those databases are extremely difficult to search by potential users outside of Japan without local Japanese searching and translation expertise.

Order	Relative Popularity*	Language	Name of database
1 (1)	100	J/E	**JICST, Japan scientific literature file**
2 (3)	87	J/E	**Nikkei Newspaper article file**
3 (2)	82	J	**Japan patent and utility model file**
4 (5)	39	E	WPI
5 (9)	35	J/E	**Asahi Newspaper article databses**
5 (6)	35	E	CA-SEARCH
7 (10)	33	J	**Trademark file**
8 (8)	31	E	CA
9 (4)	30	E	MEDLINE
10 (7)	24	J	**JICST medical magazine Japanese medical literature file**
11 (14)	20	E	CLAIMS
12 (11)	17	J	**NIKKEI file**
13 (12)	16	E	INSPEC
14 (13)	15	E	BIOSIS
15	15	J	**COSMOS 2**

Note: ( ) --Previous order ; **Japan-made databases**

* % of the replies for the most popular database;total 425 users,multiple replies

Table 2 The Most Frequently Used Databases in Japan

Adapted from: "Survey of User Awareness of Database Service", DPC, Japan. March 1991

The plight of the Japanese searcher is similarly problematical where a Japanese language translation of the foreign language database is not available. Although it must be said that it is less of a problem given the foreign language skills of the Japanese which are considerably more developed than the Japanese language skills of the non-Japanese Table 2 shows that English language databases with no Japanese translation rank highly according to a survey of user awareness carried out by the Database Promotion Center in Japan.

There were 1,546 foreign databases available in Japan in 1991. The topic of 'Natural science and technology ' is the most populated section (620 databases/40.1% of the whole), 'Business' is the second (513 databases/33.2%), 'General' is third (341 databases/22.1%) followed by 'Social and human science' (68 databases/4.4%).

According to *Information Market Indicators* [1988], the foreign databases most frequently used in Japan in the areas of Science and technology and Business were as follows:

Science and technology:	Business:
MEDLINE	PREDICASTS
CA FILE	DOW JONES
CA SEARCH	ABI/INFORM
WPI	EXCHANGE
BIOSIS	DUN'S MARKET
INSPEC	TEXT SEARCH SVC
CAS ONLINE REGISTRY	TRADE & INDUSTRY
NTIS	INVESTEXT
CLAIMS/US	COMMERCE BUSINESS DAILY
COMPENDEX	TRADEMARKSCAN

Table 3 The Most Frequently Used Databases in Science and Technology and Business in Japan

The reasons for popularity of databases are complex and the relative popularity must involve some component reflecting ease of use. In this situation it is notable that, from an analysis of the results obtained in a survey carried out by the Database Promotion Center of user opinions, the INSPEC database has a higher assessment than the JICST SCIENTIFIC FILE which is a similar database in the science and technology area and is used by three times as many people. Given such a high satisfaction it can be assumed that usage would be bound to increase, and satisfaction may be even greater, if access to INSPEC was provided in Japanese as well as English.

Name of Database or Files	Relative Popularity%	Comments Poor	O.K.	Good	Excellent
INSPEC	32	1(1.3)	27(35.5)	28(36.8)	20(26.3)
JICST SCIENTIFIC FILE	100	25(10.7)	108(46.2)	59(25.2)	43(18.4)

Table 4 A Comparison of the INSPEC and JICST Databases

1.2.2 Japanese Host Systems

The readiness to use English language systems can also be evidenced in a survey of host systems being used. The most frequently accessed Japanese host systems are JOIS, PATOLIS, NIKKEI TELECOM, STN and NEEDS-IR, as shown in Table 3.

1.2.3 Japanese Databases Accessible in Western Countries

The Japan Database Industry Association (DINA) has conducted a series of surveys of its membership and other database producers and distributors (105 members of DINA and 95 others) in Japan, in order to establish availability of Japanese database services on the overseas market, as well as to detect problems encountered by companies that are extending their services in Western countries.

Order	Relative Popularity*	Language	Name of online host system
1 (1)	100	J/E	**JOIS**
2 (2)	80	E	DIALOG
3 (3)	79	J/E	**PATOLIS**
4 (4)	77	J/E	**NIKKEI TELECOM**
5 (5)	25	J/E	**STN**
6 (6)	14	J/E	**NEEDS-IR**
7 (10)	11	J/E	**HINET**
8 (7)	11	J/E	**COSMOS**
9 (8)	10	E	BRANDY
10 (9)	10	E	TSR
10 (11)	10	J/E	**NICHIGAI-ASSIST**
12	6	E	DIALINE
12 (12)	6	J/E	**QUICK Video-I**
12	6	E	BRS
15	5	E	REUTER MONITOR

Note: ( ) --Previous order ; **Japanese host**
* % of the replies for the most popular host;total 466 users,multiple replies

Table 5 Most Popular Host Systems for Japanese Users
Source: "Survey of User Awareness of Database Service", DPC, Japan. March 1991

According to the survey conducted in August 1991, the number of Japanese databases available overseas was 226, an increase of 71 over the corresponding number in 1990. In addition some 29 databases were being planned for overseas distribution. Of the total number of Japanese databases (808) as many as 28% of them are now available overseas.

The more the quality of Japanese databases advances, the more they will need to be accessed from overseas.

1.2.4 Machine Translation

One solution to overcoming the language barrier to information exchange is to increase the number of Japanese databases translated into English. But it is very difficult for Japanese database producers and distributors because there are significant problems [Database Promotion Center 1991b], not least of which are:

1. high translation cost
2. time-lag between data creation and distribution
3. small market size in Japan for Japanese information written in English

In general current translation systems typically cannot achieve a straightforward translation from the source to the target language, though they can provide an extremely valuable first cut translation to assist professional translators. They can be cost efficient, they can be used to translate tedious texts such manuals and they can be counted on to translate vocabulary consistently throughout long documents.

Some machine translation systems are heavily used, not only in Japan but also in other countries. Their accuracy and performance, however, leave a lot to be desired, and their purpose is limited to special applications and experiments.

The intelligibility and accuracy level of state-of-the-art machine translation systems are largely determined by the characteristics of the source and target language. Although research on machine translation systems between Japanese and English has been underway for decades, the technology available today is far from perfect. Further technological advances in areas such as computer technology and natural language processing will improve the quality of future machine translation systems.

1.2.5 Multilingual Front-end Retrieval Systems

The absence of complete database translations, and the undesirable investment of effort in translation given a low hit rate on most databases, has lead to research into the application of multilingual front-end retrieval systems for foreign users searching Japanese databases.

The Database Promotion Center has indicated that Machine Translation is not seen as the only way forward to improve information exchange and was due to start a joint research project for overseas users searching Japanese databases in May 1991. The intended query languages were to include Japanese, English, Spanish, Chinese, French, German, and Russian [Database Promotion Center 1991b]. The final goals of this project are to:

1. lower the language barrier between Japanese and the user's language
2. make access to Japanese databases quicker
3. promote the accurate transfer of contents from Japanese databases.

Assistance in retrieval would also be provided using English or other languages. Overseas users would then be able to retrieve Japanese information from various fields and immediately obtain the accurate original text. A report on the progress of this project has yet to be received.The approach advocated is not clearly specified but is expected to be keyboard-based and utilise translating dictionaries. A more radical approach is proposed in the application of the MenUSE interface and intermediary system for bibliographic retrieval. A multilingual front-end for retrieval can be enhanced by coupling it to some limited machine translation system extending the model shown in Figure 1.

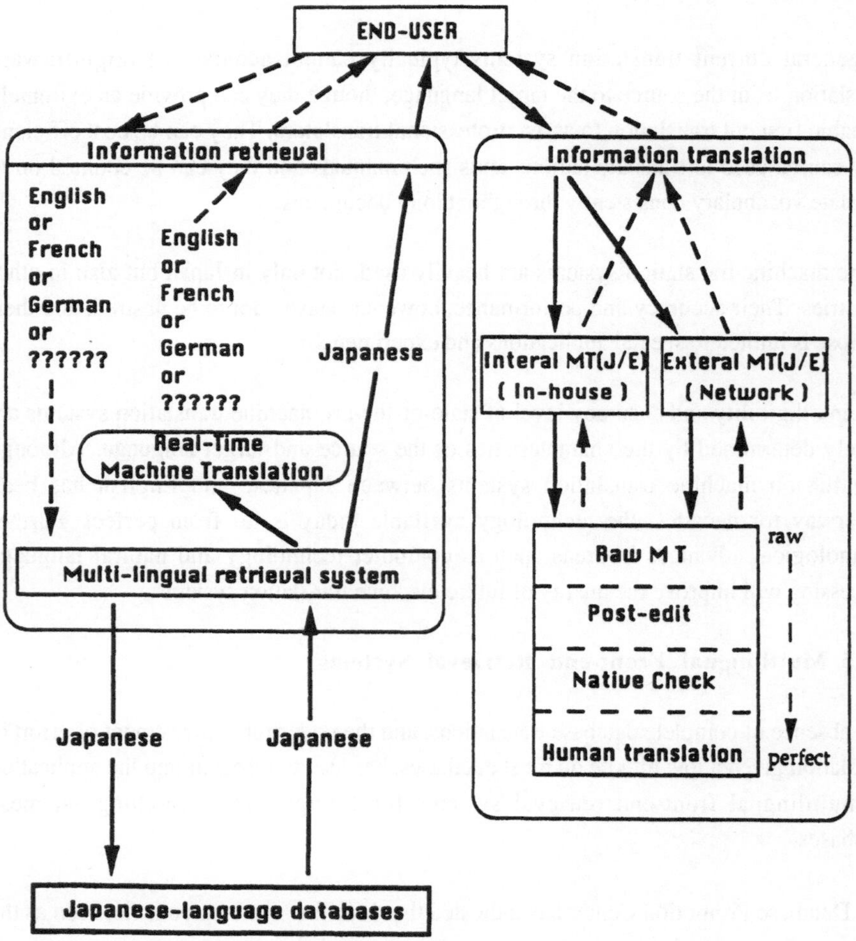

Figure 1. Machine Translation and Multilingual Front-end Retrieval Systems

1.2.6 The MenUSE Intermediary System - Background

The principles of MenUSE can be seen to be generally applicable across databases in all subject areas and efforts are now underway to continue the development and exploitation of the MenUSE ideas given its multilingual capabilities both within the European Community and globally, paying particular attention to the need to improve access to Japanese databases.

The main development platform continues to be the PC using PDC-Prolog [Smith, Pollitt & Li 1992]. However, following a British Library funded research project which developed a novel front-end for library OPACS [Murphy, Pollitt & White 1991], a second platform, the Apple Macintosh, has been investigated. A demonstration of an English/Japanese version of MenUSE has been developed using HyperCard 2.0 [Goodman 1990] on an Apple Macintosh II computer under KanjiTalk 6.0.7, a Japanese Operating System, and demonstrated on a range of Apple computers, including the PowerBook and the LC.

Work was already underway on MenUSE for Computing and Control so the issues of menu construction were not the subject of the development on this new platform. From the material presented above it can be seen that the choice of INSPEC was most appropriate.

The INSPEC database can be searched directly online on ten online host services, four in Europe, four in North America, one in Japan and one in Taiwan, providing access to the INSPEC database from most countries of the world.

1.2.7 Demonstration Development Software

Previous development of MenUSE has been carried out on PCs using Turbo-Prolog and is continuing using PDC-Prolog. This demonstration has been developed on HyperCard 2.0 using an Apple Macintosh II under KanjiTalk, a popularly used Japanese Operating System.

HyperCard provides an appropriate platform for the development of novel interfaces. As its name implies, it uses *Cards* as its system building block. Cards can contain ***fields***, *buttons* and *images* where user interaction typically involves the user in the selection of labelled command buttons using a mouse pointing device. The fields, buttons or images may be placed in the *foreground*, which is unique for one card, or the ***background***, which can be shared by a number of cards. Collections of cards are put together in *stacks*. Within a stack, many different types of cards with several backgrounds can be present next to each other. Browsing through a stack can be performed either sequentially or by following established links, by selecting buttons or lines of fields.

The programming language for HyperCard is HyperTalk, and programs are referred to as *scripts*. The execution of scripts can be governed by selecting buttons, fields or on opening cards or stacks.

KanjiTalk is a Japanese Operating System which enables both English and Japanese to be used. There is a soft switch on the upper-right corner of the screen for the user to select English or Japanese mode of input. In Japanese mode, there are five ways for the user to input Japanese characters - kanji or kana in full or half size and Roma-ji (phonetics). This last method is the one most popular with overseas users .

We exploit the layered nature of cards (foreground and background) together with the ability to layer fields on cards, to create Japanese menus as pictures behind a front field which is empty and transparent when the search interaction is with the Japanese menus. The English menus are held on a field on the bottom layer , and if the user selects English as the query language, then the English menus are transferred from the bottom layer to the front-menu field on the top layer, which is set to become opaque, so hiding the Japanese menus.

2 Multilingual MenUSE for INSPEC

2.1 The MenUSE Intermediary System

MenUSE can provide a means of access to databases in many subject areas. The INSPEC Computer and Control Abstracts Database has been selected for demonstrating a Japanese version of multilingual MenUSE given that it is currently in use in Japan, and can be seen to be part of the technological information base on which Japan has built its current prosperity. The generic nature of MenUSE can extend to the selection of databases and a top level menu as shown in Figure 2.1 which indicates the range of databases that might be accessed in this way.

In the multilingual demonstration, both English and Japanese menus have been created. On running the demonstration program, the user can select English or Japanese as the query language for his/her information searching. The query language selection can be made by using a mouse pointing device to activate the *Languages* button. A pull-down menu appears below the button and the user selects the required language for the interaction in the same way (Figure 2.2). After selecting *Japanese*, all menus are changed to Japanese. Figure 2.3 is a Japanese menu equivalent to English menu Figure 2.2.

The user is presented with the size of each database in a column headed *Refs* and the number of terms in the thesaurus used to access the database, in the column headed *Terms*. This browsing feature is retained through all the MenUSE screens at all levels and will allow the user to appreciate the amount of material in the database and the extent of the vocabulary which can further describe the subject matter in the database.

In this demonstration the user selects the entry for INSPEC Computer and Control Abstracts and the top-level menu of the database is presented (Figure 2.4).

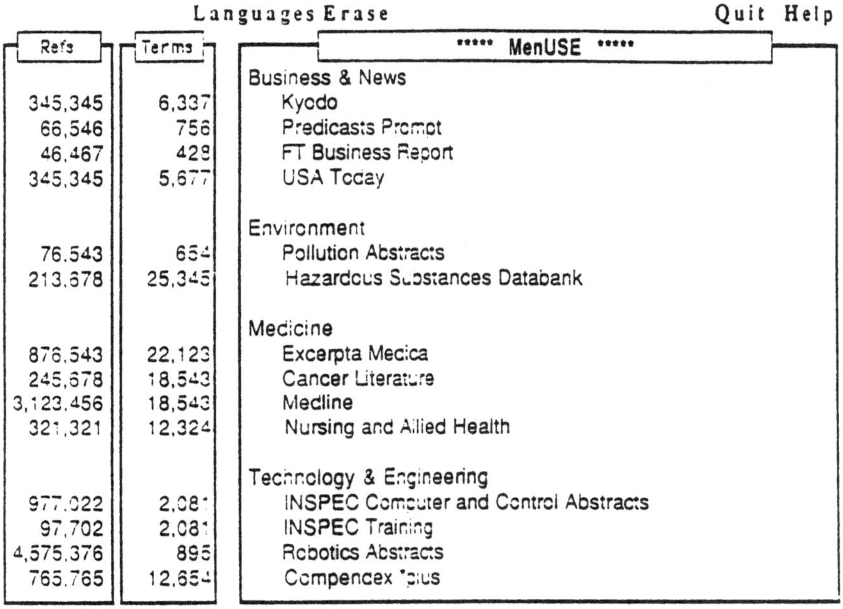

Languages Erase
Quit Help
Refs
Terms
***** MenUSE *****
Business & News
345,345 6,337 Kyodo
66,546 756 Predicasts Prompt
46,467 429 FT Business Report
345,345 5,677 USA Today
Environment
76,543 654 Pollution Abstracts
213,678 25,345 Hazardous Substances Databank
Medicine
876,543 22,123 Excerpta Medica
245,678 18,543 Cancer Literature
3,123,456 18,543 Medline
321,321 12,324 Nursing and Allied Health
Technology & Engineering
977,022 2,081 INSPEC Computer and Control Abstracts
97,702 2,081 INSPEC Training
4,575,376 895 Robotics Abstracts
765,765 12,654 Compendex *plus

Figure 2.1 Top level menu in MenUSE

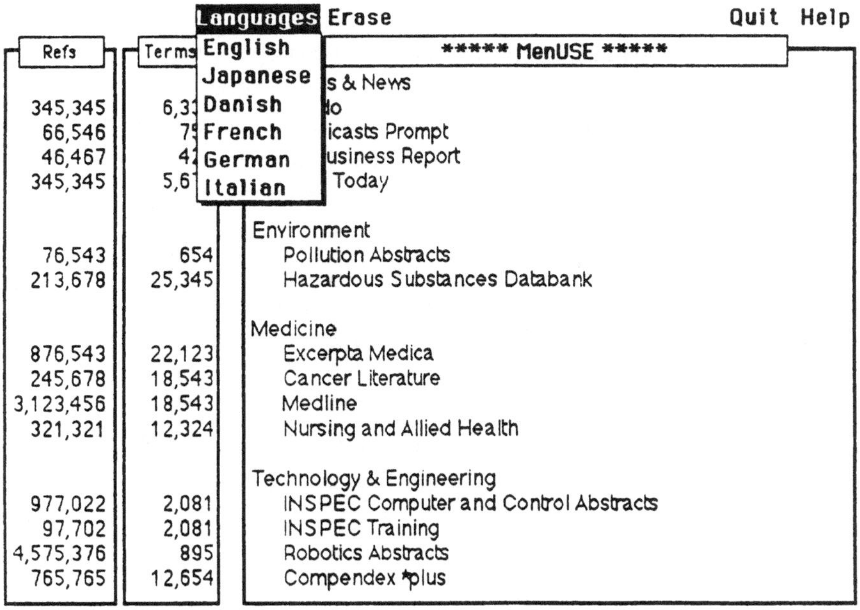

Figure 2.2 Selecting language

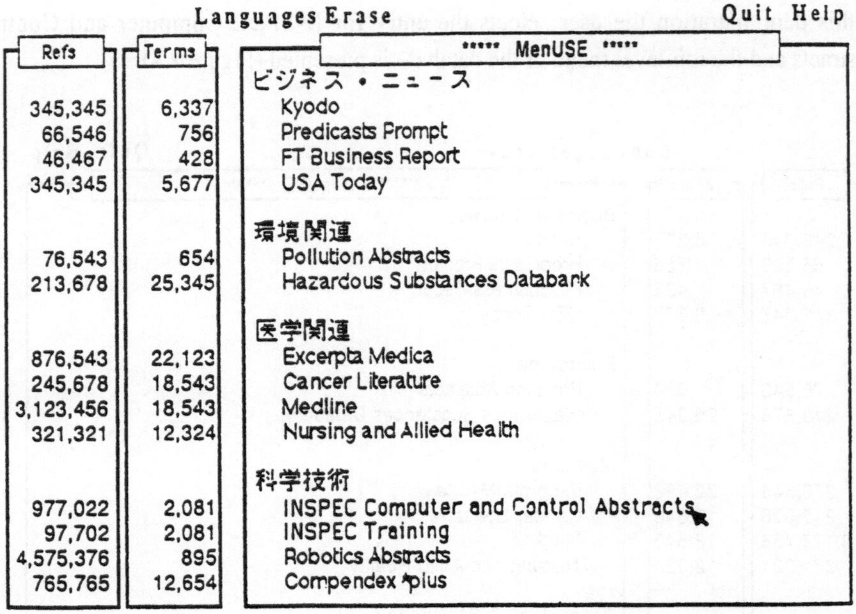

Figure 2.3 The top level menu in Japanese

2.2 An Example Search

The central feature of MenUSE is the presentation of concepts to the user for selection. These concepts are determined in the thesaurus for the database and the subject area covered by the complete database is presented on the top-level menu. Figure 2.4a shows the top-level menu of MenUSE for the INSPEC Computer and Control Abstracts Database. A concept of interest can be explored by the user selecting the appropriate descriptor.

The number in the column headed *Terms* is the count of the number of terms within that concept, e.g. there are 106 terms which describe the concept of *Computer software - techniques and systems* in more detail.

The number in the column headed *Refs* is the result of searching INSPEC for all the terms under the corresponding concept or term. For example, there are a total of 156,002 references to be found in the INSPEC database on some aspect of *Computer software - techniques and systems*. These figures are an accurate record of the contents of the database when incorporated into the demonstration (November 1991).

The equivalent Japanese menus are shown below the English all through the demonstration.
The following example shows the principles of the MenUSE retrieval system to search for references on: **Prolog and Information Retrieval Systems**

The user selects the concept *Computer software -- techniques and systems* as the first step to specifying the programming language Prolog. The screen then changes to the menu which expands the *Computer software -- techniques and systems* concept.

At the level immediately beneath *Computer software -- techniques and systems* (Figure 2.5), there are seven main concepts with twelve sub-concepts below them. *Languages* is one of the main concepts which is expanded to more specific terms; *Formal languages, Natural languages, Programming languages, Query languages, and Specification languages.* The sub-concepts are indicated by indentation on the screen. The user then selects *Programming languages.*

Prolog can be found indented under High level languages and is selected by the user (Figure 2.6), no subconcepts are available under *Prolog* (i.e. Terms = 1), so the system indicates the selection of a concept/term for the search by marking the entry with an asterisk (*) (Figure 2.7).

The menu above the current level will show the addition of a marker (>) against the selected term *Programming* to indicate that the user has chosen a sub-concept within programming. (Figure 2.8). The user may move back up to this menu by selecting the *Previous* button at the top of the screen. Alternatively the user can return to the top level of the database by selecting *Top-Menu* (Figure 2.7 or 2.8 to Figure 2.9).

The user now selects *Information science and documentation* as a first step to specifying the second concept in the query, and moves to an expansion of the terms under that concept (Figure 2.10). Selecting *Information retrieval systems* causes the latter to be marked as a concept for this search (*) and the two sub terms, *Bibliographic Systems* and *Information retrieval system evaluation* to be marked as sub-concepts (+)(Figure 2.11).

Selecting *Search* will cause MenUSE to perform a search on all combinations of concepts and display summary descriptions with the resulting set of references. (Figure 2.12). The user selects a description, in this case *prolog and all information retrieval systems* to see the titles for the references in the retrieved set (Figure 2.12).Figure 2.13

shows a menu of the titles for selection for the selected description. Figure 2.14 shows the full reference and abstract for the selected title.

3. Summary

According to Japanese MITI's *Database Directory* issued in October 1991, there are 738 databases accessible in Japan on the subject of Natural Science and Technology. Only 118 databases (16% of whole) are produced by Japanese producers, the other 620 databases are foreign. This figure shows that the present state of Japanese database industry is still lagging behind Western countries especially on the subject of Natural Science and Technology. The database products of Western companies have a broad market in Japan, but few will be translated into Japanese in the immediate future. On the other hand more and more Japanese information is needed by Western companies and organisations. Most (i.e. 88%) of the 808 databases provided by Japanese institutions in 1991 are not available in English.

The language barrier is a bottleneck which seriously impedes the information exchange between Japan and other countries.

MenUSE applies current technology and information retrieval know-how to provide a multilingual information retrieval system which is a practical and efficient way to overcome the language barrier both for foreign users searching Japanese databases using their own languages and Japanese users searching non-Japanese databases using Japanese. It will also provide a more effective and efficient way for the Japanese to search their own databases.

Acknowledgements

We would like to express our appreciation to Christopher Dillon, Head of the Japanese Information Service at the British Library, for his most helpful assistance. We wish also to thank Patricia Nelson, researcher of the Research Policy Institute, at Lund University in Sweden, for passing much useful information to us. Thanks are also due to IEE INSPEC for the provision of current manuals on the INSPEC database. We are also grateful to Radio-Suisse Data Star for supporting the costs of database searching.

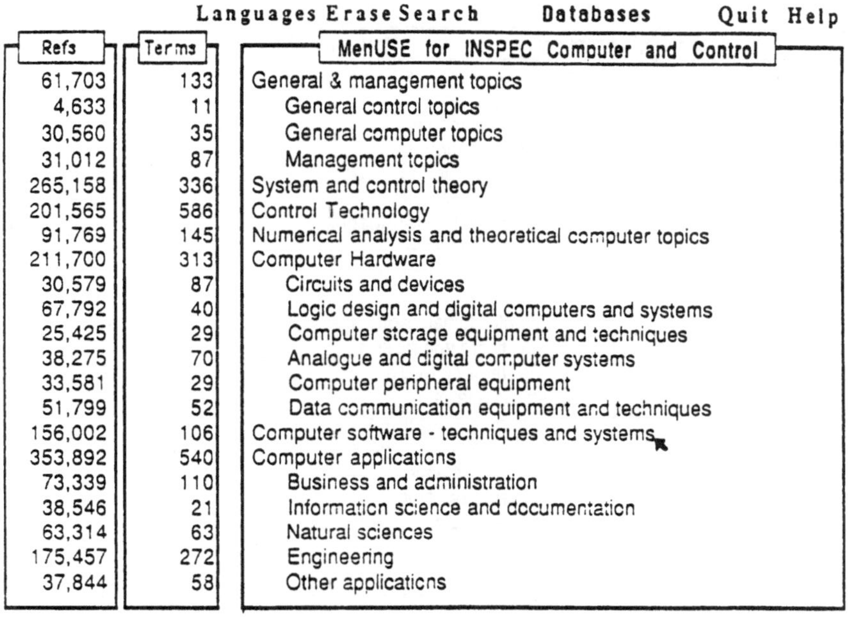

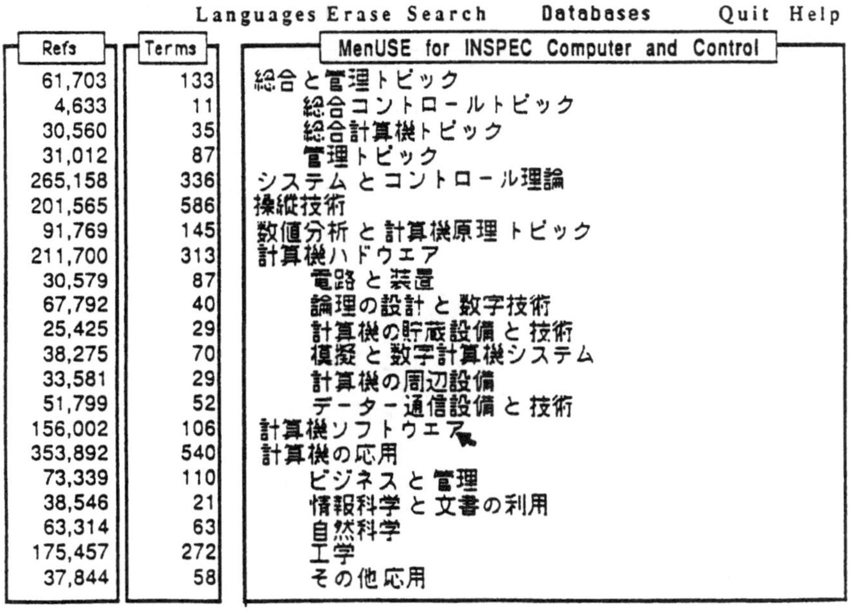

Figure 2.4 The top-level menu of MenUSE for INSPEC

Languages Erase Search Previous Top-Menu Quit Help

Refs	Terms	***** MenUSE *****
156,002	110	Computer software - techniques and systems
42,854	35	Languages
4,207	6	Formal languages
3,621	1	Natural languages
21,806	29	Programming languages
1,576	1	Query languages
2,491	1	Specification languages
84,745	43	Computer software
698	1	Integrated software
509	1	Macros
137	1	Public domain software
25,153	10	Software engineering
54,403	28	Systems software
8,954	4	Systems analysis
21,828	5	Database management systems
22,188	2	Knowledge based systems
16,872	1	Expert systems
1,386	2	Multimedia systems
1,026	1	Hypermedia
64,832	18	Programming

Languages Erase Search Previous Top-Menu Quit Help

Refs	Terms	***** MenUSE *****
156,002	110	コンピュータソフトウェアシステム
42,854	35	言語
4,207	6	公式の言語
3,621	1	自然の言語
21,806	29	プログラム言語
1,576	1	質問言語
2,491	1	説明言語
84,745	43	コンピュータソフトウェア
698	1	インテグタテド-ソフトウェア
509	1	マークロス
137	1	公用のソフトウエア
25,153	10	ソフトウエア工学
54,403	28	システム ソフトウェア
8,954	4	システム解析
21,828	5	データベース管理システム
22,188	2	知能システム
16,872	1	専門家システム
1,386	2	マルチメデイアシステム
1,026	1	ヘポーメデイア
64,832	18	プログラムイング

Figure 2.5 Computer Software - Techniques and Systems

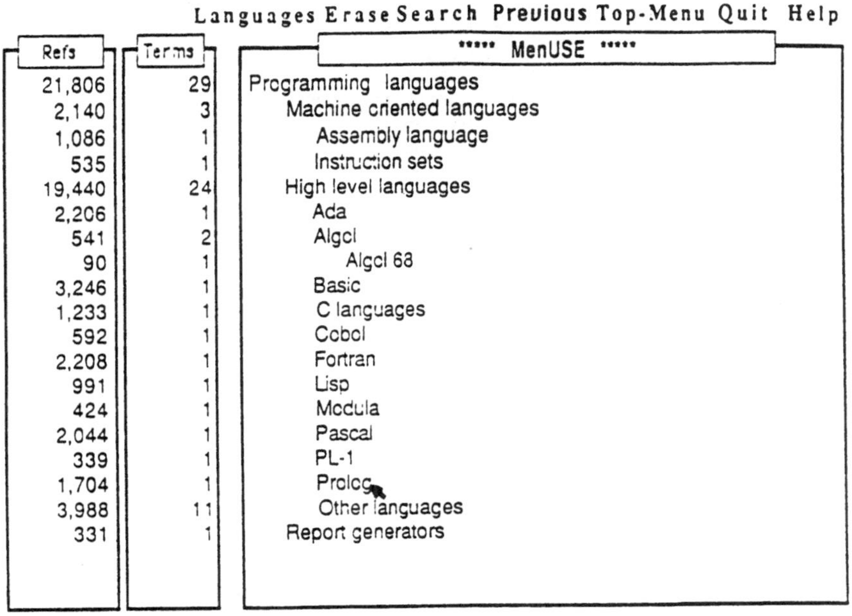

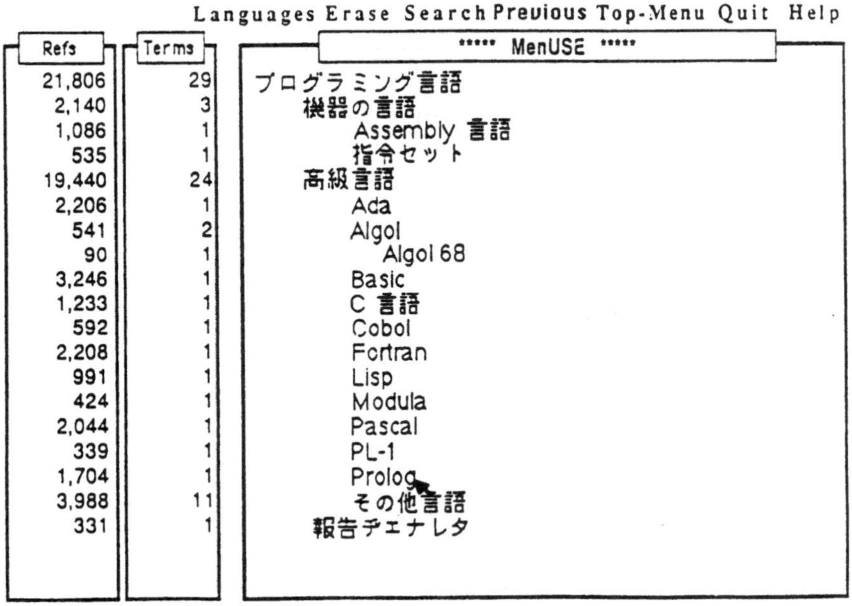

Figure 2.6 Programming Languages

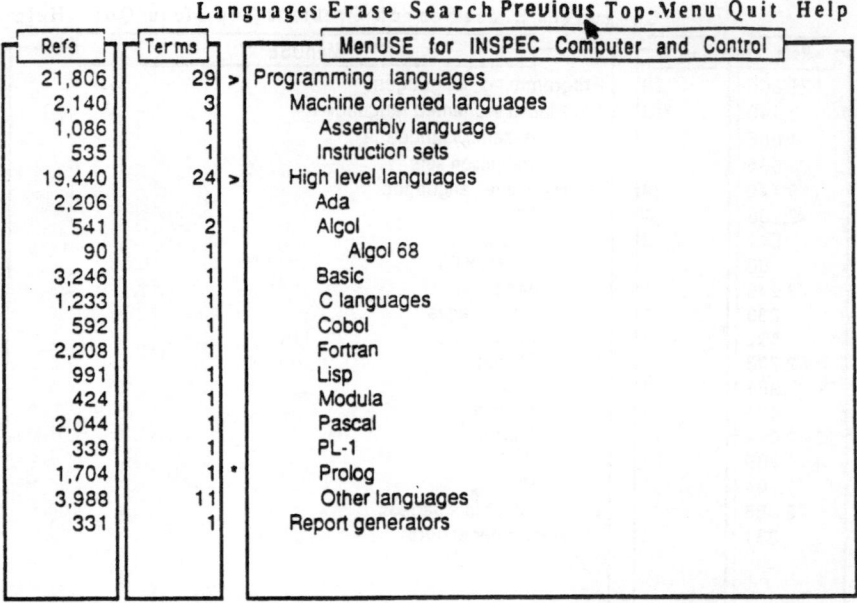

Languages Erase Search Previous Top-Menu Quit Help

Refs	Terms		MenUSE for INSPEC Computer and Control
21,806	29	>	Programming languages
2,140	3		Machine oriented languages
1,086	1		Assembly language
535	1		Instruction sets
19,440	24	>	High level languages
2,206	1		Ada
541	2		Algol
90	1		Algol 68
3,246	1		Basic
1,233	1		C languages
592	1		Cobol
2,208	1		Fortran
991	1		Lisp
424	1		Modula
2,044	1		Pascal
339	1		PL-1
1,704	1	*	Prolog
3,988	11		Other languages
331	1		Report generators

Languages Erase Search Previous Top-Menu Quit Help

Refs	Terms		MenUSE for INSPEC Computer and Control
21,806	29	>	プログラミング言語
2,140	3		機器の言語
1,086	1		Assembly 言語
535	1		指令セット
19,440	24	>	高級言語
2,206	1		Ada
541	2		Algol
90	1		Algol 68
3,246	1		Basic
1,233	1		C 言語
592	1		Cobol
2,208	1		Fortran
991	1		Lisp
424	1		Modula
2,044	1		Pascal
339	1		PL-1
1,704	1	*	Prolog
3,988	11		その他言語
331	1		報告ヂエナレタ

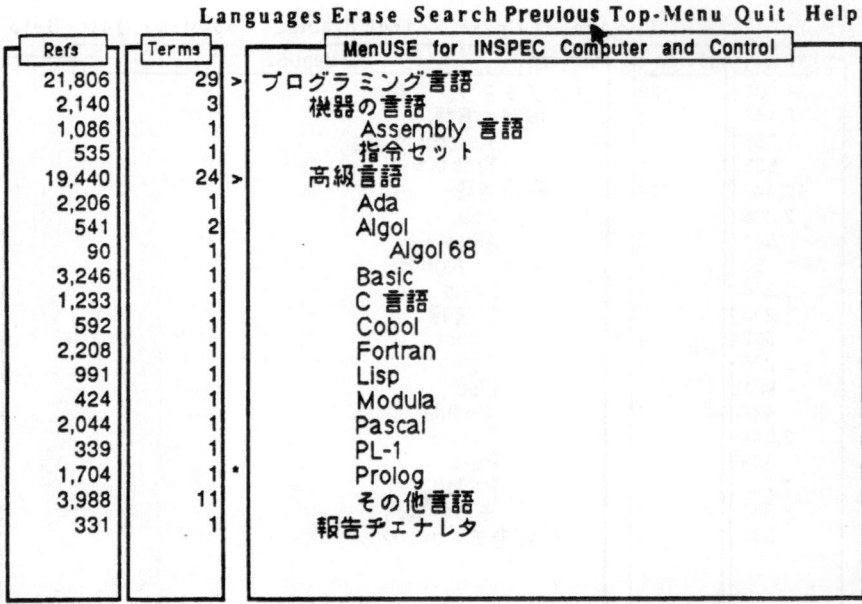

Figure 2.7 Programming Languages with Prolog selected

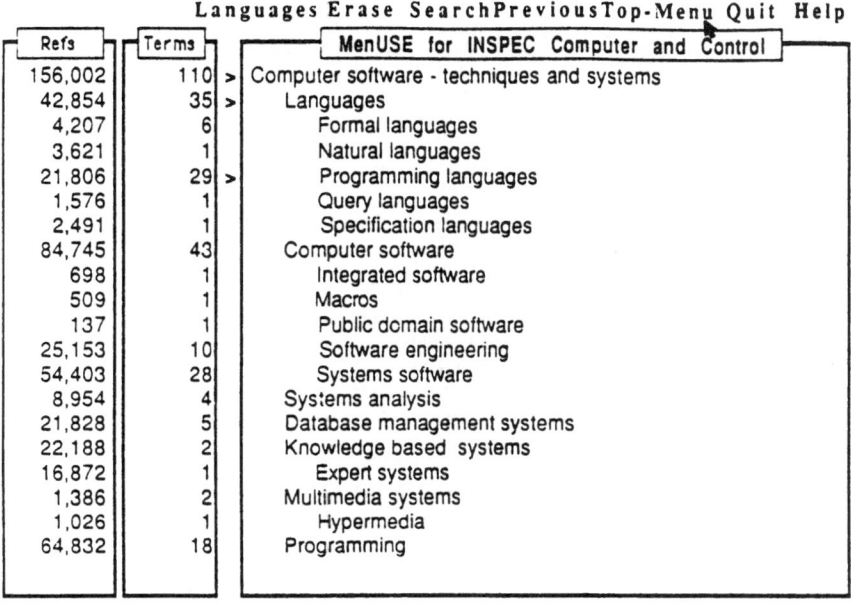

Languages Erase SearchPreviousTop-Menu Quit Help

Refs	Terms		MenUSE for INSPEC Computer and Control
156,002	110	>	Computer software - techniques and systems
42,854	35	>	Languages
4,207	6		Formal languages
3,621	1		Natural languages
21,806	29	>	Programming languages
1,576	1		Query languages
2,491	1		Specification languages
84,745	43		Computer software
698	1		Integrated software
509	1		Macros
137	1		Public domain software
25,153	10		Software engineering
54,403	28		Systems software
8,954	4		Systems analysis
21,828	5		Database management systems
22,188	2		Knowledge based systems
16,872	1		Expert systems
1,386	2		Multimedia systems
1,026	1		Hypermedia
64,832	18		Programming

Languages Erase SearchPreviousTop-Menu Quit Help

Refs	Terms		MenUSE for INSPEC Computer and Control
156,002	110	>	コンピュータソフトウェアシステム
42,854	35	>	言語
4,207	6		公式の言語
3,621	1		自然の言語
21,806	29	>	プログラム言語
1,576	1		質問言語
2,491	1		説明言語
84,745	43		コンピュータソフトウェア
698	1		インテグタテド-ソフトウェア
509	1		マークロス
137	1		公用のソフトウエア
25,153	10		ソフトウエア工学
54,403	28		システム ソフトウェア
8,954	4		システム解析
21,828	5		データベース管理システム
22,188	2		知能システム
16,872	1		専門家システム
1,386	2		マルチメデイアシステム
1,026	1		ヘボーメデイア
64,832	18		プログラムイング

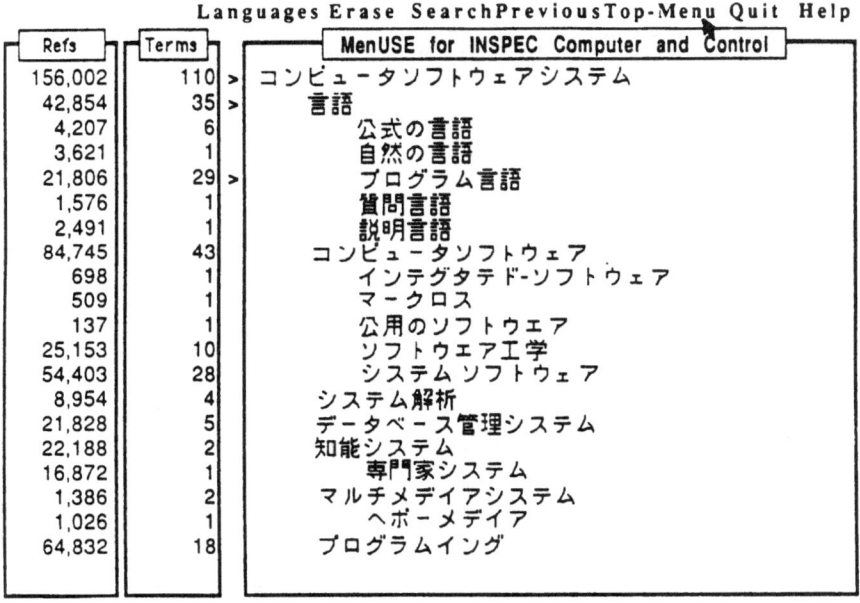

Figure 2.8 Computer Software - Techniques and Systems (Previous)

Languages Erase Search Databases Quit Help

Refs	Terms		MenUSE for INSPEC Computer and Control
61,703	133		General & management topics
4,633	11		General control topics
30,560	35		General computer topics
31,012	87		Management topics
265,158	336		System and control theory
201,565	586		Control Technology
91,769	145		Numerical analysis and theoretical computer topics
211,700	313		Computer Hardware
30,579	87		Circuits and devices
67,792	40		Logic design and digital computers and systems
25,425	29		Computer storage equipment and techniques
38,275	70		Analogue and digital computer systems
33,581	29		Computer peripheral equipment
51,799	52		Data communication equipment and techniques
156,002	106	>	Computer software - techniques and systems
353,892	540		Computer applications
73,339	110		Business and administration
38,546	21		Information science and documentation
63,314	63		Natural sciences
175,457	272		Engineering
37,844	58		Other applications

Languages Erase Search Databases Quit Help

Refs	Terms		MenUSE for INSPEC Computer and Control
61,703	133		総合と管理トピック
4,633	11		総合コントロールトピック
30,560	35		総合計算機トピック
31,012	87		管理トピック
265,158	336		システムとコントロール理論
201,565	586		操縦技術
91,769	145		数値分析 と 計算機原理 トピック
211,700	313		計算機ハドウエア
30,579	87		電路 と 装置
67,792	40		論理の設計 と 数字技術
25,425	29		計算機の貯蔵設備 と 技術
38,275	70		模擬 と 数字計算機システム
33,581	29		計算機の周辺設備
51,799	52		データー通信設備 と 技術
156,002	106	>	計算機ソフトウエア
353,892	540		計算機の応用
73,339	110		ビジネス と 管理
38,546	21		情報科学 と 文書の利用
63,314	63		自然科学
175,457	272		工学
37,844	58		その他応用

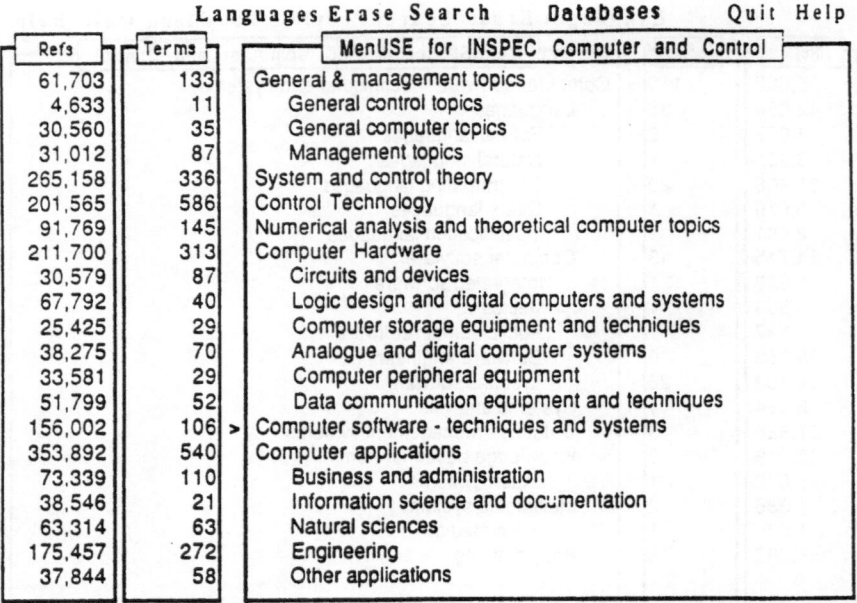

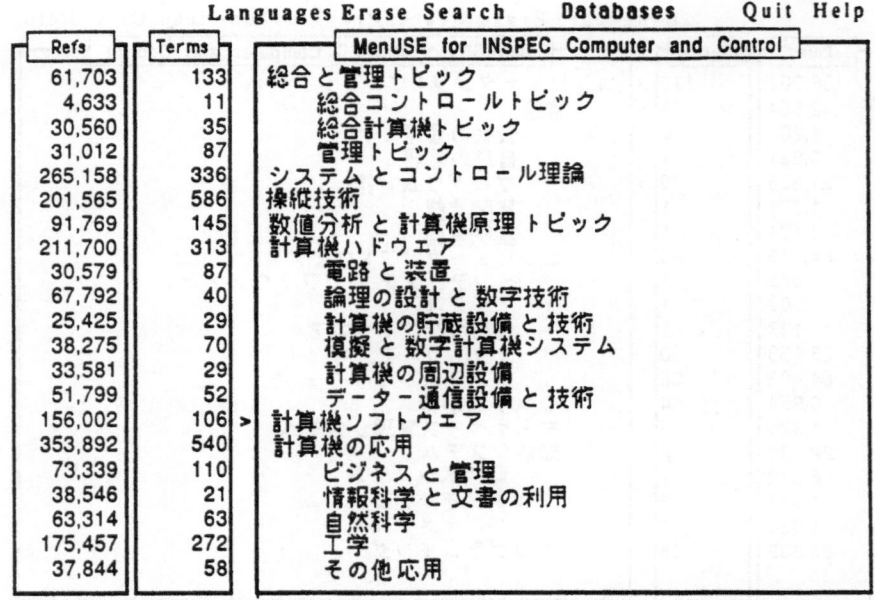

Figure 2.9 The top-level menu of MenUSE for INSPEC

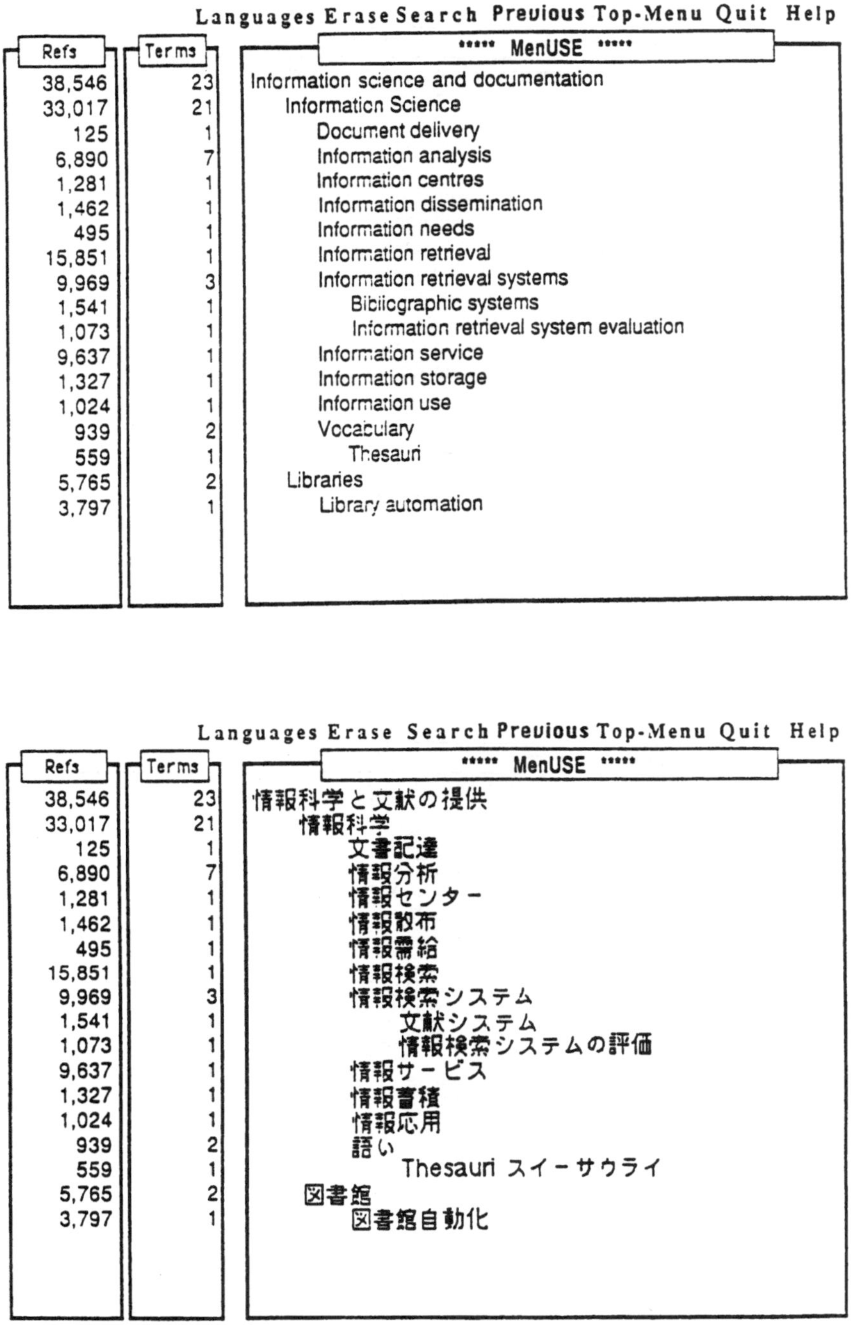

Figure 2.10 Information Science and Documentation

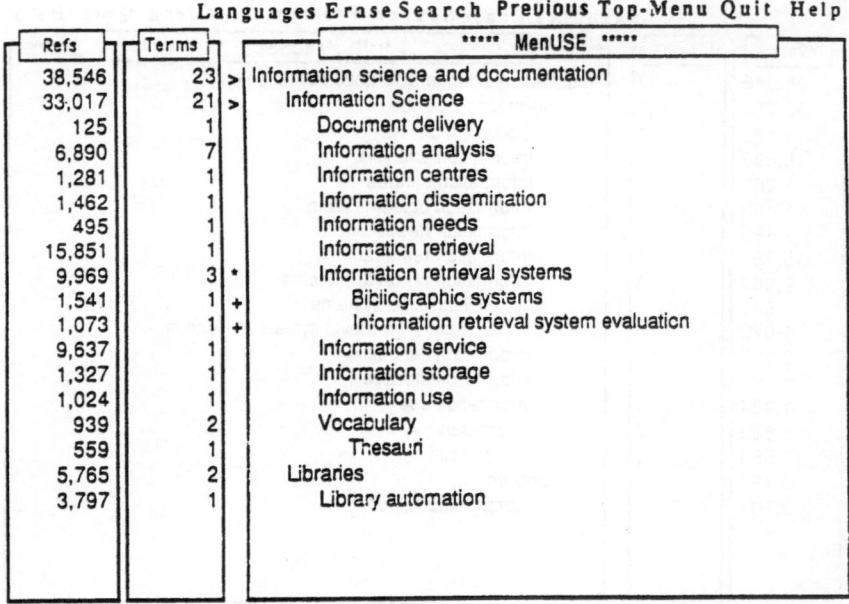

Languages Erase Search Previous Top-Menu Quit Help

Refs	Terms		***** MenUSE *****
38,546	23	>	Information science and documentation
33,017	21	>	Information Science
125	1		Document delivery
6,890	7		Information analysis
1,281	1		Information centres
1,462	1		Information dissemination
495	1		Information needs
15,851	1		Information retrieval
9,969	3	*	Information retrieval systems
1,541	1	+	Bibliographic systems
1,073	1	+	Information retrieval system evaluation
9,637	1		Information service
1,327	1		Information storage
1,024	1		Information use
939	2		Vocabulary
559	1		Thesauri
5,765	2		Libraries
3,797	1		Library automation

Languages Erase Search Previous Top-Menu Quit Help

Refs	Terms		***** MenUSE *****
38,546	23	>	情報科学と文献の提供
33,017	21	>	情報科学
125	1		文書配達
6,890	7		情報分析
1,281	1		情報センター
1,462	1		情報散布
495	1		情報需給
15,851	1		情報検索
9,969	3	*	情報検索システム
1,541	1	+	文献システム
1,073	1	+	情報検索システムの評価
9,637	1		情報サービス
1,327	1		情報蓄積
1,024	1		情報応用
939	2		語い
559	1		Thesauri スイーサウライ
5,765	2		図書館
3,797	1		図書館自動化

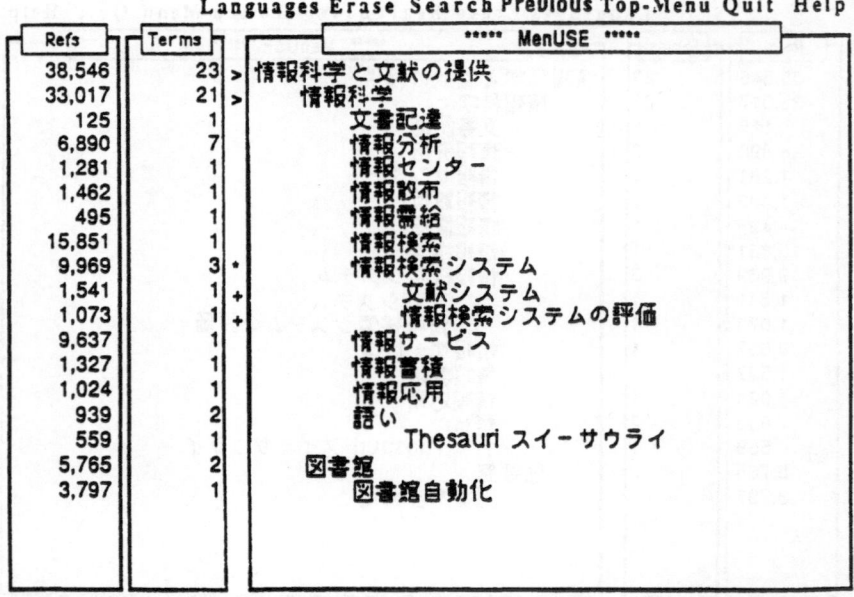

Figure 2.11 Information Retrieval Systems - selected

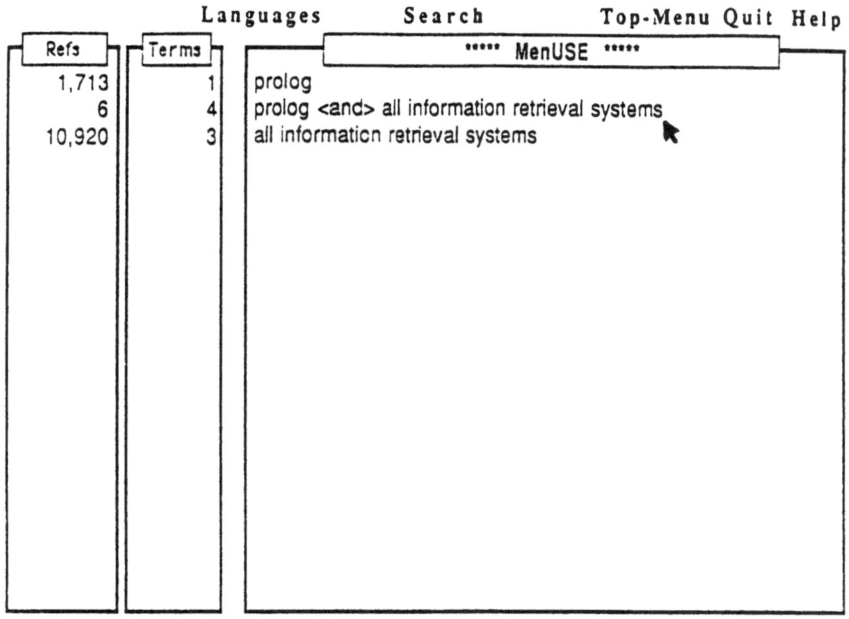

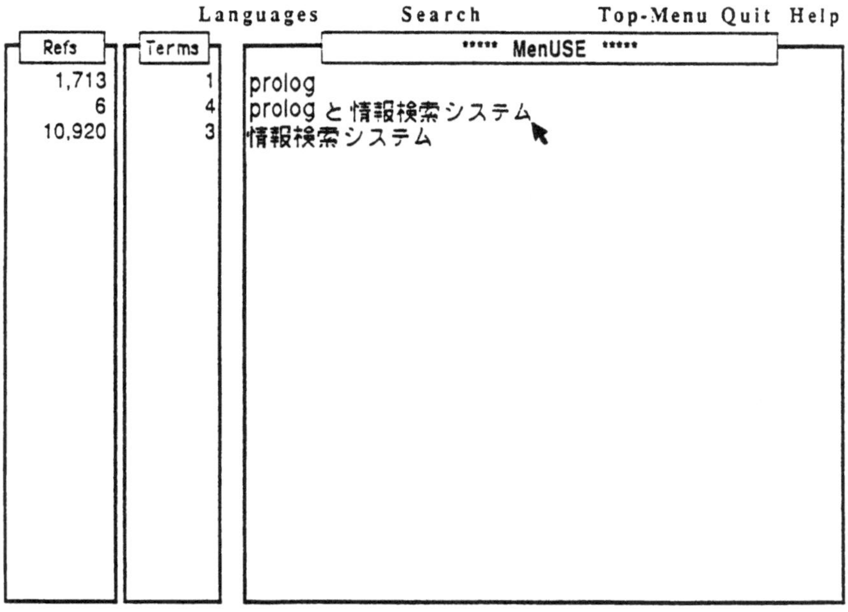

Figure 2.12 Search results - Summary Descriptions

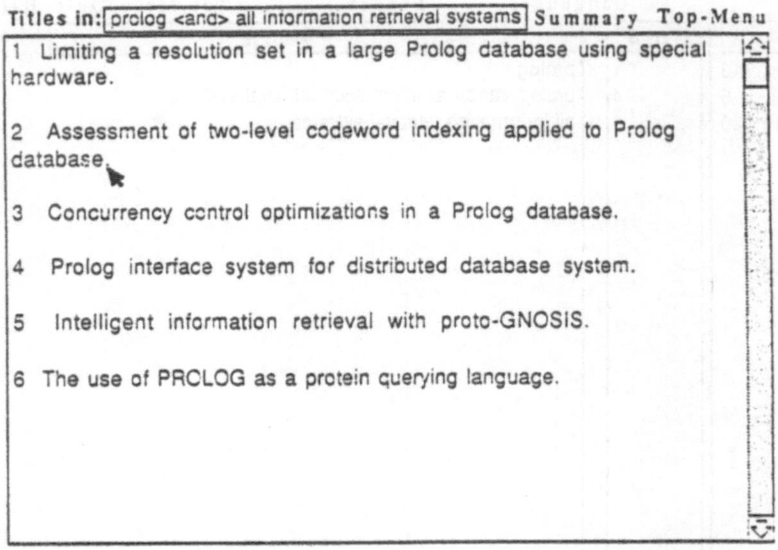
Titles in: prolog <and> all information retrieval systems
Summary
Top-Menu
1 Limiting a resolution set in a large Prolog database using special hardware.
2 Assessment of two-level codeword indexing applied to Prolog database.
3 Concurrency control optimizations in a Prolog database.
4 Prolog interface system for distributed database system.
5 Intelligent information retrieval with proto-GNOSIS.
6 The use of PROLOG as a protein querying language.

Figure 2.13 Titles for Prolog and All Information Retrieval Systems

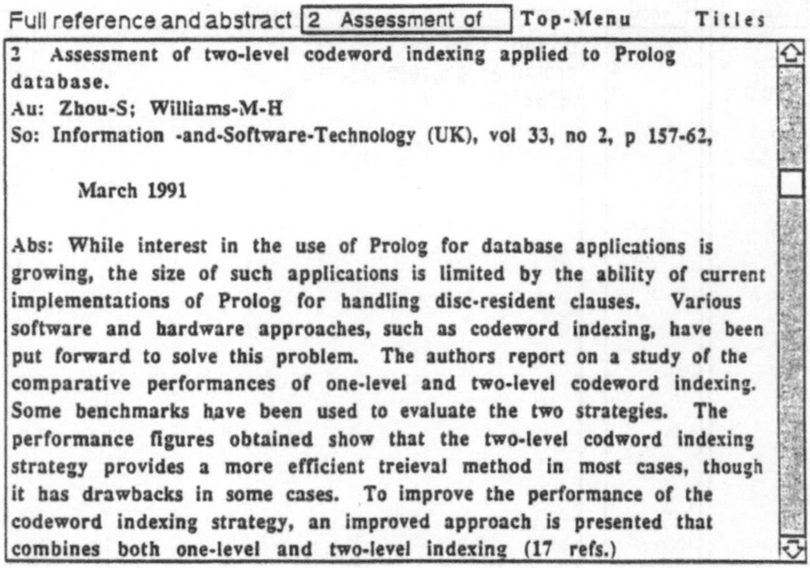
Full reference and abstract
2 Assessment of
Top-Menu
Titles
2 Assessment of two-level codeword indexing applied to Prolog database.
Au: Zhou-S; Williams-M-H
So: Information -and-Software-Technology (UK), vol 33, no 2, p 157-62,
March 1991
Abs: While interest in the use of Prolog for database applications is growing, the size of such applications is limited by the ability of current implementations of Prolog for handling disc-resident clauses. Various software and hardware approaches, such as codeword indexing, have been put forward to solve this problem. The authors report on a study of the comparative performances of one-level and two-level codeword indexing. Some benchmarks have been used to evaluate the two strategies. The performance figures obtained show that the two-level codword indexing strategy provides a more efficient treieval method in most cases, though it has drawbacks in some cases. To improve the performance of the codeword indexing strategy, an improved approach is presented that combines both one-level and two-level indexing (17 refs.)

Figure 2.14 Full reference for selected title

References

Database Promotion Center (1991a) Database in Japan 1991. Database Promotion Center, Japan.

Database Promotion Center (1991b) Proposal for Joint research project of Retrieval systems for overseas users of Japanese databases, Database Promotion Center, Japan, 15th May, 1991

Goodman, D. (1990) The Complete HyperCard 2.0 Handbook, Bantam Computer Books.

Greatrex, R. (1990) Japanese Machine Translation in the 1990s: The European User's Perspective. Japanese Information Science, Technology and Commerce, Proceedings of the 2nd International Conference, IOS, Amsterdam, Netherlands.

King, S. and Sassoon, J. (1989) Review of Japanese databases and their usage in Europe. Proceedings of the 13th International Online Information Meeting. Learned Information Ltd.

Li C S, Pollitt A S & Smith M P (1992) Multilingual MenUSE for Searching Bibliographic Databases: A feasibility study of Japanese MenUSE, The Polytechnic of Huddersfield, March 1992.

Matsumura, T. (1990) The Japanese information scene: Today and tomorrow. Information Service & Use 10 (1990), Elsevier Science Publishers.

Murphy F. J., Pollitt, A. S., White, P. R. (1991). Matching OPAC User Interfaces to User Needs. British Library R&D Report No. 6041, The Polytechnic of Huddersfield.

Nelson, P. (1991) Breaching the language barrier: Experimentation with Japanese to English machine translation. Proceedings of the 15th International Online Information Meeting, Learned Information Ltd.

Pollitt A S (1988) A common query interface using MenUSE - a Menu-based User Search Engine. 12th International Online Information Meeting, Vol II, pp 445-457, London, December 1988.

Smith M P, Pollitt A S , Li C S (1992) An evaluation of concept translation through menu navigation in the MenUSE intermediary system. 14th BCS IRSG Research Colloquium in Information Retrieval, University of Lancaster, April 1992.

An Evaluation of Concept Translation Through Menu Navigation in the MenUSE Intermediary System.

M P Smith, A S Pollitt, C S Li
The Polytechnic of Huddersfield, U.K.

Abstract

The MenUSE (Menu-based User Search Engine) intermediary system was developed as a front-end for end-user searching of bibliographic databases as a follow-on to CANSEARCH. Although initial MenUSE development concentrated on improving access to MEDLINE, the principles underpinning its design are generally applicable across all databases. The CANSEARCH interface, providing a hierarchy of linked menus of concepts and terms which enables the user to specify the subject of a search, is retained but redesigned. However, the initial domain dependent rule-base for search statement generation has been replaced by a simpler algorithm, searching all combinations of concepts and presenting the user with descriptions and postings for the resulting sets. This makes it easier and quicker to create MenUSE systems for different subject areas, in different databases. MeSH (Medical Subject Headings), a very well developed thesaurus with a high specificity, was used to automatically create the menus in the original prototypes which accessed MEDLINE. This paper looks at applying MenUSE to access the Computer and Control Abstracts in the INSPEC database, an area where the vocabulary is not as well developed as in Medicine. A new prototype, with menus derived from the INSPEC Thesaurus, is described together with the findings of a preliminary experiment to evaluate how easily users are able to translate concepts through menu navigation.

1.Introduction.

The MenUSE (Menu-based User Search Engine) intermediary system [Pollitt 88],was developed as a front-end for end-user searching of bibliographic databases as a follow-on to CANSEARCH [Pollitt 86,87]. Although initial MenUSE development concentrated on improving access to MEDLINE, the principles underpinning its design are generally applicable across all databases. The CANSEARCH interface, providing a hierarchy of linked menus of concepts and terms which enables the user to specify the subject of a search, is retained but redesigned. However, the initial domain dependent rule-base for search statement generation has been replaced by a simpler algorithm, searching all combinations of concepts and presenting the user with descriptions and postings for the resulting sets. This makes it easier and quicker to create MenUSE systems for different subject areas, in different databases.

The research into MenUSE has received a boost through research funding provided by the Polytechnic of Huddersfield, and a research team is now working on applying MenUSE to access different databases using two development platforms. The original prototypes were developed using Turbo-Prolog on the PC, this software is being rewritten in PDC-Prolog on the same platform, making sure that the interface is compliant with the Common User Access (CUA) guidelines promoted by IBM [IBM 89] as part of their Systems Application Architecture (SAA), and recognised as a standard for interface design within industry. The second platform is the Apple Macintosh and PowerBook using HyperCard. This development is aimed initially at demonstrating the multilingual capabilities of MenUSE, where Japanese can be selected as the language of interaction between the user and MenUSE, with English language searching of the database. This development is described in a paper presented at this research colloquium [Li, Pollitt & Smith 92]. This paper looks at applying MenUSE to access the Computer and Control Abstracts in the INSPEC database, an area where the vocabulary is not as well developed as in Medicine. A new prototype, with menus derived from the INSPEC Thesaurus, is described together with the findings of a preliminary experiment to evaluate how easily users are able to translate concepts through menu navigation. A fuller description of the search process with an example search through the MenUSE for Computer & Control menus is provided in the paper on Japanese MenUSE [Li, Pollitt & Smith 92].

2. Menu Construction in MenUSE for Computer & Control Abstracts

MeSH (Medical Subject Headings), a very well developed thesaurus with a high specificity, was used to automatically create the menus in the original prototypes which accessed MEDLINE. The tree structures in MeSH are divided into fifteen categories and take advantage of the natural hierarchical breakdown of concepts to more specific terms, such as in the extract from the Anatomy category shown in Figure 1.

Terms can be duplicated in different places within the tree structures as shown in Figure 2 where the terms EYEBROWS and EYELASHES have been repeated in a second hierarchical arrangement. This duplication with trees is essential when the view taken by the user of the subject matter can map to different hierarchical sets. For example, disease names can be found in the hierarchy according to the site of the disease (such as BILE DUCT NEOPLASMS beneath BILE DUCT DISEASES) or the type of the disease (BILE DUCT NEOPLASMS beneath BILIARY TRACT NEOPLASMS). In MenUSE the same terms may be found through users taking different routes according to their perception of the concept. The terms in the selected hierarchy should then expand on the chosen concept.

ANATOMY
- **BODY REGIONS**
  - ....
  - **HEAD**
    - **EAR**
    - **FACE**
      - **CHEEK**
      - **CHIN**
      - **EYE**
        - **EYEBROWS**
        - **EYELIDS**
          - **EYELASHES**
      - **FOREHEAD**
      - **MOUTH**
        - **LIP**
      - **NOSE**
  - **NECK**

Figure 1. Extract from MeSH Tree Structure ANATOMY - HEAD

ANATOMY
- **BODY REGIONS**
  - ....
  - **HEAD**
  - ....
  - **SKIN**
    - **HAIR**
      - **EYEBROWS**
      - **EYELASHES**
    - **NAILS**
  - ....

Figure 2. Extract from MeSH Tree Structure - ANATOMY - SKIN

The INSPEC thesaurus is not divided into convenient categories in the same way as MeSH and has a large number of relatively low-level top terms. There is some duplication of terms within different hierarchies but the terminology and its arrangement is by no means well established as can be seen in Figure 3 which shows the two hierarchies beneath the top terms **computer software** and **programming.** The menus for INSPEC could not be generated automatically, as with the MeSH menus, and had to be created manually by using a mixture of the thesaurus and classification scheme. The INSPEC classification scheme (Figure 4), which is used to arrange the printed INSPEC Computer and Control Abstracts into sections, was employed to group the (relatively low) top terms from the thesaurus into appropriate higher level concepts.

computer software programming

. integrated software
. macros
. public domain software
. software engineering
. . formal specification
. . programming environments
. . project support environments
. . software maintenance
. . software metrics
. . software portability
. . software reliability
. . software reusability
. . software tools
. systems software
. . computer bootstrapping
. . interrupts
. operating systems
. ...
. program processors
. . program assemblers
. . program compilers
. . program interpreters
. utility programs

. analogue computer programming
. application generators
. automatic programming
. functional programming
. hybrid computer programming
. interactive programming
. logic programming
. microprogramming
. object-oriented programming
. parallel programming
. program testing
. . program verification
. software tools
. structured programming
. system documentation
. . decision tables
. visual programming

Figure 3. Extract from the INSPEC Hierarchical List of Terms

General and Management Topics.

System and Control Theory.

Control Technology.

Numerical Analysis and Theoretical Computer Topics.

Computer Hardware.

Computer Software

Computer Applications.

Figure 4. The INSPEC Classification headings for Computers & Control

The classification provides its own hierarchy with divisions beneath the headings shown in Figure 4 such as for Computer Software as illustrated in Figure 5.

Computer Software

Software Techniques and Systems

Systems analysis and programming

....

Programming support

File organisation

Data handling techniques

....

Programming languages

....

Systems software

....

Computer communications software

Database management systems (DBMS)

Expert systems

User Interfaces

....

Simulation techniques

Figure 5. The INSPEC Classification subheadings for Computer Software

File Edit Goto Search Print Options Help

Refs	NoT	Inspec computing and control
61730	134	General and management topics
4633	11	General control topics
30560	35	General computer topics
31012	87	Management topics
265158	336	Systems and control theory
201565	586	Control technology
91769	145	Numerical analysis and theoretical computer topics
211700	308	Computer hardware
30579	87	Circuits and devices
67792	40	Logic design and digital techniques
25425	29	Computer storage equipment
38275	70	Analogue and digital computer systems
33581	29	Computer peripheral equipment
51799	52	Data communication equipment and techniques
156002	110	Computer software - techniques and systems
353892	462	Computer applications
85102	115	Business and administration
38546	23	Information science and documentation
63314	63	Natural sciences
175457	272	Engineering
37844	58	Other applications

F1-Help F2-Save F3-Exit F4-Load F5-Erase F6-Top F7-Previous F8-Review F9-Search.

Figure 6. The top-level menu in MenUSE for Computers & Control

The top two levels of the classification hierarchies were used to group the terms from the thesaurus and provided the top-level menu presented in Figure 6.

The number of terms underneath each classification grouping is given in the NoT column on the screen, and the number of references/postings, as if a search was made ORing all the terms in that particular hierarchy, is shown by the Refs column. These figures were accurate as of the end of November 1991. The next level menus were then the result of marrying the INSPEC Classification with the term hierarchies. Figure 7 shows the menu for Computer Software - techniques and systems.

```
      File      Edit      Goto      Search      Print      Options      Help
 Refs    NoT    Computer software - techniques and systems
156002   110  Computer software - techniques and systems
 84745    43     Computer software
 64832    18     Programming
 42854    39     Languages
  4207     6        Formal languages
  3621     1        Natural languages
 21806    29        Programming languages
  1576     1        Query languages
  2491     1        Specification languages
   221     2     Computer communications software
    68     1        Network operating systems
  8954     4     Systems analysis
 25342     8     File organisation
  7221     5     Computer graphics
   875     3     User interfaces
  7682    13     Data handling
 21828     5     Database management systems
 22188     2     Knowledge based systems
 16872     1        Expert systems
  1386     2     Multimedia systems
  1026     1        Hypermedia
F1-Help F2-Save F3-Exit F4-Load F5-Erase F6-Top F7-Previous F8-Review F9-Search.
```

Figure 7. The menu for Computer software techniques and systems

Lower level menus were created by using the term hierarchies. The lower level menu for **programming** is shown in Figure 8, a direct copy of the thesaurus entry - see Figure 3.

```
      File      Edit      Goto      Search      Print      Options      Help
 Refs    NoT                        Programming
 64832    18  Programming
    41     1     Analogue computer programming
   548     1     Application generators
  1348     1     Automatic programming
   598     1     Functional programming
    64     1     Hybrid computer programming
   976     1     Interactive programming
  3091     1     Logic programming
  2609     1     Microprogramming
  2907     1     Object-oriented programming
  4080     1     Parallel programming
  4619     2     Program testing
  1681     1        Program verification
  6555     1     Software tools
  1710     1     Structured programming
  1169     2     System documentation
   286     1        Decision tables
   144     1     Visual programming
F1-Help F2-Save F3-Exit F4-Load F5-Erase F6-Top F7-Previous F8-Review F9-Search.
```

Figure 8. The menu for Programming

The system gives the user a view of the database and presents them with a top down way of selecting terms, considered by many, notably Thompson [71], to be the most natural way of thinking. The use of menus as a means of selection is also considered to be the best type of interface for new/intermittent users of a system [Geller & Lesk 83] who would be the main users of this type of system.

The 80+ menus produced, by hand, gave us a sufficiently large set of menus so that a preliminary evaluation could take place of the ease of user navigation when searching for particular concepts. Such an evaluation could be expected to indicate alternative user classifications not adopted by INSPEC so that MenUSE for Computers & Control could be extended to accommodate different user perceptions of the subject area.

3 The Method of Evaluation.

It was decided that two types of task should be tested with a range of experimental subjects. The first type was to search the hierarchies for a term which could be found in the menus, the second type was to derive terms or concepts from titles of articles extracted from the database and search for those terms which could be matched by synonyms. Ten terms (Figure 9) were selected from the lower level menus and included both end (narrow/very low level) and intermediate (broad but not top) terms. Ten titles (Figure 10) were extracted from the March edition of Computer and Control Abstracts. Selection of both the titles and the terms depended on their perceived level of difficulty as far as the user might be concerned. A title such as 'Traffic Control - Beat The Jam Electronically' may be considered ambiguous/obscure and would not be used in such an exercise as terms cannot easily be derived to search for in the menus.

The access routes within MenUSE for the single terms and terms derived from titles are included as an appendix.

Public domain software.
Law administration.
Natural sciences computing.
Smalltalk listings.
Multiprogramming.
Logic arrays.
Parallel architectures.
Home computing.
Algol 68.
Code division multiple access.

Figure 9. The ten terms to be found in the menus.

Each subject was given a random mixture of five of the ten terms and a random mixture of five of the ten titles; the randomness was introduced to check the effect of a subject remembering where a term was in the menus.

'A digital optical implementation of RISC'.

'A specification based approach to maintenance'.

'Object oriented analysis'.

'Knowledge directed query processing in expert database systems'.

'Knowledge based desk top publishing with expertpage'.

'Indexing and compressing full text databases for cd rom.'

'Multilingual indexing and retrieval in bibliographic systems'.

'Software tools for students in higher education'.

'An intelligent geographic information system - IGIS1'.

'FTP file transfer program'.

Figure 10. The ten titles from which concepts were chosen

A minimal amount of instruction was given to each subject prior to their participation in the experiment and no particular approach to their identification of concepts/terms from titles was offered to make this as genuine a test of end-user behaviour as possible. For example the title :

'An Object Oriented Implementation of an Intelligent Information System'

could be broken down into :

Object oriented , Knowledge based , Information system

The user would then search through the menus to find either these terms or their synonyms. They would also say whether they would pick any terms found in the menus which they had not previously considered. It is important to note here that when deciding which titles to choose from the printed abstracts for the exercise, we noted the INSPEC descriptors assigned to each paper; each term used could be found in the menus. The titles themselves did not necessarily contain these terms, as it is the content of the actual paper and not the title which determines the entries in the descriptor field. The user might typically identify three concepts/terms for each title.

4 The Users

Sixteen users volunteered to participate in the experiment, at very short notice. These comprised final year HND students, final year BA(Hons) Computing in Business students, technicians, computing researchers, the computing librarian and members of the teaching staff. This cross section of users had varying levels of subject knowledge and reflected candidate end-users of the eventual MenUSE for Computers & Control system.

Each subject was asked to relate exactly what they were thinking as they navigated the menus, and to give reasons for any decisions taken. This provided the core data for the experiment which would explain why failures to find concepts/terms occurred.

Although no strict data gathering occurred in respect of the time taken to scan menus and select entries, problems which led to what were thought to be excessive amounts of time spent in scanning and navigation were noted.

The requirement for successful navigation in this system is, of course, the user's ability to interpret the broad/top level terms and to be able to say that the term that they are looking for is in a particular part of the term hierarchy. In an ideal navigation, a subject should be able to recognise and select associated broad level terms in the first scan although failure to do this does not, in itself, indicate a failed navigation, as long as the system can subsequently be navigated without undue wasted time.

Using test queries chosen at random did tend to test the user rather than the system on a number of occasions. In general the HND students had the greatest difficulty in navigating through the menus simply because they sometimes did not know what a term was and therefore could not associate any broad terms with it. Some HND students (alas) did not know that 'Algol 68' was a programming language. Hopefully, this sort of problem would not be encountered when the subject of the search originated with the user.

5 Findings of the Evaluation.

Although the evaluation exercise was intended as a preliminary study, the findings have provided valuable input to the further design activities needed prior to evaluating an online version.

5.1 Choice of Navigation Path

All subjects used a system of eliminating subject areas. - "It is not in A. It might be in C but my first choice is B". If a term cannot be found in B then C will be checked. If the term cannot then be found the subject reverts to browsing through the menus.

Browsing usually takes place after a second choice route has failed. The first choice browsing route is usually down a 'catch all' path such as 'Other applications' or 'Computer software - techniques and systems'. If these fail then the subject browses in an ad hoc way.

Some subjects take their time and read the menus carefully and assess every option on the screen before making a considered decision, others 'scan' until they find the first applicable option. The former is more likely to find the term and will also remember a menu so that if they need a term from that menu they will go straight to it. The latter is least likely to remember where they have seen a term before, if they saw it at all when they were on a particular menu. The latter is also likely to miss out on synonyms for terms they were looking for. The result is that this type of subject took marginally longer to do the evaluation than the careful menu navigator.

5.2 Level of Computing Knowledge

The successful search for a term was dependent on the computing knowledge of the subject, and comment has been made regarding the testing of the users rather than the system in the previous section.

It is interesting to note that having additional knowledge of a subject can cause problems when navigating through a menu. One subject, when looking for 'Smalltalk listings', stated that "Smalltalk is used in the natural sciences and so I will look in there". Needless to say that route did not lead to the required term although their logic in searching was reasonable, even if a little misdirected.

Familiarity with concepts may leave the user wanting a more specific vocabulary to match. When looking for 'optical R.I.S.C. computing' one subject, who knew the area well, found 'R.I.S.C.' but decided that there must be something more detailed and did not pick 'R.I.S.C.' and 'Optical logic' (which was on another menu), instead they looked for 'Optical R.I.S.C.' - they expected more detail from the menus and were reluctant to select less specific concepts/terms.

User knowledge and expectation is going to affect their ability to navigate MenUSE successfully, too little knowledge leads naturally to an inability to navigate, too much (if there is such a thing) will lead to the user creating additional paths for navigation.

This evaluation has shown that using test questions with subjects who are not fully appreciative of the subject area, or where the questions are ambiguous, hampers search statement formulation . When the fully working prototype is written an evaluation of the system will take place with subjects who will search for terms corresponding to their own queries.

5.3 User Perceived Classification Errors

Although the general comment was that the menus were easy to work through, there were one or two problems associated with what users saw as a classification error. For example 'Smalltalk listings' was placed in 'Other applications' rather than 'Computer software - techniques and systems' and was therefore missed by many subjects. This problem caused some loss of confidence in the system so that when a term was not in the place expected, then the user anticipated failure on searching for the next term and didn't choose what would have otherwise been their first choice path.

It was also felt that many broad terms used in the thesaurus did not necessarily point to narrower terms on lower level menus. An example of this being 'social sciences computing', a broad term for 'educational computing' which is on a menu at the next level down.

Some terms were considered ambiguous or covered a large subject area which caused problems, an example being 'Computer software'. One possible solution to this problem may be to give examples of narrower terms at the top level menu, a technique adopted in the top level menu for MEDLINE. The most ambiguous terms were naturally considered to be those at a high level in the hierarchy of menus.

A general impression conveyed by especially the more knowledgeable users was that the terminology used was outdated and too oriented towards the technical side of computing rather than giving an overall impression of todays computing terminology.

5.4 The Use of the 'Number of Terms' and 'References' Information

The **Refs** (number of references/postings) and **NoT** (number of terms), information on the screen can be a great aid to users when searching for terms. The figure in the NoT Column was used by many to see how detailed a term was. A number of users realised that they had gone down the wrong path simply because the figure in the NoT column on their chosen route was 1.

The Refs column was used by some as an indicator of when they should narrow a search statement. After selecting only three of the four concepts from a title, one subject decided that this would be enough as the numbers in the Refs column indicated that selecting the fourth term might create a zero or low result ie. the fourth term would narrow the search too much. This would not actually be the case with MenUSE, given that it provides all combinations of sets, but clearly, there is a trade-off between specifying all the concepts and scanning retrieved sets of references that will need careful study when the online version is evaluated.

It appears that these two columns of information are needed and indeed are used in an intelligent way by many users. It was suggested by some that they 'cluttered up the screen' but as we see they, add richness to the information already presented.

5.5 HCI Aspects, Depth of Hierarchy and Information Overload

As would be expected the deeper into the menus a term was, the harder it was to find and of course the longer it took to find. The reasons for this are that the top/broad terms are usually very broad in meaning and are therefore not always the first choice starting points in a search. The effect of menu depth in MenUSE needs to be established in further evaluations, though it is evident that we need to balance the depth of menus with the amount of detail per menu, an issue addressed by Shneiderman [87]. The maximum number of lines on each menu, given the extensive use of indentation, was set by the number of lines available on the character-based screen; menus built using a smaller maximum have not been tested.

The volume of information displayed and the layout of screens caused some problems. Some users complained that the indentation used to signify broad-narrow term relationships was not sufficient. Some complained about there being too much on the screen to "scan", leading to terms being missed. The effect of the highlight bar on a term to be selected, was thought by more than one user to "hide" the term directly below the bar.

5.6 Translating Titles into Concepts

The second part of the evaluation, title-concept translation, caused more problems than the first, simply because the users were not sure what concepts to choose from the titles, given that some of the titles were ambiguous. The concepts that were chosen were, by and large, similar to the controlled vocabulary terms chosen by the database indexers. The problem was that after choosing a term, a subject had difficulty finding the actual term or its synonyms. This can again be seen as a failure brought about by the nature of the experiment, testing the knowledge of the users, rather than their ability to navigate for concepts with which they are familiar..

6. Conclusions.

Many users stated that the system was easy to use, although sometimes not all that easy to navigate through. Navigation was, on the whole, thought to be satisfactory, although there is still a lot of work to be done to enhance the menus and address some of the problems identified above. Work is continuing to fully develop the prototype to query the INSPEC Computer and Control database. When this is completed then a series of evaluations is scheduled to take place involving users in real situations.

As might be expected more experienced users can be expected to use the system more immediately with greater success than less experienced users, which is what you might expect, although the issue of wanting to over specify a concept will need to be tackled, probably by means of a better introduction to using the system.

Of wider concern are the implications of this preliminary study and the menu building difficulties for the existing term hierarchies in INSPEC. The hierarchies should be extended to a higher level and further duplication of terms in different hierarchies considered, to offer the user their own view of the subject matter wherever possible, without compromising the task of the indexer. Similarly the role of the terms and the classification need to be reconciled along the lines of MeSH.

We now have some experience of the target audience for MenUSE and how they might conceivably interact with the MenUSE system and will hopefully make use of this experience in our continuing development.

Acknowledgements

We would like to thank INSPEC for providing the necessary documentation on INSPEC. Thanks must go to Radio-Suisse and INSPEC for supporting us in respect of the costs of searching the INSPEC database on Datastar. Thanks must also go to staff and students at the Polytechnic of Huddersfield for their help and participation in the evaluation.

References

Geller V J & Lesk M E (1983) User Interfaces to Information Systems : Choices Vs Commands. Proceedings of the sixth annual International ACM SIGIR Conference on Research and Development in Information Retrieval. Maryland USA, June 1983.

IEE(1991) INSPEC Thesaurus 1991 ISBN 0 85296 489 7

IEE (1992) A classification scheme for the INSPEC database. ISBN 0 85296 497 8

IBM Corp. (1989) IBM Systems Application Architecture Common User Access Advanced Interface Design Guide. IBM Corp. SC 26-4582.

Li C S, Pollitt A S & Smith M P (1992) Multilingual MenUSE for Searching Bibliographic Databases: A feasibility study of Japanese MenUSE. School of Computing & Mathematics, The Polytechnic of Huddersfield, Research Report no. 92/1, March 1992

National Library of Medicine (1990a) Medical Subject Headings, Tree Structures, 1990

National Library of Medicine (1990b) Medical Subject Headings, Annotated Alphabetic List, 1990

Pollitt A S (1986) A rule-based system as an intermediary for searching cancer therapy literature on MEDLINE. in Davies R (ed) Intelligent Information Systems: Progress and

Prospects pp82-126, Place of publication : Ellis-Horwood.

Pollitt A S (1987) An Expert Systems Approach to Document Retrieval. Information Processing and Management, Vol 23, No 2, pp119-138.

Pollitt A S (1988) A common query interface using MenUSE - a Menu-based User Search Engine. 12th International Online Information Meeting, Vol II, pp 445-457, London, December 1988.

Pollitt A S (1990) Intelligent interfaces to online databases. Expert Systems for Information Management, Vol 3 No 1, pp 49-69.

Shneiderman B (1987) Designing the User Interface - Strategies for Effective Human Computer Interaction. Place of publication : Addison Wesley.

Thompson D (1971) Interface Design for an Interactive Information Retrieval System, Journal of the American Society for Information Science,Vol 22 pp361-373.

Appendix

SECTION A. - THESAURUS TERMS AND ROUTES

1. - Public domain software.
Computer software - techniques and systems -> computer software -> public domain software.

2. - Law administration.
Business and administration -> law administration.

3. - Natural sciences computing. (Broad term)
Natural sciences -> natural sciences computing.

4. - Smalltalk listings.
Other applications -> complete computer programs -> more computer programs -> smalltalk listings.

5. - Multiprogramming (Broad term).
Computer software - techniques and systems -> computer software -> systems software -> multiprogramming.

6. - Logic arrays.
Circuits and devices -> logic circuits -> logic arrays.
OR
Circuits and devices -> digital circuits -> logic circuits -> logic arrays.

7. - Parallel architectures (Broad term).

Logic design and digital techniques - > distributed processing - > parallel architectures.

OR

Logic design and digital techniques - > distributed processing - >
multiprocessing systems - > parallel architectures.

OR

Analogue and digital systems - > multiprocessing systems - > parallel architectures.

OR

Computer software - techniques and systems - > computer systems - >
systems software - > multiprogramming - > parallel architectures.

OR

Logic design and techniques - > computer architecture - > parallel architectures.

8. - Home computing.

Other computing - > personal computing - > home computing.

9. - Algol 68.

Computer software - techniques and systems - > formal languages - > algol 68.

OR

Computer software - techniques and systems - > programming languages - > algol 68.

10. - Code division multiple access.

Data communication equipment and techniques - > protocols - >
code division multiple access

OR

Analogue and digital computer systems - > multi-access systems - >
code division multiple access.

SECTION B. - TITLE -> CONCEPT TRANSLATION AND ROUTES

1. - A digital optical implementation of RISC.

Logic design and digital techniques - > signal processing - >
optical information processing.

Logic design and digital techniques - > signal processing - >
optical information processing - > optical-logic.

Logic design and digital techniques - > computer architecture - >
reduced instruction set computing.

2. - A specification based approach to maintenance.

Computer software - techniques and systems - > computer software - >
software engineering - > formal specification.

Computer software - techniques and systems - > computer software - >
software engineering - > software maintenance.

Computer software - techniques and systems - > programming - > object-oriented programming.

Computer software - techniques and systems - > specification languages.

3. - Object oriented analysis.

Computer software - techniques and systems - > programming - > object-oriented programming.

Computer software - techniques and systems - > computer software - > software engineering.

Computer software - techniques and systems - > systems analysis.

4. - Knowledge directed query processing in expert database systems.

Computer software - techniques and systems - > Knowledge based systems.

Computer software - techniques and systems - > Knowledge based systems - > expert systems.

Computer software - techniques and systems - > database management systems - > deductive databases.

Information science and documentation - > information retrieval.

5. - Knowledge based desktop publishing with expertpage.

Computer software - techniques and systems - > Knowledge based systems.

Other applications - > desk top publishing.

6. - Indexing and compressing full text databases for cd rom.

Information science and documentation - > information analysis - > indexing.

Information science and documentation - > information retrieval.

Computer software - techniques and systems - > file organisation - > data structures.

Computer storage equipment - > read only storage - > CD ROMs.

OR

Computer storage equipment - > optical storage - > CD ROMs.

Logic design and digital techniques - > signal processing - > data compression.

7. - Multilingual indexing and retrieval in bibliographic systems.

Information science and documentation - > information analysis - > indexing.

Information science and documentation - > information analysis - > thesauri.

Information science and documentation - > information retrieval.

Information science and documentation - > information retrieval systems - > bibliographic systems.

Other applications - > humanities data processing - > language translation.

8. - Software tools for students in higher education.

Computer software - techniques and systems - > computer software.

Other applications - > social sciences computing - > educational computing.

Other applications - > software packages.

9. - An intelligent geographic information system - IGIS-1.

Computer software - techniques and systems - > file organisation - > data structures.
Computer software - techniques and systems - > file organisation - > deductive databases.
Computer software - techniques and systems - > user interfaces.
Computer software - techniques and systems - > knowledge based systems.
Computer software - techniques and systems - > programming languages - > prolog.
Computer software - techniques and systems - > natural languages.
Other applications - > Geographic information systems.

10. - FTP-file transfer program.

Computer software - techniques and systems - > file organisation.
Data communication equipment and techniques - > computer networks.

ISIR: An Integrated System for Information Retrieval

Yonggang Qiu
Department of Computer Science
Swiss Federal Institute of Technology (ETH) Zurich, Switzerland

Abstract

In this paper, we will present an Integrated System for Information Retrieval ISIR. ISIR is an experimental Information Retrieval (IR) system serving as a testbed for the integration of modern (IR) methods. Our first approach allows the user to issue queries as weighted descriptors. ISIR is connected to a commercial database service (Data-Star) containing millions of information items. The current version of ISIR establishes automatically a Data-Star session and submits Boolean queries that have been derived from the weighted query descriptors which may be put together by means of the information structures. In order to help the user formulate queries, an interface to various thesauri is available, which can help the user browse through the thesauri in three different views. ISIR is based on the X-Window and X-Widgets.

1 Introduction

Many commercially available IR systems have been in operation for a long time. They have very useful extensive databases covering a wide range of subject areas. The commercial database service *Data-Star* developed by Radio Schweiz AG is one of the successful IR systems which consists of more than hundred databases, e.g., INSPEC, MEDLINE, etc. Each database contains millions of documents. The current searching system is, however, based upon very traditional IR principles, and as a result, is difficult to use and not suitable for processing queries precisely. Since Data-Star is well established and contains a great deal of crucial information, an experimental IR system incorporating modern IR methods to access the Data-Star databases is under development.

When users use IR systems to retrieve information items, it might be hard for them to formulate queries expressing their information needs. Using search terms which are too broad in queries may not help them find relevant items. Generally, the quality of the output provided by an IR system is related to the number of appropriate search terms. The retrieval effectiveness can be improved by using more precise search terms. For these reasons, thesauri which describe terms and relationships between the terms are integrated into our system [STR86] and a graphical thesaurus browser to various thesauri is provided. Different kinds of thesauri, e.g., ERIC [ERI87], INSPEC [INS88] and MeSH [MES89], are in use in ISIR. These thesauri have their own formats. Supporting different interfaces for the different format thesauri will inconvenience the user. In order to use the same tool to browse through the thesauri, we convert the thesauri into a common format without loss of important information.

There are many well-known drawbacks in conventional Boolean retrieval systems [RAD88], [LOS88]. ISIR allows the user to issue a query as weighted descriptors. The weighted query is translated into Boolean queries by representing every Boolean expression as a disjunction of conjunctions called Elementary Logical Conjuncts (ELCs) [ARN62], [FRE91]. An ELC contains every search term either positive or negative. The set of documents resulting when an ELC is submitted as a query to a Boolean IR system is called the answer set of the ELC. Since the documents in the answer set of an ELC are similar with respect to the search terms, we could assume that documents in the same answer set have a similar meaning. Therefore, the ranking of the set of retrieved documents can be substituted by ranking the ELCs according to the similarities between the ELCs and the weighted query.

The remainder of the paper is organized as follows. We first describe different thesauri (e.g., INSPEC and MeSH) and how they can be browsed through in the same way. We then present the retrieval methods. Section 4 shows ISIR's functions and architecture and the user interface. Finally, we conclude with the features of ISIR and future works.

2 Thesauri

2.1 Thesauri and Their Formats

A thesaurus describes a set of terms and relationships between the terms. The thesaurus can be constructed either manually or automatically. In information retrieval, thesauri are used for the following purposes:

1) manual indexing;
2) automatic indexing;
3) finding additional search terms for the users;
4) being used by a retrieval function.

Here, we concentrate on the third function. In a traditional IR system, the user may have difficulty finding appropriate search terms to compose (or enhance) her/his query. Usually, the user needs a specialist who helps when formulating a query. Since the thesaurus specifies a set of terms with their meanings and the term dependencies between the terms, the user can easily find appropriate search terms when a thesaurus browser is available. The user can pick up terms from a thesaurus to strengthen the queries. Before describing the thesaurus browser, we first study the formats of thesauri.

In our system, three thesauri ERIC [ERI87], INSPEC [INS88] and MeSH [MES89] are used. The thesauri offered by various information centers have different formats. The format of INSPEC is shown as Fig. 2.1. It shows the different fields with their codes.

420	Thesaurus Term
422	'Used for' Term(s)
424	Scope Notes
430	Narrower Term(s)
440	Broader Term(s)
450	Related Term(s)
460	Top Term(s)
470	Related Classification Code(s)
480	Prior Term(s)
481	Date of Introduction

Fig. 2.1: The format of the INSPEC thesaurus

The format of ERIC is similar to the format of INSPEC (for details see [ERI87]). The MeSH thesaurus is more complex and contains a more detailed description than the INSPEC thesaurus. It consists of the MeSH main headings and subheadings and chemical terms. The format of the MeSH main headings is shown as Fig. 2.2 which shows the different fields with their codes.

MH MeSH Heading (Descriptor)
MS MeSH Scope Note
BX Backward Cross Reference(s) with Cross Reference Type(s)
FX Forward Cross Reference(s)
MN MeSH Tree Number(s)
AN Annotation
AQ Allowable Topic Qualifiers (Subheadings)
DA Date of Entry
OL On-line Note
HN History Note
PI Previous Indexing
... Other information about the descriptor (term)...

Fig. 2.2: The format of the MeSH thesaurus

The Backward Cross Reference (BX) identifies "used for" terms (when the cross reference type is 1), narrower terms (when the cross reference type is 2) and related "referred from" terms (when the cross reference type is 3) of the term. The Forward Cross Reference (FX) identifies related "designation" terms of the term (The Forward Cross Reference directs the user from a term to a related term usually in a different category or subcategory in the tree structures [MES89]). From a structural point of view, both the BX with type 3 and the FX specify the related relationships between the terms. The MeSH tree number is the alphanumeric string that designates the position of the term in the tree structures (for details see [MES89]). The hierarchical relationships between the terms can be derived from the MeSH tree numbers. An example entry of MeSH is shown in Fig. 2.2.1.

MH SOCIAL WORK
MS The use of community resources, individual case work or group work to promote the adaptive capacities of individuals in relation to their social and economic environments; includes social service agencies.
BX SOCIAL WORKERS::1
SOCIAL SERVICE::1
FX COMMUNITY HEALTH SERVICES
MN I1-880-792
N2-421-849
AN SPEC: SPEC qualif CATALOG: /geog /form
AQ CL EC ED HI IS LJ MA MT OG SN ST TD
OL use SOCIAL WORK to search SOCIAL SERVICE back thru 1966
HN 78; was SOCIAL SERVICE 1963-77
......

Fig. 2.2.1: An example entry of the MeSH thesaurus

From INSPEC, ERIC and the points made about the MeSH thesaurus, we can follow that there remain only three kinds of relationships between the terms. They are synonymous (used for, use), related and hierarchical (broader and narrower) relations. Therefore, we can convert thesauri into a common format in order to be able to use the same tools. We call the format *thesaurus browser format.* It consists of two parts, *relation part* which specifies the relationships between terms and *information part* which describes the meanings and other information about the terms. The format is shown in Fig. 2.3 and Fig. 2.4.

The reason to store the tree numbers of the MeSH thesaurus is that some domain experts know the tree structures quite well and they would like to browse through the MeSH thesaurus by the tree numbers. Moreover, we can display the tree structures by using the tree numbers. Converting the INSPEC thesaurus into the thesaurus browser format is simple. The fields 420, 422, 430, 440, and 450 are converted into the relation part of the thesaurus browser format of

```
'T'   Term
  'F'   Used For Term1
        ...
        Used For Termf
  'R'   Related Term1
        ...
        Related Termr
  'B'   Broader Term1
        ...
        Broader Termb
  'N'   Narrower Term1
        ...
        Narrower Termn
  'M'   Tree Number1
        ...
        Tree Numberm
or
'T'   Term
  'U'   Use Term
or
'M'   Tree Number
  'T'   Term
```

Fig. 2.3: The relation part of the thesaurus browser format

```
'T'   Term
  'S'   Scope Note
  'A'   Annotation
  'Q'   Allowable Topic Qualifiers (Subheadings)
  'D'   Date of Entry, or Date of Introduction
  'O'   On-line Note
  'H'   History Note
  'P'   Top Term(s)
  'I'   Previous Indexing, or Prior Term(s)
  'C'   Related Classification Code(s)
  ... other information about the term ...
```

Fig. 2.4: The information part of the thesaurus browser format

the INSPEC thesaurus. The fields 420, 424, 460, 470, 480 and 481 are converted into the information part of the thesaurus browser format of the INSPEC thesaurus. In the following subsection, we describe the translation rules converting the MeSH thesaurus into the thesaurus browser format.

2.2 Converting the MeSH Thesaurus into the Thesaurus Browser Format

From the format of the MeSH thesaurus described in the last subsection, we know that the MH paragraph identifies a term t_i and only BX, FX and MN paragraphs draw the relationships between the term t_i and other terms. Since the hierarchical structures of the MeSH thesaurus can be derived from the tree numbers, the backward cross references with type 2 are redundant and ignored. For consistency [SCH89], a term t_j with the "use" relationship to the term t_i, which has a "used for" relationship to t_j, is added to the thesaurus. In order to map a tree number to a term quickly, an index on the field tree number is built into the thesaurus. Therefore, we can have the following translation rules from the MeSH thesaurus format into the thesaurus browser format for the relations:

MH	fi	'T'
BX (type: 1)	fi	'F'
BX (type: 3)	fi	'R'
FX	fi	'R'
MN	fi	'M'
f (MN)	fi	'B' and 'N'

MH ti BX(type:1) tj	⇒	'T' tj 'U' ti
MH ti MN tn	⇒	'M' tn 'T' ti

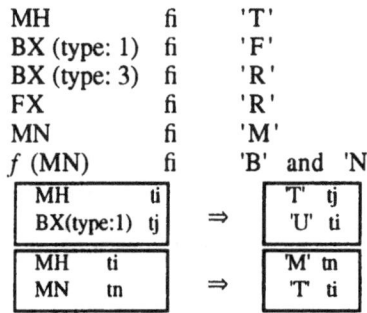

Fig. 2.5: Translation rules for the relations

In Fig. 2.5, f is a function which maps a tree number of a term into broader and narrower terms of the term. A term t_k is a broader term of the term t_i if and only if the tree number of t_k is a substring of the tree number of t_i and t_k is located only one level higher than t_i in the tree structures. The location level of a term can be calculated from the tree number of the term. For example, the term "SOCIOLOGY" with the tree number "I1-880" is a broader term of the term "SOCIAL WORK" with the tree number "I1-880-792". Conversely, A term t_k is a narrower term of the term t_i if and only if the tree number of t_i is a substring of the tree number of t_k and t_k is located only one level lower than t_i in the tree structures.

Other fields of the MeSH thesaurus are converted into the information part of the thesaurus browser format. The translation rules are shown as Fig. 2.6:

MH	fi	'T'
MS	fi	'S'
AN	fi	'A'
AQ	fi	'Q'
DA	fi	'D'
OL	fi	'O'
HN	fi	'H'
PI	fi	'I'
......		

Fig. 2.6: Translation rules for the information

With a common format, the same browsing software can be applied to different thesauri. Therefore, a user can browse through the MeSH thesaurus and the previously mentioned ERIC and INSPEC thesauri using the same thesaurus browser (see Section 4).

3 Retrieval Methods

3.1 Boolean Retrieval

The commercial database service Data-Star is based on Boolean logic. In our system, we also provide a facility for Boolean retrieval. A Boolean query is a Boolean expression of search terms or term stems combined by operators (e.g., "and", "or", "not", "xor", "same", "with" and "adj"), and parentheses. The retrieval status value for the Boolean query q and the document d_j is:

$$RSV(q, d_j) = \begin{cases} 1 & \text{if } d_j \text{ satisfies the Boolean query q} \\ 0 & \text{otherwise} \end{cases} \qquad (1)$$

3.2 Weighted Retrieval

There are many well-known drawbacks in conventional Boolean retrieval systems [LOS88], [RAD88]. First of all, the search terms in a query cannot be expressed in a weighted way. Users need to know the Boolean logic, otherwise they cannot formulate queries expressing their information needs. Even search specialists often complain the difficulty of formulating Boolean queries. Secondly, Boolean retrieval systems divide the document collection into two sets, the set of retrieved documents (answer set) and the set of not retrieved documents. Documents in the answer set are not ranked. If the queries are formulated by using too broad search terms, the answer set will be too large. Finally, it is impossible for the systems to incorporate automated, efficient relevance feedback process.

Experiments show that the assignment of weights to terms can improve ranking results and the retrieval effectiveness [SAL88]. A weighted query q is represented by a vector q = $(a_1, a_2, ..., a_m)$. A document d_j is represented by a vector $d_j = (b_{1j}, b_{2j}, ..., b_{mj})$. Here, the a_is and b_{ij}s imply the importance of the index terms (t_is) in the query q and the document d_j, respectively, and m is the number of terms in the collection. The retrieval function we use here is the simple scalar vector product:

$$RSV(q, d_j) = \sum_{i=1}^{m} a_i \cdot b_{ij} \qquad (2)$$

ISIR is built to be connected to the Boolean retrieval system Data-Star which does not support term-weighting schemes. Not even the term frequencies are available. Hence, our system provides the following 3 simple optional term weighting schemes for the query terms.

∂_{q1}) The weight of search term t_i indicated by the user is assigned to the query vector q:

$$a_i = \begin{cases} weight_u(t_i): & \text{if } t_i \text{ is a search term in the weighted query q} \\ 0: & \text{otherwise} \end{cases}$$

∂_{q2}) Since the well-known inverse document frequency (idf) can be used to improve the retrieval effectiveness, the inverse document frequency is taken into account for weighting the term:

$$a_i = \begin{cases} weight_u(t_i) \cdot idf(t_i): & \text{if } t_i \text{ is a search term in the weighted query q} \\ 0: & \text{otherwise} \end{cases}$$

∂_{q3}) $idf(t_i)$ is assigned to the query vector q. The user does not have to determine the weight for the term:

$$a_i = \begin{cases} idf(t_i): & \text{if } t_i \text{ is a search term in the weighted query } q \\ 0: & \text{otherwise} \end{cases}$$

where:

$weight_u(t_i)$ represents the weight of search term t_i indicated by the user;

$idf(t_i) = \log(\frac{|D|}{df(t_i)})$ is the inverse document frequency,

$|D|$ is the number of documents in the collection D,

$df(t_i)$ is the number of documents $d \in D$ containing t_i.

Two optional weighting schemes for the document terms are given:

∂_{d1}) The existing binary weighting scheme in the Boolean retrieval system is used:

$$b_{ij} = \begin{cases} 1: & \text{if } t_i \text{ is a term in the document } d_j \\ 0: & \text{otherwise} \end{cases}$$

∂_{d2}) $idf(t_i)$ is used to approximate the weight of the term t_i in the document d_j:

$$b_{ij} = \begin{cases} idf(t_i): & \text{if } t_i \text{ is a term in the document } d_j \\ 0: & \text{otherwise} \end{cases}$$

The weighting schemes for the query terms ∂_{q1}) - ∂_{q3}) and for the document terms ∂_{d1}) - ∂_{d2}) are combined for evaluating the similarities between queries and documents. There are six possible combinations. With the weighting schemes, the retrieval function in formula (2) can be rewritten as formula (3):

$$RSV(q, d_j) = \sum_{(t_i \in q) \text{ and } (t_i \in d_j)} a_i \cdot b_{ij} \qquad (3)$$

As Data-Star is unable to process weighted queries directly, they are translated into Boolean queries. Using Boolean algebra, every Boolean expression can be represented as a disjunction of conjunctions called Elementary Logical Conjuncts (ELCs) [ARN62]. Hence, our system translates a weighted query automatically into ELC queries [FRE91]. The set of documents resulting when an ELC is submitted as a query to a Boolean IR system is called the *answer set* of the ELC. The documents in the answer set of an ELC are indistinguishable with respect to the search terms. More precisely, all the documents retrieved by the same ELC contain all the positive search terms and none of the negated (NOTed) search terms in the ELC. It is clear that the documents retrieved by the same ELC have the same retrieval status value in accordance with the formula (3). Therefore, the ranking of the documents can be substituted by ranking the ELCs according to the weights of the ELCs with respect to the weighted query. The weight of an ELC_k with respect to the weighted query q is calculated as follows:

$$\sum_{t_i \in q} a_i \cdot b_{ik} \qquad (4)$$

where, a_i is same as above and b_{ik} is given as follows:

∂_{d1})

$$b_{ik} = \begin{cases} 1: & \text{if } t_i \text{ is a positive term} \\ 0: & \text{if } t_i \text{ is negated} \end{cases}$$

∂_{d2})

$$b_{ik} = \begin{cases} idf(t_i): & \text{if } t_i \text{ is a positive term} \\ 0: & \text{if } t_i \text{ is negated} \end{cases}$$

The ELCs can be ranked according to their descending weights before the ELC queries are submitted. The ranked ELCs are then sequentially submitted to Data-Star until the number of retrieved documents is at least equal to the number the user requested.

4 ISIR System

4.1 Architecture

The architecture of ISIR is shown as Fig. 4.1.

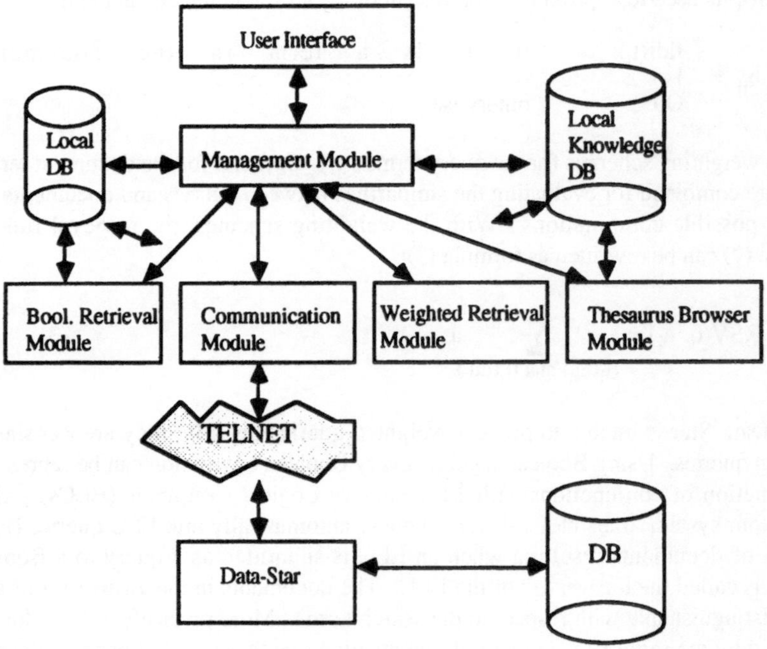

Fig. 4.1: Architecture of ISIR.

The Management Module is the main body of the system. It coordinates the requests issued by the user and also deals with any special requests and messages arriving from any of the remote connections. It starts and manages the processes that handle the individual remote connections.

Boolean Retrieval, Weighted Retrieval, Thesaurus Browser and Communication Modules are the modules for the individual applications.

The Local Database manages the storage and retrieval of queries, result lists and retrieved documents. It is also used to reduce the data to be transferred to improve the performance.

The Local Knowledge Database manages the storage and retrieval of information structures: thesauri and concept spaces, application profiles, etc.

The User Interface allows fast and independent response to user actions with requests and responses being exchanged with the Management Module.

The current version of ISIR has the following functions:

1) automatically log into and log out the Data-Star via TELEPAC or TELNET;
2) browse through thesauri in different views, including the semantic view;
3) process Boolean queries;
4) process weighted queries;
5) support effective help for the user.

4.2 Thesaurus Browser

The thesaurus browser module is self-contained. With the thesaurus browser, the user can browse through as many thesauri as she/he wants simultaneously in different windows. The thesaurus browser also allow the user to browse through a thesaurus in different views, original text, alphabetical order and semantic views simultaneously in different windows. The tree number in MeSH defines a unique tree structure which can be displayed. The user can pick up terms and/or tree numbers from the thesauri as search terms to compose (or enhance) queries. The semantic view of the MeSH thesaurus is shown in Fig. 4.2. Here, the current term is "SOCIAL-WORK". The term occurs in two different positions in the tree structures. The tree number of the term is "I1-880-792" in one position and "N2-421-849" in another position. It has a broader term "SOCIOLOGY" in the first position and a broader term "HEALTH-SERVICES" in the second position. The terms in the two positions refer to the same narrower term "SOCIAL-WORK-PSYCHIATRIC". If a term occurs in more than two positions in the tree structures, the button "<<" and ">>" can be used to scroll the broader and narrower terms. The user can browse through a thesaurus by (typing in and) highlighting a term (or tree number) anywhere and then clicking the button "Select_Term" (or "Select_TreeNumber").

4.3 The User Interface for Weighted Queries

Using ISIR, the user can pop up a window shown in Fig. 4.3 for weighted queries. He can move the mouse to where terms and their weights may be specified, or pick up the terms from a thesaurus to formulate queries, then "submit" to the Data-Star and "show" the retrieved documents. The "options" button can be used to change the retrieval algorithm to be applied to the weighted queries (see "Algorithm:" field in Fig. 4.3). It is also used to set the number of documents to be retrieved (see Fig. 4.3, where it is set to 25), and to choose the displayed paragraphs of the retrieved documents (see "Paragraph:" field in Fig. 4.3). Here, the search terms are RELEVANCE, FEEDBACK, TERM, FREQUENCY and INFORMATION-RETRIEVAL. Their weights indicated by the user are 1.0, 0.7, 0.2, 1.0 and 0.1, respectively. The top first ranked document with the title "Experiments with a component theory of ..." is displayed in the window. When using the interface, the user can easily reformulate the query by picking up terms from the displayed documents or deleting terms from the term subwindow.

Fig. 4.2: Semantic view of the MeSH thesaurus

5. Conclusions

The design and implementation aspects of ISIR have been presented in this paper. In summary, it has the following main features:

- The system can automatically log into and log out from the Data-Star.
- Information structures (thesauri) are integrated into the system. The user can browse through different kinds of thesauri in different views via the same thesaurus browser, and find additional search terms to enhance her/his queries.
- The system provides a facility for weighted retrieval. By using the system, the user can easily formulate queries without knowing the complicated Boolean logic to access the Data-Star databases which contain much crucial information.

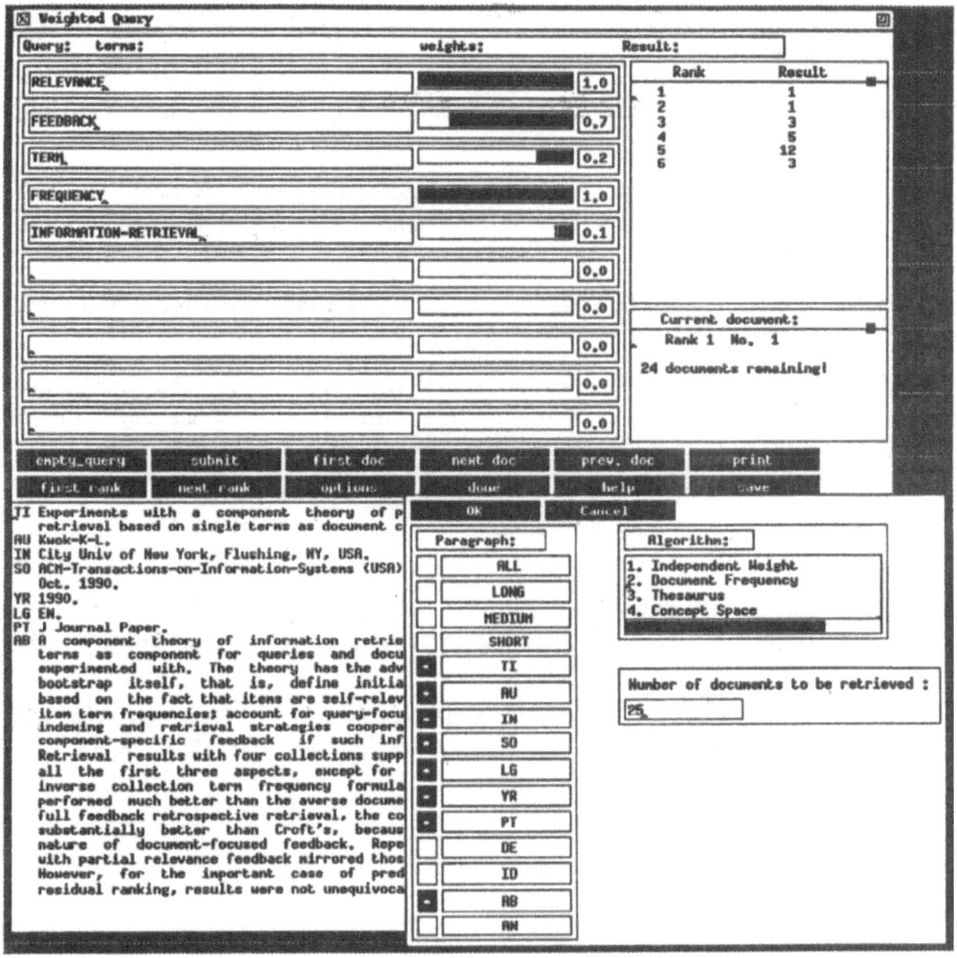

Fig. 4.3: Weighted query window.

We are going to study and integrate more modern IR methods. The integration of relevance feedback and information structures into IR algorithms and the improvement of information structures by using relevance information will be studied.

Acknowledgements

I would like to thank Prof. H.P. Frei for guiding and helping me; Dr. P. Schäuble and S. Meienberg for comments, ideas and discussions.

References

[ARN62] Arnold, B.H., *Logic and Boolean Algebra.* Englewood Cliffs, NJ: Prentice-Hall, 1962.

[ERI87] *Thesaurus of ERIC Descriptors.* Oryx Press, Phoenix, Arizona, 1987.

[FRE91] Frei, H.P., Meienberg, S., Evaluating Weighted Search Term as Boolean Queries. *Informatik-Fachberichte*, Nr. 289, pp. 11-22, Springer-Verlag, Berlin, 1991.

[INS88] *INSPEC Thesaurus*. The Institution of Electrical Engineers, Herts SG5 1RG, U.K., 1988.

[LOS88] Losee, R.M., Integrating Boolean Queries in Conjunctive Normal Form with Probabilistic Retrieval Models. *Information Processing & Management*, Vol. 24, No. 3, pp. 315-321, 1988.

[MES89] *Medical Subject Headings*. National Library of Medicine, Bethesda, Maryland, 1989.

[RAD88] Radecki, T., Trends in Research on Information Retrieval - The Potential for Improvements in Conventional Boolean Retrieval Systems. *Information Processing & Management*, Vol. 24, No. 3, pp. 219-227, 1988.

[SAL88] Salton, G., Buckley, C., Term-weighting Approaches in Automatic Text Retrieval, *Information Processing & Management*, Vol. 24, No. 5, pp. 513-523, 1988.

[SCH89] Schäuble, P., *Information Retrieval Based on Information Structures*. D.Sc. Thesis ETH, No. 8784, Reihe Informatik-Diss. Nr. 15, vdf-Verlag, Zürich, 1989.

[STR86] Strong, G.W., Drott, M.C., A Thesaurus for End-User Indexing and Retrieval, *Information Processing & Management*, Vol. 22, No. 6, pp. 487-492, 1986.

WING: An Intelligent Multimodal Interface for a Materials Information System

Jutta Marx, Stephan Roppel
Linguistic Information Science
University of Regensburg, Germany
P.O. Box 10 10 42
W-8400 Regensburg
Tel.: ++49 941 943 3588
Fax.: ++49 941 943 2305
e-mail: roppel@vax1.rz.uni-regensburg.dbp.de

Abstract

The development of a prototypical multimodal interface in the domain of materials databases is described. The project WING-IIR focusses on a blending of the two natural modes of interaction, natural language and direct manipulation and a combination of different retrieval-strategies. Multimodality is seen as the key to avoiding the inherent disadvantages of the individual modes. Besides the question of multimodality the integration of intelligent help components and techniques of Intelligent Information Retrieval form another main point of interest.

1 Introduction

The following paper deals with the empirically derived integration and coordination of multiple retrieval strategies based on Direct Manipulation and Natural Language interface techniques. The development of a prototypical multimodal interface in the domain of materials databases is the goal of the project **WING-IIR** (**W**erkstoff**I**nformationssystem mit **N**atürlichsprachlicher/ **G**raphischer Benutzeroberfläche und **I**ntelligentes **I**nformation **R**etrieval [= Materials Information System with Natural Language/Graphical User Interface and Intelligent Information Retrieval]) of the Linguistic Information Science Department, Regensburg University, granted by the German Ministry for Economics.

2 Methodology and Application Domain

The scientific aim behind our multimodal approach is to combine the two basic modes Human Computer Interaction (HCI) favoures today: graphical user interfaces and natural language. However, analysing these two basic modes covers only part of the decisions and components necessary for human computer interaction (HCI). The problem of database search can - independently from the chosen modality - be modelled in completely different ways, e.g. as a mapping of cognitive task structures or on the basis of a computer centered data model (e.g. SQL). Thus in WING-IIR several different types of interaction have been taken into account and combined instead of two basic modes only.

In addition to the development of an adequate user-interface ideas from the domain of Intelligent Information Retrieval should be considered in the context of improving materials information systems as a whole (cf. Krause 1992). The terms 'IIR' (cf. Brooks

1987, Croft 1987) or 'expert systems for information retrieval' (cf. Hawkins 1988) articulate the intention to make accessible ideas, methods and techniques of AI. IIR means to improve traditional information systems by adding AI components like user modelling or active help systems and its integration should be considered parallel to the design of the interface itself.

Decisions of how to combine different search modes in an interface of a given application domain depend heavily on empirical results. Therefore we adopted a rapid prototyping strategy, iteratively testing and redesigning versions of the interface.

Within WING-IIR, our industrial partner is MTU GmbH (Motor and Engine Union), a major manufacturer of aircraft engines and heavy Diesel motors. Since 1988, a department of MTU is responsible for building up and servicing a relational database containing facts on relevant materials, especially nickel and titanium alloys (cf. Womser-Hacker 1990). This database has been implemented in DB2 under the operating system MVS on a central mainframe computer. Our interface prototypes are based on a structurally complete subset of this database. It contains about 30 tables with data on some 200 materials and 2.000 sets of measurement data, the structure of which can be described in terms of its level of generality:

a) General information covering essential properties of a certain material, also providing a great deal of textual information,

b) Specific measurement data gained from materials tests and containing great amounts of data series on nineteen different material properties, e.g. stress-strain curves or information on high cycle fatigue.

The database is used for various tasks (materials selection, damage analysis or cost calculations) by different departments of MTU (as a whole about 40 users), a fact that points to the need to adapt the interface to different groups of database users.

3 'Natural' Interaction Modes: Graphics and Natural Language

One of the basic ideas in WING-IIR is the combination of 'natural' modes of interaction, namely graphics and natural language. Even though there are several ways these two modes may be actually implemented, a brief discussion of their general characteristics should precede the presentation of the different database access types in WING-IIR.

3.1 Natural Language

The 'naturalness' of natural language interaction is established by the fact that the need to learn new ways of interacting, as in command-oriented systems, is eliminated by the user's familiarity with language interaction.

However, no natural language interface covers the whole range of human communication. Thus the question is, whether the partial solution designed for WING-IIR´s NL-interface meets the requirements of the actual retrieval situation. In the worst case the advantages of taking over knowledge from human communication get lost, if the handling of the implemented language subset requires learning and recalling efforts comparable to those of formal-language alternatives.

Tests of a simulated natural language component have already shown that materials experts, when talking to the computer, use natural language utterances different from those in human communication. These 'computer talk' phenomena have been confirmed empirically for the domain of materials data (cf. Marx 1991, Krause 1991). They are being considered in the necessary modifications of the present natural language input component (cf. Oesterle/Wenger 1989).

3.2 Graphical User Interfaces (GUIs)

Apart from the use of icons, pull-down menus, and windows the strengths of GUIs are characterized by two features: underlying metaphors and direct manipulation (cf. Shneiderman 1982). However, the analogical nature of metaphors implies that every metaphor will at some point be violated. The electronic world is equal to the real world only in so far as there are analogies with a lot of details that help the user in becoming familiar with the functions of the software.

Both primary modes for the design of 'natural' user interfaces have implicit deficiencies that can't be avoided, given the present state of the art in system development as well as theoretical considerations. A reasonable combination of these two modalities, however, might eliminate parts of their respective weaknesses.

4 Types of Interaction in WING-IIR

Though our working hypothesis is that natural language and GUIs should serve as the core of a multimodal database interface, we tested several modes of interaction, the most of which include at least some elements of one of the two basic modalities. Almost any style of interaction may be embedded in a GUI and it is often hard to judge whether the advantages e.g. of a GUI-based hypertext system rely on the hypertext features as such or stem from the working environment of the GUI in general.

Different access modes have first been developed and tested in parallel. This parallel development was restricted to the first stages of prototyping, where the tests of the single modes disclosed their respective strengths and weaknesses and provided the basis for the blending of the different query modes.

The single modes considered in WING-IIR are:

1) **Hierarchically organized search paths**
2) **Hypertext structures**
3) **Cognitively motivated interface structuring**
4) **Query-By-Example**
5) **Natural language interaction**
6) **Formal Language (SQL)**

4.1 Hierarchical Search Paths

The present form of access to the MTU-database is built upon a hierarchical structure. A query is made up by a sequence of individual selections from menus. Both, entrypoints into the network of relations between generic and specific terms and the ordering of query stages are determined by the system. Different types of materials names constitute the bottleneck which every user must pass in order to access materials data.

4.2 Hypertext Relations

Since information concerning specific materials and their properties is contained in the database on different levels and in different contexts (overview vs. measurement data), it seemed promising to connect these levels by means of a hypertext tool. The functional kernel of a hypertext based interface are links between detailed and condensed types of information in a so-called datasheet, a typical information medium of materials experts.

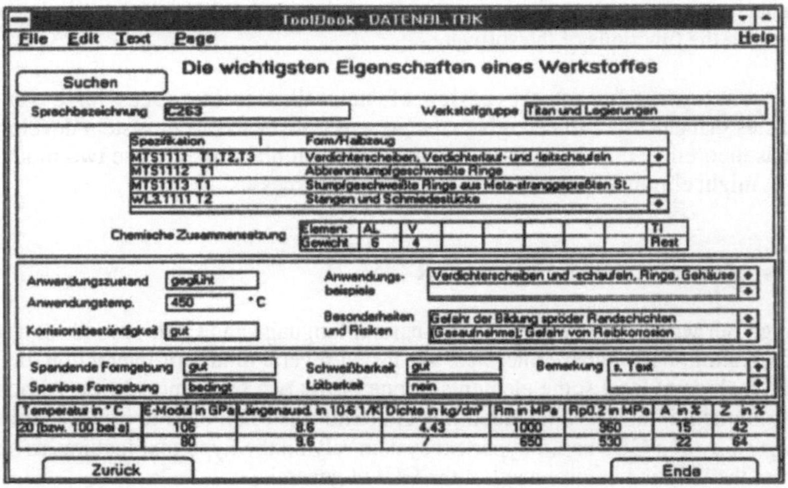

Fig. 1: The Datasheet offering Hypertext-Links

4.3 Cognitively Motivated Interface Structuring

Cognitively motivated interface structuring tries to choose the users' view of the application domain as the starting point for design: Potential problem patterns of materials experts were analyzed, using data from an empirical study on materials database users (cf. the literature and test protocols cited in Wolff 1990). The resulting functional query options that match with the expert problem solving patterns form the structure of the cognitive graphical query mode. The following problem types were modelled:

a) naming problems
b) information about specific materials (already known by name),

c) search of materials by specification profile,
d) display of general properties of materials,
e) comparison of materials.

Search type e) in particular underlines the idea of modeling an interface according to the users' cognitive representation of the domain. The user simply selects the materials and specifications to be compared from two lists into a search matrix. A conversion of this cognitively adequate process into an equivalent SQL-query is a highly complex task unlikely to be solved as easily by non-expert users.

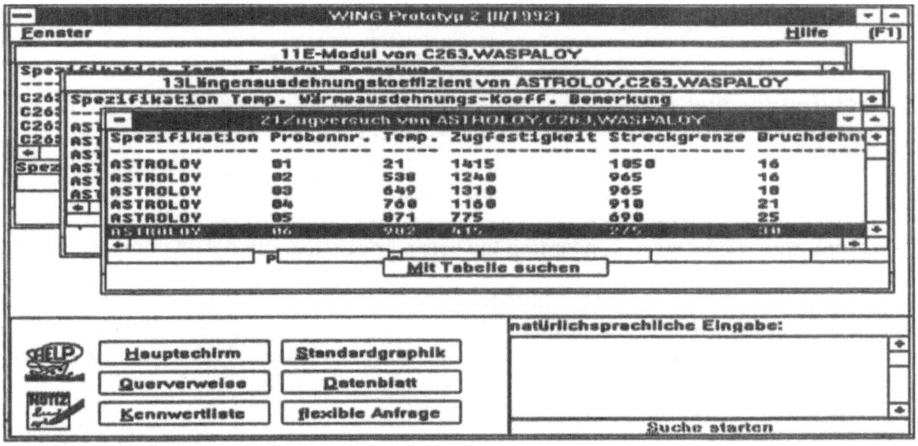

Fig. 2: the result of a materials comparison

4.4 Natural Language

NL-access in WING-IIR allows the users to formulate queries in their native tongue (in this case, German) without having to adapt to conceptual violations caused by system functionality, nevertheless certain restrictions (grammatical correctness, no vague expressions like "higher", "better") have to be observed.

As the DCG-based natural language interface, developed by the Centre for Information and Language Science at Munich University (cf. Wenger/Oesterle 1989), is only currently being adapted to the application domain, this access mode was tested in a hidden operator experiment where a human expert simulated the computer.

4.5 Query-By-Example (QBE)

Since tables containing materials facts are the main content of the database, the QBE mode, where the information need has to be entered into a query form determined by the database table structure (cf. Zloof 1975), was also tested.

5 Prototyping and Empirical Testing

After the preliminary prototyping phase the different access modes were tested separately. User tests on a larger scale were carried out for the cognitively structured, the hierarchical, hypertext, and natural language mode only, as preliminary tests had shown that the other access modes were not going to be integrated into the multimodal prototype on a large basis.

The results obtained determined the role of the single modes and the way of combining them in the multimodal prototype. The first multimodal system itself has been tested only recently and is currently being adapted again according to the findings of the last test.

5.1 Test Design and Testing

Ten MTU materials experts from different departments and with different technical background tested the systems. Each test consisted of three phases:

- a pre-search interview, concerning the user's prior experience with computers and the database in question
- the test itself: The users were introduced to the system and asked to solve typical problems as well as prefabricated tasks, using the 'thinking aloud' technique.
- a post-search interview during which the subjects were asked to comment the systems tested.

Since the natural language parser has not yet been adapted, both the previous stand-alone version and the component that forms part of the actual multimodal prototype were simulated in a hidden-operator experiment.

5.2 Test Results

Among the single modes tested, the cognitive-graphical mode was considered most adequate because its structure and interface offered the broadest and most natural adaptation to the functional needs of the materials domain.

The hierarchical system was favored by users exclusively looking for data of specific materials already known because of clear system guidance and their familiarity with this query structure.

As to hypertext, the easy access to textual information was considered an advantage. Experts praised the high flexibility of the system in general, although it doesn´t support clear-cut retrieval strategies.

The natural language system (the simulated 'ideal parser') was judged to be adequate for novice users in particular because no special knowledge is necessary. Syntactic as well as lexical peculiarities of the materials-domain could be determined.

6 The Multimodal Prototype

These results provided the basis for the construction of a multimodal system integrating each mode's most advantageous features into a powerful user interface along the following lines:

The functional structure of cognitive-graphical access mode serves as the basic working environment of the interface. It offers a good adaptation to the different retrieval problems of materials experts.

Hypertext functionality is not globally available but exclusively employed where nonlinear association of textual information is appropriate or links can be interpreted unambigously. This is especially the case for relating general information, collected in the datasheet, to specific measurement data in property-tables.

In spite of the hierarchical access mode's limited retrieval-capabilities, its high level of system-guidance provided by a stepwise construction of queries was taken as a design guideline throughout the system.

Query by example can be used as a follow-up query-technique, where previous results have been presented as tables.

The natural language component is employed on different levels and for several tasks: on the one hand the user is presented with a seperate window, where natural language input with syntactical and lexical restrictions is possible, on the other hand direct-manipulation input in certain query-windows can be completed by means of natural-language formulations, e.g. parameters for a profile search.

The integration of a (commercial) document retrieval component using descriptors and boolean logic may become important as the database will be extended and contain greater portions of (long) texts.

Although formal language access (e.g. SQL) has been ruled out as a significant part of a multimodal interface for the cognitive overhead of learning a formal language, additional (graphically supported) formal language facilities may be included as an adaptable add-on component for expert users.

A preliminary evaluation of the test of the first multimodal prototype confirms the chosen coordination of the cognitively-based, hypertext and QBE modes, although some software-ergonomic adjustments are still necessary. Natural language was rarely used as an independent input mode, in most cases the test persons employed language only when entering certain parameters in graphical query windows. The reluctance to use natural language as an input mode for complete query formulation stems from the users´

unwillingness to type long portions of texts, a fact that could only be remedied by the integration of speech recognition instead of merely parsing typed input.

7 Intelligent Help Components

The development of cognitively adequate interfaces designed according to the standards of software ergonomy does not dispense with the need to provide the users with help in problematic situations that are caused by the complexity of the interface itself or task-specific problems. Therefore, parallel to the design of the interface, an adaptive active help system WINGHELP (cf. Obermaier/Roppel 1991) providing suggestions of how to improve or continue a dialog has been integrated into the prototype. Additionally, suggestions for the integration of processes that offer domain specific help based on domain knowledge and query context have been worked out and will be added after the next stage of prototyping. Both, the interaction and the domain specific help components employ techniques developed in the context of AI and can be subsumed under the notion of Intelligent Information Retrieval

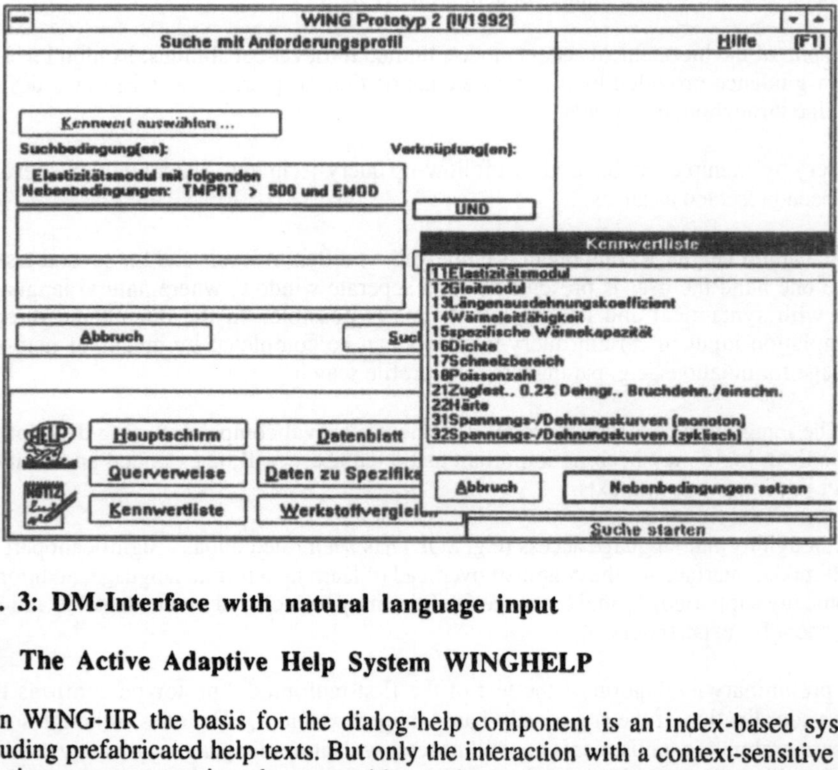

Fig. 3: DM-Interface with natural language input

7.1 The Active Adaptive Help System WINGHELP

In WING-IIR the basis for the dialog-help component is an index-based system including prefabricated help-texts. But only the interaction with a context-sensitive and adaptive component, using plan recognition to detect the user´s goals, allows for help in situations, where the user is unaware of his problems or unable to express his needs.

During work with the materials information system WINGHELP observes the user's actions and associates them with predetermined user plans. Possible plans might be "Comparison of two materials" or "Entering the parameters for a profile search", typical actions are e.g "Activate dialog box x" or "Choose item y from the presented list". The plans match the functional structure of the interface and have also been confirmed empirically by user tests. The user's action-sequences are classified as optimal, incorrect or inefficient, relative to the underlying plan. At the same time potential misconceptions to be corrected by help-messages are detected.

There are two cases for WINGHELP to intervene in the dialog: In case the user requests help during the interaction, WINGHELP offers help specific for the recognized plan, usually information of how to continue successfully from the present state to fulfill the plan. With no plan actually recognized, the main index of the passive help-system is presented.

The actual structure of the prototype - typical problem patterns are modelled as functional units - facilitates plan-recognition and the user tests showed that situations where the user had not made a mistake but did not know the next steps to accomplish a plan are likely to be the most frequent occasion for providing help.

In case the user's action are assessed as incorrect or obviously inefficient WINGHELP automatically intervenes with a help-message that mentions the reasons for the interruption, corrects misconceptions and offers viable alternatives.

In both cases the user can directly access extended information concerning the actual plan and actions mentioned in the help-message.

7.2 Task-related Help Components

Besides context-sensitive help that deals with the dialog component of the interface an intelligent information system must also incorporate components that provide the user with task-specific help, taking into account the actual query content, as well as drawing on information about previous query formulations, database-context and domain knowledge.

On the one hand such processes may already support the user during the phase of query formulation, on the other hand they may provide him with viable alternatives in response to an unsatisfactory query-result.

To illustrate the first case - supporting the query formulation - the system will, in contrast to a merely syntactical process, check whether numerical conditions concerning materials properties are compatible with general domain-knowledge, with other conditions previously entered or match with limits set by database-content. As another example, the parameters that determine the comparability of different materials (e.g. measurement conditions) could be provided before actually starting the process of materials comparison. In these examples, domain-knowledge, query-context as well as database-contents are employed to guide the user in building a consistent and promising query.

Given a consistent query-formulation the search result may still not contain the data specified by the user, because it is not available as such in the database. Such "gaps" are very frequent in the case of materials, as hardly any material has entries for all properties theoretically provided by the database.

In those cases the system should try to help develop strategies for retrieving similar or adjacent data or adjusting the query in such a way as to broaden the scope of search.

Similarity between materials can be defined on different levels by materials science as the criteria for adequate and allowable substitutes depend very much on the application context and the user´s goals. Again, domain-knowledge has to be combined with information from query context and a user model, in order to give intelligent support to the user.

The development of task-related retrieval aids as discussed in this section will build on the plan recognition methods that have so far been employed in WINGHELP. The building of a domain knowledge base concerning mainly the problem of gaps and similarity as well as a generic user-model will be done in close cooperation with the MTU materials department.

8 Implementation

The prototype is implemented using MS-Windows SDK and Asymetrix ToolBook in a PC / MS-Windows 3 environment, connecting different modules by a DDE-communication. It serves as a front-end to the relational DBMS SqlBase, the knowledge-based components will be implemented in KAPPA-PC.

9 Outlook

Multimodality seems to be a viable design principle for information systems in complex application domains. The test and integration of different access modes for a materials information system reveals the effects and benefits of multimodalitiy in a real word application. A first multimodal prototype, supplemented by intelligent help components, has been developed and tested and will undergo further prototyping.

In the future, graphical query techniques, allowing the user to formulate his problem by manipulating property charts, and components of intelligent information retrieval will complement the multimodal system.

Bibliography

AAAI (ed.) Workshop Notes from the Ninth National Conference on Artificial Intelligence (AAAI-91). Workshop on Intelligent Multimedia Interfaces, Anaheim/CA., July, 15, 1991.

Bauer, G. (1991). Überlegungen und Vorschläge zur Verbesserung des Umgangs mit der mtu-Datenbank auf der Basis von IIR-Verfahren. Regensburg University, Linguistic Information Science, project WING-IIR, research paper 11, January 1991.

Brooks, H. M. (1987). Expert Systems and Intelligent Information Retrieval. Information Processing & Management, Vol.23 No.4, 367-382. Vol.23 No.4, 249-254.

Hanne, K.H., Hoepelman, J.P. (1988). Man Computer-Interfaces Combining Graphic- and Natural Language-Interaction. In: Bullinger et al. (eds.). EURINFO '88. Proceedings of the First European Conference on Information Technology for Organisational Systems. Athens, Greece, Amsterdam et al. S. 410-415.

Hawkins, D. T. (1988). Applications of Artificial Intelligence (AI) and Expert Systems for Online Searching. Online, Jan., 31-43.

Krause, J. (1990). Zur Architektur von Wing: Modellaufbau, Grundtypen der Informationssuche und Integration der Komponenten eines intelligenten Information Retrieval. Regensburg University, Linguistic Information Science, project WING-IIR, research paper 7, October 1990.

Krause, J.; Bauer, G.; Lutz, J.; Roppel, S.; Wolff, C.; Womser-Hacker, C. (1990). WING - The Research Prototype of a multimodal Materials Information System, Comprising Natural Language- Graphical/Direct Manipulation and Knowledge Based Components. In: Herget, J.; Kuhlen, R. (edd.) Pragmatische Aspekte beim Entwurf und Betrieb von Informationssystemen. Proc. 1.International Symposion on Information Science, Konstanz, Germany, Oct. 17-19 1990. (= Konstanzer Schriften zur Informationswissenschaft Bd.1)

Krause, J. (1991). The Combination of two "natural" modes of human-computer interaction: natural language and graphics. In: AAAI (1991), 47-52

Krause, J. (1992). Intelligentes Information Retrieval. Rückblick, Bestandsaufnahme und Realisierungschancen. In: Kuhlen, R. (ed.). Festschrift für Gerhard Lustig. Konstanz: Universitätsverlag (= Konstanzer Schriften zur Informationswissenschaft Bd.3).

Marx, J. (1991). Benutzertests zur natürlichsprachlichen Komponente von WING-IIR. Testaufbau, Ergebnisse und Anforderungsprofil für den Parser. Regensburg University, Linguistic Information Science, project WING-IIR, research paper 18, October 1991.

Marx, J.; Roppel, S.; Wolff, C. (1991). Der erste multimodale Systementwurf für den WING-Prototyp. Regensburg University, Linguistic Information Science, project WING-IIR, research paper 21, December 1991.

Obermaier, C.; Roppel, S. (1991). WINGHELP. Eine aktive adaptive Hilfekomponente für den Prototypen WING eines multimodalen Werkstoffinformationsystems.

Regensburg University, Linguistic Information Science, project WING-IIR, research paper 16, July 1991.

Oesterle, J.; Wenger, C. (1989). Abschlußbericht für das Projekt 'Natürlichsprachliche Zugangssysteme zu Werkstoffdatenbanken'. Universität Tübingen, Seminar für Natürlichsprachliche Systeme.

Schmauks, D., Reithinger, N. (1988). Generierung multimodaler Ausgabe in NL Dialogsystemen - Voraussetzungen, Vorteile und Probleme. Universität des Saarlandes, SFB 314 (XTRA), Memo Nr. 24.

Shneiderman, B. (1982). The future of interactive systems and the Emergence of Direct Manipulation. Behaviour and Information Technology 1, 237-256.

Tyler, S.W.; Schlossberg, J.L.; Cook, L.K. (1991). "CHORIS: An Intelligent Interface Architecture for Multimodal Interaction." In: AAAI (1991), 99-106.

Wolff, C. (1990). Die graphische Benutzeroberfläche des Forschungsprototyps WING und der kognitiv-graphische Zugangsweg WING-KOGRA.. Regensburg University, Linguistic Information Science, project WING-IIR, research paper 5, July 1990.

Wolff, C. (1991). Der Prototyp 2 des kognitiv graphischen Zugangswegs von WING-IIR. Regensburg University, Linguistic Information Science, project WING-IIR, research paper 17, July 1991.

Womser-Hacker, C. (1990). Die Motoren- und Turbinen-Union als Anwendungsbereich von WING-IIR. Regensburg University, Linguistic Information Science, project WING-IIR, research paper 1, June 1990 [with the cooperation of W. Buchmann, mtu].

Zloof, M.M. (1975). "Query by Example". In: AFIPS National Computer Conference, No. 44. New York. 431-437.

Dialogue Management in a Pragmatics-Based Natural Language Information System

William J Black,[1] Nancy Underwood, Kristiina Jokinen and Hamish Cunningham

Centre for Computational Linguistics,
UMIST,
UK.

Abstract

This paper reviews the problem of providing pragmatic based natuarl language interaction. A system is introduced, DIAL, which aims to provide this form of interaction by paying close attention to the concept of robustness and working within the framework of pragmatic principles developed by Grice.

1 Introduction

Natural language access to computer-based information systems has been the subject of experimentation for some 25 years, and of commercial software products for ten, but with the same failure to fulfil promise that characterises other natural language applications like machine translation. Early systems such as Rendezvous and LIFER recognized the importance of the design goal of robustness, and of some pragmatic dialogue phenomena such as ellipsis, but totally ignored linguistic generalisations. Work in the 1980s pursued the opposite tendency: Since computationally-oriented linguistic formalisms were beginning to mature, many seemed to propose that better grammars would suffice to produce effective natural language interfaces. It was sometimes argued that human users were more intelligent and adaptable than computers, so there was no need to build fail-soft or ergonomic features into query systems. However, it is our contention and that of our partners in the PLUS project[2] that natural language interfaces will not be acceptable unless they are robust, and they cannot be made robust without due attention to the principles of pragmatics.

The goal of the PLUS project is the production of a robust natural language dialogue system integrating linguistic and non-linguistic knowledge in a principled way, based on the pragmatics theories of Grice and Searle, and using results in knowledge-base management systems and logic programming for the maintenance of dynamic contextual knowledge bases.

The principal characteristic of such a system is robustness in a wide range of situations: the system should be capable of dealing with extragrammatical input (such as 'elliptical' fragments and misspellings), and flexible enough to allow a real dialogue with the user. In order to demonstrate the capabilities of the PLUS system on a realistically sized application, an interactive Yellow Pages Information Service has been chosen as the demonstrator.

These robustness problems can very well be tackled in a non-pragmatic way. For example, a spelling corrector can be invoked in a context-independent way, as it is in a word processor, but this will generate many nonsensical corrections, as well as missing

[1] We gratefully acknowledge the financial support of Brother International PLC and of the Commission of the European Communities' ESPRIT programme (Project No. P5254).

[2] CAP Gemini Innovation, Paris, CAP Gemini SCS, Hamburg, Omega Generation, Bologna, and the universities of Bristol, Gothenburg, Paris (LIMSI), Pisa, and Tilburg (ITK).

completely cases where a misspelling has produced a different but unintended word. Similarly, ellipsis can be tackled in a non-pragmatic way, by seeking to pattern-match on the syntactic or semantic representation of a previous sentence. From a pragmatic point of view, however, elliptical utterances are not deviant or vestigial, and in a dialogue are perfectly appropriate to the situation.

The approach taken to the construction of a pragmatic natural language understanding system in the PLUS project is based on a fruitful interaction of theory, empirical study, and software design. In this paper, we report work done to date along the way, in each of these aspects.

2 Theory

The principal theoretical claim in PLUS is that language understanding and use is not just an act of decoding, encoding or translation, but of rational purposive action exactly like non-linguistic action. This notion is based on the theory of the Co-operative Principle by Grice and developed by Allwood in his theory of Communication Activity theory (Allwood 1976, 1984).

Grice's work is of course only the stimulus for a great deal of more recent efforts at explaining communication in rational terms. Some work, such as that of Leech (1983) has explored further maxims of the same general nature. Other recent work, such as Sperber and Wilson (1986) has attempted to be more reductionist, seeking to replace the set of maxims with a single principle of relevance. Allwood's theory of Linguistic Communication as Action and Co-operation (1976, 1992) extends Grice's notion with a more thorough account of communication at various levels, *viz:* contact, perception, understanding and evoked attitudes, and gives an explanatory account of communication following from general principles of rationality, motivation, agency, etc. combined with a linguistic analysis of the semantic content of utterances including those that are described in other theories as having pragmatic but not semantic content (Allwood, Nivre and Ahlsén, 1992).

Grice's Co-operative Principle (CP) provides a basis for an explanatory account of the principles on which everyday linguistic communication operates. Grice proposed four maxims under the CP: *quality* (be truthful), *quantity* (or an economy principle - say as much but only as much as is needed to communicate the message), *manner* (politeness), and *relation* (an utterance must have a perceivable relation with its predecessors in a discourse)

An example of his is the following short dialogue between two strangers:

(A) My car is out of gas.
(B) There's a gas station around the corner.

Quantity, quality and relation are all at work in this example dialogue between A and B. By the maxim of Quality, the above conversants can be said to communicate that A intends B to believe that A's car is out of gas, and that B intends A to believe that B believes there is a gas station around the corner.

However, much more is communicated even in such a trivial dialogue. For example, B indicates to A that he has accepted a task of helping A to rectify A's lack of gas, that he believes the gas station around the corner to be open, and that he presumes it is shared knowledge that a gas station sells gas, etc. This list of inferences could be extended still further, but they suffice to indicate the principles behind what Grice calls a 'conversational implicature.' This is the name he gives to an inference which is not simply based on deductive laws and explicitly asserted premises, but on such contextual sources as accumulated beliefs about the dialogue partner that have arisen during the conversation, background knowledge, and the Gricean principles themselves.

B's utterance has to be relevant to A's, for it to make sense as communication under the CP. This is what entitles A to implicate that B indeed believes the garage to be open, and the implicature is confirmed via the quantity maxim - since the implicature is derivable, it is not necessary to add "and I believe it is open, and I expect you could buy some gas there."

The status of maxims is often a subject of confusion: Grice's explanation of them is often read as a set of moral imperatives, but this is not the case. He intended the maxims of conversation subsumed by the CP to be read as Kantian preconditions for communication to be possible at all. For example, the Maxim of Quality, is rendered 'be truthful'. This should not be interpreted as a prescriptive rule of behaviour, but rather as an observation that if people did not behave truthfully when talking most of the time, communication would be impossible, and even occasional lies could not work.

To operationalise the notion of an implicature, we need at least the following elements in an architecture for a pragmatic natural language understanding system: a *knowledge base* of generally known facts and relations about the external world that will be conversed about, a *contextual model* which will store, amongst other things, beliefs of the system about the dialogue partner and some *attentional organisation* so that the system deals with initiatives it has not yet responded to fully in an appropriate sequence.

3 Software Design

The various theoretical accounts of rational communication, supported by analysis of the dialogue corpus show the necessity of both background knowledge of the the external world and a dynamic contextual model of the mental states of the dialogue partner. These elements are reflected in corresponding functional components and knowledge bases in the software architecture. They also clearly influence the kinds of analysis (and generation) that are appropriate ways of handling linguistic events in the system. A more conventional approach to the construction of a database interface is to view the problem as one of translation to a query language, which is then evaluated against an extensional database or a knowledge base. Typically, a logical form is computed compositionally by annotating grammar rules and lexical entries with semantic information, and the content part of such a representation is directly mapped to attributes in the database. The crucial difference in a pragmatics-based system is that a literal meaning computed in this way does not exhaust the meaning of a message to the system. We therefore compute not just a literal meaning of the utterance, but also the attitudes (beliefs and intentions) of the dialogue partner. Some of these are derivable from the literal meaning directly, but further implicated attitudes can also be derived taking into account the context.

Besides the constant modelling of the attitudes of the dialogue partner, another important aspect is the dialogue status of utterances, for example as an initiative or response, clarification question, etc. For example, an initiative places an obligation on an addressee to respond or at least acknowledge, and in the exchange structure of utterances in dialogue, we observe that the topic of both the initiative and response in an exchange remain identical. Given that we model attitudes, it can be argued that some of this analysis of dialogue structure is redundant, but one important use of a hierarchical record of the exchange structure is that it constrains the search for dialogue antecedents for referring expressions and elliptical utterances, from amongst all the attitudes.

One important aspect of a natural language component is the workload needed to integrate natural language interaction in a new application. For some NL systems everything has to be re-built from lexicon to semantic representation and semantic evaluation.

The PLUS architecture clearly differentiates what is specific to the language (lexicon, grammar), what is specific to the application (application model) and what is independent of both language and application (basic knowledge), such as conversational rules and deductive mechanisms. This minimises the cost of building a new application. Only the part specific to the application needs to be developed. Language specific components and basic knowledge need only extensions or additions. This modularity reduces also the cost of adding a new language to the capabilities of the system, making the evolution towards a multilingual tool feasible.

3.1 Architecture

The functional architecture is arranged as indicated in Figure 1. One thing this clearly shows is that the natural language engine is designed as a completely isolated part of the system, which has its own linguistic resources, but is not integrated with the pragmatic interpretation parts of the system. Another, not mentioned in the theoretical discussion is the KBMS. It is intended that the context model as well as the world model is managed in a KBMS known as CML (Stanley, 1987), which was developed earlier by a member of the consortium (Haidan and Meyer, 1990) in an earlier project. This is an object-oriented conceptual modelling environment supported by reasoning tools capable of supporting non-monotonic updates of knowledge bases, as well as abductive reasoning (a method of dealing with implicatures that is being actively pursued in the project, and attitudes modelling. Not all of these reasoning tools were available in CML at the outset of the project, but the PLUS project is motivating extensions to the reasoning tools that we expect to be of wider interest.

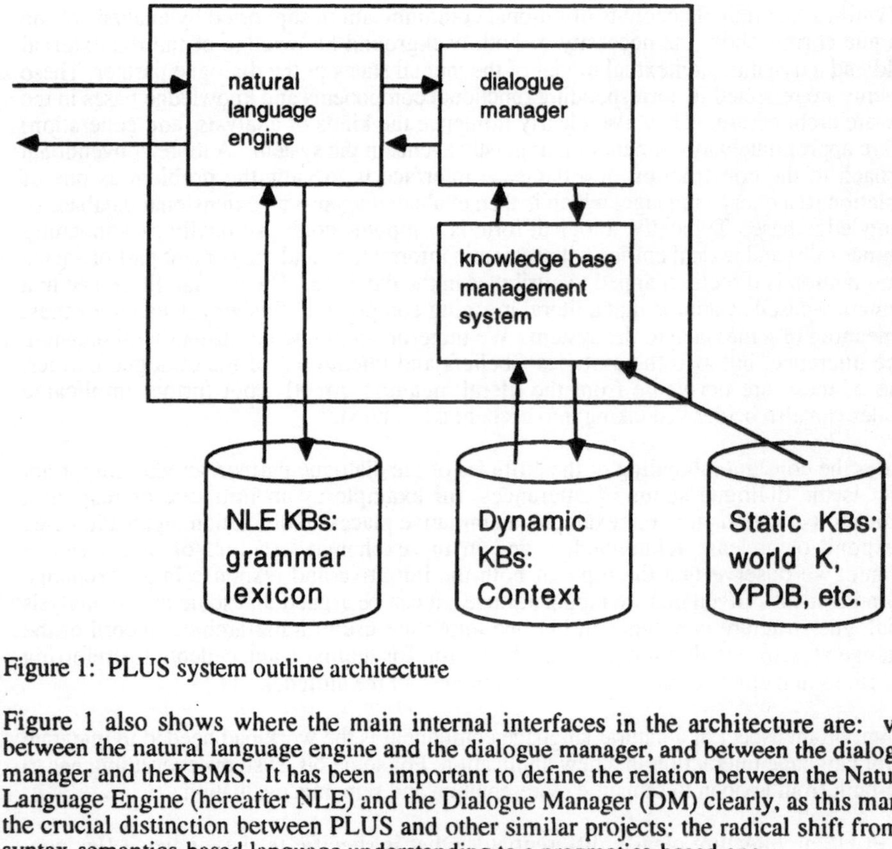

Figure 1: PLUS system outline architecture

Figure 1 also shows where the main internal interfaces in the architecture are: viz. between the natural language engine and the dialogue manager, and between the dialogue manager and theKBMS. It has been important to define the relation between the Natural Language Engine (hereafter NLE) and the Dialogue Manager (DM) clearly, as this marks the crucial distinction between PLUS and other similar projects: the radical shift from a syntax-semantics-based language understanding to a pragmatics-based one.

It is proposed that ideally the NLE would operate symmetrically with respect to analysis and generation. This means that the static data stored in the knowledge bases could be the same for both tasks: the NLE would use the same grammar and dictionary for parsing and generation. The formalism being used for this purpose in PLUS is HPSG (Pollard and Sag, 1987). The grammar and the dictionary are 'private' to the NLE, and the other KBs (including the remaining static knowledge bases and the dynamic knowledge bases) are private to the DM, via its Problem Solver interface.

The Dialogue Manager is further decomposed into three principal subcomponents, and the Natural Language Engine into two. These are:
in the Dialogue Manager, the Cognitive Analyser (CA), the Goal Formulator (GF) and the Response Planner (RP); and in the Natural Language Engine, the Parser and Surface Generator.

3.2 The Natural Language Engine

The main distinguishing feature of the parser from the type widely described in the literature of natural language interfaces is that we require it to produce a rather underspecified yet still formal literal semantic and pragmatic meaning representation, in particular abstaining from such operations as spelling correction, sense disambiguation, pronoun resolution, modifier and quantifier scope disambiguation, because these all belong to the domain of contextual, pragmatic, analysis. The mirror image of this, in the surface generator, is that the latter accepts a relatively complete specification of the form and content of the generated utterance, exercising no real choices, which are all made in the pragmatic component: the Response Planner (RP),which deals with theissues that belong to both strategic and tactical generation as usually described. The surface generator is therefore able to use much of the recently reported work on generation from logical form with unification grammars, and not require the more complex procedural notions of the more traditional systemic generators.

3.3 The Dialogue Manager

The Cognitive Analyser is responsible for all interpretation of the utterance of the dialogue partner, including inferring the user's intentions and beliefs. The Goal Formulator is responsible for deciding on a strategy for responding, including making enquiries from the Yellow Pages database in order to have the information to respond, and determining what kind of dialogue act is an appropriate way to respond. The Response Planner is responsible for what is described as both Strategic and Tactical Generation in the literature, including rhetorical planning, anticipating implicature and presupposition derivation, sequencing, partitioning into linguistic units, focusing, sentence type choice and planning of referring expressions (not necessarily in that order).

3.4 Cognitive Analyser

The cognitive analyser can be conceptualised as a function from 'literal meanings,' background knowledge states and contexts to contexts. Thus its inputs include all the knowledge bases in the architecture with the exception of the natural language engine's grammar and dictionary. The dynamic KBs that comprise the context, being updated during the dialogue, are the dialogue history and the belief model.

The task of the Cognitive Analyzer is to find the most relevant utterance meaning to the context, using its world knowledge (which for the present discussion we will regard as subsuming the application-specific knowledge). The CA analyses the dialogue partner's turn in accordance with the dialogue grammar and pragmatic rules, and tries to find out the communicative intention of the dialogue partner who used the particular expression.

The output of the CA is a set of new system beliefs that are to be incorporated into the Attitudes Model. The output of the CA thus goes to the contextual knowledge bases and triggers the knowledge base updating procedures.

The internal structure of the Cognitive analyser is based on the elaboration of the meaning from literal to contextual in what can be conceived as three stages. Firstly, the content part of the meaning has to be mapped from the literal predicates of the literal meaning logical form language to the conceptual level language. Secondly, the intended pragmatic force must be determined, and finally additional implicatures/inferences are derived as necessary for the coherent incorporation of the new beliefs into the Attitudes Model.

3.5 Goal Formulator

The goal formulator decides what to do next at a given moment of the dialogue. It plans the strategy of responding to the communicative act of the dialogue partner utterance. It has an ultimate goal that is determined by the application model (in the YP application: 'give a name/address/telephone number to the user'), and it solves the problem of how to reach the ultimate goal within the limits given by the world model and the current, updated dialogue history and belief model, assuming the Gricean maxims of quality and relevance. The goal formulator plans the steps or sub-goals to attain the main goal. It 'knows' about the preferences among the sub-goals, and relying on general problem solving techniques, it passes the selected goals with an indication of priority to the Response Planner.

The Goal Formulator maps from a context to a specification of system goals. The input is a knowledge base representing the context derived from the application of the output of the Cognitive Analyser to the previous context (the "initial context"). This represents the context as created by the dialogue partner input (the "amended context").

The output is a specification of a new goal context representing a state of affairs the system will strive to reach. The difference between the amended context and the goal context represents the system's goals as determined by the effect of the dialogue partner input on the initial context. These goals are output to the Response Planner.

3.6 Response Planner

The RP is responsible for planning the literal meaning of the next system utterance in reaction to the current dialogue situation. It also has access to the results of the Goal Formulator's enquiries to the Yellow Pages Database. This computation incorporates the following functions: Planning, critiquing of plans, evaluation of effects on dialogue partner, deep generation and dialogue history update. The effects and needs of the Response Planner implies that it can access the all knowledge sources excluding the application database.

3.7 KBMS

The operational KBMS is built using a CML (Haidan and Maier, 1990) subsystem which permits access to a set of loaded knowledge bases (generated by the CML Support System) and perform the operations needed by the PLUS system.

A given data base can be interfaced to a KB such that part of the factual knowledge in this KB physically resides in the data base but can be accessed by the same KBMS access operation that are used for the knowledge bases. This mechanism is used to interface the Yellow Pages Data Base to the Application KB for retrieval of its factual contents.

On top of the basic functions of query and update of knowledge bases (with consistency checking), a set of higher level meta-reasoning mechanisms are built, including abduction, temporal reasoning, planning, reasoning about beliefs, tracing and explanation.

Meta reasoning is used as well to access and reason about different KBs, their informational contents and their interrelations e.g. compatibility of knowledge contained in them or capability to help solving a given problem. It is based on concepts of provability and mutual knowledge.

As well as the internal reasoning mechanisms, the KBMS service has well-defined interfaces both to the Dialogue Manager and to the application database.

4 Empirical Study

4.1 Corpus Collection and Analysis

Corpus collection and analysis has been carried out within the PLUS project to provide relevant information for the design of system components and to provide useful information for test and evaluation of the resulting system. The above dialogue is an idealised version of one of the actual dialogues (with the place names changed), which we are using as a focus for the design and construction of the first prototype of the system at an early stage in the project (the 18th month of 48).

In the corpus collection task, dialogues were collected in three languages, partly because of the commercial interests of some partners in the project, and partly because of our interest in how much pragmatic reasoning is independent of language and cultural norms. The languages concerned are English, French and Swedish.

Dialogue type was also varied: human-human dialogues were collected for contrastive purposes, but the majority of data collected and analysed was of so-called Wizard-of-Oz terminal dialogues, where the subject interacts through a terminal with what he believes to be a computer system. This is the closest we can reasonably get in an empirical experiment to the kind of dialogue that will be possible with the completed system.

Scenarios were given to the subjects to prompt them to search for information in the areas of the Yellow Pages that we had prepared information about, and which were agreed as the subject matter of the initial world model for at least the first prototype system. The scenarios chosen were car hire, restaurants, and personal insurance.

The dialogue corpora collected in PLUS are first subjected to a preliminary analysis and subsequently to a more detailed analysis within the work packages devoted to pragmatics, natural language engine and knowledge base management.

Analysis of the dialogues with regard to pragmatic phenomena gives useful information for designing such components as dialogue grammars and rules of conversation. Analysis of syntactic and semantic aspects of the corpora is being used in designing the parts of the system analyzing and generating language, specifically in producing grammars and lexica. Information from the corpus analysis has also contributed to the modelling of the application.

4.2 A Sample Dialogue.

The following dialogue is one that was derived from the corpus collection work. It has been simplified for expository purposes, to focus on the essential pragmatic phenomena the PLUS system deals with.

PLUS(1): Welcome to the Pages Jaunes information service.
How may I help you?

USER(2): I need a car for tommorrow afternoon.

PLUS(3): Do you want to rent or buy one?

USER(4): rent

PLUS(5): In which area?

USER(6): Atalante

PLUS(7): Where is Atalante?

USER(8): In Rennes

PLUS(9): There are 30 car rental companies in Rennes.
Here are the first 5.

....

This dialogue shows a number of the distinctive ways in which the PLUS system analyses its inputs and plans its own responses. You may have noticed the misspelling in USER(2). The PLUS parser has no problem with this because it is designed to cope with content words not in its lexicon. A literal meaning is computed whereby need, car, tommorrow and afternoon are all predicates. When the analyser of contextual meanings takes over, it does not find a mapping to a concept in the world knowledge base for the literal predicate tommorrow, and it finds two concepts for car (the second as in restaurant car).

The kind of contextual and background knowledge that the system uses to derive contextual meanings includes the background knowledge that the system believes that the user believes the system is only able to supply telephone directory information, and not for example to book hire-cars directly. This enables a contextual meaning to be derived as follows:

INTEND(U,BELV(U,SETOF(X,$XŒCompany:$YŒCar:supplies(X,Y)))

in other words, the user intends to know (believe) the value of the set of companies that supply cars. (The notation is simplified, but illustrates the essentials. The actual formalism being used in the project is a development of EL/F, described in Bunt, 1985). In the world model, supply is a generalisation of such actions as sell, rent etc., which does not map directly to a directory heading. In passing, we also note that the problem with interpreting tommorrow did not even need to be resolved, since the time of the needing of the car is irrelevant to the provision of the information. (Of course it could have been relevant in a case like a courier service).

As well as updating the attitudes model with both the more literal interpretation concerning the need for a car, and the derived interpretation about the want of information about companies, we must also update the dialogue structure record to show an initiative, with the above propositional content, and with topic car.

At this point, the system having interpreted the user's input, it must decide how to react. Its contextual meaning representation concerning the want of information about companies who supply cars is a logically well-formed query, but cannot be satisfied in the Pages Jaunes database, which does not have a concept of a generic car supplier. It does have service descriptions corresponding to the sale and hiring of cars. It could therefore generate a clarification question: "Which service do you want:car distributors, dealers and agents, or car and van hire services? However, we want our system to respond as felicitously as possible, and produce a response with a topic shift (McCoy and Cheng, 1991) that is clearly related to the previous utterance. Since car was the topic of USER(2), it is appropriate to generate a referring expression that relates to car in the response (and since it is a needed car rather than one already in existence, the chosen referring expression is a one-anaphor).

Successive utterances in this dialogue could be commented at equivalent length, but for reasons of space, we simply list some of the points they illustrate.

USER(4): rent - this ellipsis has to be resolved by reference to the context model's record that the most recent system goal was an intentional to know which of two actions: {buy, rent} was desired by the user;

SYSTEM(5): In which area? - the system's responses also exploit ellipsis, in this case it is sanctioned by the salience of a previous but not fully satisfied goal.

USER(6): Atalante - like USER(4), but the system's expectation was open ended.

SYSTEM(7): Where is Atalante? - Atalante is not known to the system - it isn't in the KB or database or lexicon. The system's previous goal, however, was to know the location of a desired event, so it implicates a belief that the unknown word denotes a place.

USER(8): In Rennes. - Similar to (6), but not a problem this time.

SYSTEM(9): There are .. etc. The original question was some while back, so it is appropriate to explain the content of the answers offered.

5 Conclusion

The PLUS project is currently focussed on an architecture for dialogue management that is characterised by modularity, partly so that partners at nine sites can simultaneously work on components of the system, but more importantly because of the importance we attach to general principles of pragmatic reasoning in natural language interfaces. If the architecture cannot accommodate replacement of application-specific knowledge bases and language-specific grammars and dictionaries, we will have failed to demonstrate our claims about the generality of the reasoning mechanisms at work in natural language dialogue. The present stage of the work is that the construction of a first integrated prototype is well under way, but that this prototype does not yet demonstrate all aspects of the pragmatic approach. However, it is at a relatively early stage in the life of the project and the modular architecture will allow progressive incorporation of more rational pragmatic inferencing, and also enable experimentation to reveal the true extent of redundancy between partly overlapping representations such as our attitudes model and the dialogue exchange structure.

References

Allwood, J. (1976). Linguistic Communication as Action and Cooperation. GML 2, Dept of Linguistics, University of Gothenburg.

Allwood, J. (1984). On Relevance in Spoken Interaction. In Backman & Kjellmer (eds.) Papers on Language and Literature, pp. 18-35, Acta Universitatis Gothoburgensis.

Allwood, J. (1992). On Dialogue Cohesion. Gothenburg Papers in Theoretical Linguistics 65, Dept. of Linguistics, University of Gothenburg.

Allwood, J., Nivre, J., and Ahlsen, E. (1992). On the Semantics and Pragmatics of Linguistic Feedback. In Journal of semantics 9, 1-29.

Bunt, H.C. (1985). Mass terms and model-theoretic semantics. Cambridge University Press, Cambridge, UK.

Estival, D. (1991) Declarativeness and Linguistic Theory. In: Proc. of the First In. Conf. on Knowledge Modelling and Transfer, Sophia-Antipolis, April 1991. IOS Press, Amsterdam.

Gallaire, H., Minker, J. and Nicolas, J-M. (1984). Logic and Databases: A deductive Approach. Computing Surveys, No.2, Vol.16.

Haidan, R. and R. Meyer (1990). Requirements Modelling and System Specification in a Logic-based Knowledge Representation Framework. DAIDA (P892) Project Report.

Kowalski, R.A. (1979). Logic for Problem Solving. North-Holland

Leech, G. (1983). Principles of Pragmatics. Longman, London.

McCoy, K. and Cheng, J. (1991). Focus of Attention: Constraining what can be said next. In: Natural Language Generation in Artificial Intelligence and Computational Linguistics, Eds. Paris, Swartout and Mann, pp. 103 -124, Kluwer.

Pollard, C. and Sag, I. (1987) Information-Based Syntax and Semantics. CSLI, Stanford.

Poole, D.L. and Goebel A.R. (1986) Gracefully Adding Negation and Disjunction to Prolog. Proc. 3rd Int. Conf. on Logic Programming, Springer, 1986

Sergot, M. and Kowalski, R(1986) A Logic-Based Calculus of Events. New Generation Computing, 4:57-95.

Sperber, D. and Wilson, D. (1986). Relevance. Basil Blackwell, Oxford.

Stanley, M. T. (1986) CML: A Knowledge Representation Language with Application to Requirements Modelling. PhD Thesis, Dept. of Computer Science, University of Toronto.

Performance Comparisons of Boolean and Ranked Output Retrieval

E Michael Keen,
Department of Library and Information Studies,
University College of Wales Aberystwyth,
U.K.

Abstract

This paper presents a series of experiments which compare boolean and ranked output retrieval systems. The scope of current experiments to evaulate these systems are considered and new analyses presented.

1 Introduction

Non-Boolean ranked output retrieval techniques have been explored by researchers for the last thirty years. Interactive Boolean retrieval systems have become the norm: they require the searcher to devise one or more exact match query statements using search terms and appropriate Boolean operators. Ranked output systems provide algorithms for automatically combining the supplied search terms which provide variable levels of match so that the records may be inspected in an order of decreasing match with the query. Some variable match algorithms result in a weakly ordered output with sizable groups of records matching to an equivalent level. Others use methods of weighting the terms to compute more refined match levels and give a stronger ranking. Both Boolean exact match and ranked variable match systems can incorporate relevance feedback techniques to enhance the choice of query terms.

Tests comparing the performance merit of Boolean versus Ranked systems have not been plentiful. One reason for this may be that controlling and conducting iterative and interactive Boolean search tests requires a lot of effort. Another reason may be that very few ranked output systems have gone beyond laboratory simulations to provide a user-searchable system to test. A further reason may be that comparing the retrieval effectiveness of Boolean exact match systems with ranked output variable match systems poses methodology problems of ensuring a valid and fair comparison of systems that are rather different in nature. Even in the well-defined application of a selective dissemination service Evans (1981) regarded the comparisons he attempted as unsatisfactory. Keen (1992b) used a case of Boolean versus Ranked as an example of a difficult performance comparison even though some laboratory controls were used. In spite of this the literature does contain some useful comparison tests, and reference will now be made to some of these along with some recent work conducted at Aberystwyth.

2 Comparisons Using Recall and Precision

Though the Recall and Precision Ratios do not provide an exclusively valid or complete performance metric, their use in comparisons is held still to be the most useful starting point in IR evaluation. Some eight projects have been identified which used these measures to compare Boolean and Ranked, and Figure 1 is a composite Recall/Precision graph which plots some 18 Recall/Precision pairs from these projects. Each result represents system performance either at the conclusion of the searches or at a point which is a laboratory simulation of a sensible search stopping-point. Each system pair is boxed-in on the graph to show which result set is comparable: where these lines slope upwards to the right, from the origin of the graph towards the perfect performance area of 100% Recall and Precision, the upper system is clearly describable as better that the lower one. Where the slope is the other way, one system is better in Recall but worse in Precision than the other. The results from the eight projects considered roughly in their chronological order will now be briefly commented upon and sources for full information identified.

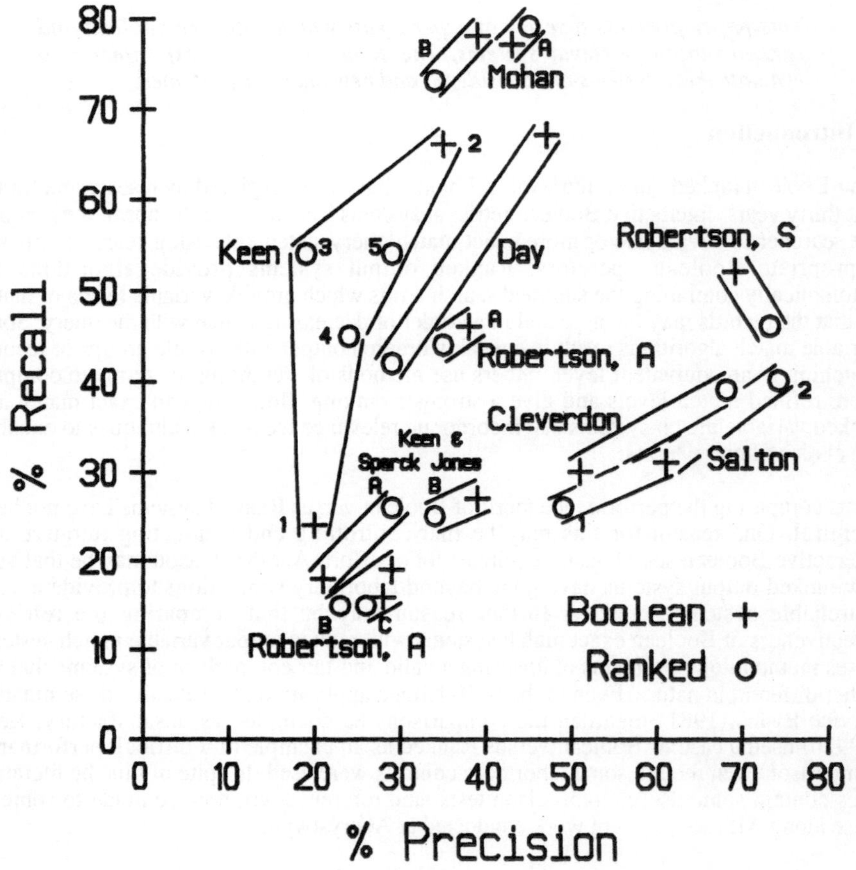

Figure 1: Composite Recall/Precision graph showing 18 comparisons of Boolean and Ranked systems from 8 named projects which are identified in the text.

The comparison marked Cleverdon was first published in 1971 but Cleverdon (1984) is the most accessible source. Some 14 selective dissemination profiles were tested on a database in precision engineering comparing Boolean and Quorum in a non-interactive batch processed system. The Quorum method was called Coordination Levels in the second Cranfield Project: it is simply an overlap score of the number of query terms which match each record, hence it provides only a very weak ranking. The result at just

Quorum level 4 is plotted in Figure 1, though there are some problems with the way this laboratory data was aggregated. However, this result showing a clear advantage for Quorum has played an important role in making people aware of the possibility that an alternative to Boolean can perform well. Two other selective dissemination services tested Quorum as well, though the data they obtained is not so readily plottable on the graph: Evans (1981) testing INSPEC found a much smaller performance gap, and Hartley, D. (1976) testing UKCIS found Boolean to be better by a large amount. Selective dissemination profiles contained many query terms, sometimes hundreds in number, and retrieval effectiveness in these circumstances may well pose a different problem to the typical retrospective query with its concise requirement in a single topic area.

Salton's SMART project has included many methods of output ranking from simple Quorum to sophisticated schemes of term weighting and feedback. Salton (1972 and 1975 page 105) reports a small non-interactive Boolean comparison with a weighted Ranked result using a thesaurus (result 1) and a relevance feedback option (result 2). These tests used a subset of MEDLARS, and Boolean performed somewhere between the two Ranked results. Two pairs of laboratory comparisons have been included from tests by Keen (Boolean) and Sparck Jones (Weighted Ranked), as described in Keen (1972 and 1981, Fig. 8.3) and Sparck Jones (1974). The passage of time has made some details unclear but Figure 1 includes results just at low Recall and high Precision. Result pair B used a more interactive Boolean scheme.

Robertson, S. identifies the results of the Cirt system developed to permit weighted feedback searching on an operational search service. Robertson, S. E. (1987) gives full details and results, and a briefer paper with no measures included is Robertson, S. E. (1990). As a front-end to a Boolean service Cirt implemented Ranking locally by sending a series of Boolean statements to cover all the combinations needed, but this did mean that Ranked searches could not contain more than about eight terms. This project used over 90 independent searches in each system and did not use matched pairs as all the other tests have done. Performance measurement used Precision and relevant retrieved, so an estimate of Recall level has been used in Figure 1. This test showed Boolean better in Recall, and Ranked better in Precision, by a small amount.

The next result by Mohan is reported in Al-Hawamdeh (1988) and used Sheffield University's INSTRUCT system to explore both Boolean and Ranked output using inverse collection frequency weights and relevance feedback. Two different methods of applying the search cutoff were tried to make this difficult comparison: result A used a method based on the Ranked result which slightly favoured that system, and result B used the Boolean cutoff as the control variable which again favoured that system. A later test using full-text paragraphs on INSTRUCT presented a similar comparison (Al-Hawamdeh 1989) with equally small differences in both directions as judged on an effectiveness measure that combines Recall and Precision. INSTRUCT was also used for the Ranked results recently obtained by Robertson, A (1990) but the Boolean system was Tome Searcher, an automated expert system front-end which constructs standard Boolean expressions from a natural language query. The three pairs of results shown are based on variants in test collection and query set, and in all cases there was a very small superiority for the automated Boolean.

The work by Day (1991) simulated Quorum on a published CD-ROM Boolean system, so the term combinations method used again limited queries to no more than eight terms. The 14 searches were done by the same person as a matched replica set. His measure of relevant retrieved has again been converted to Recall by estimation. This result shows the largest superiority for Boolean in Figure 1. In the ongoing work by Keen on Ranking by term proximity, a set of Quorum search results at all levels down to three terms was used as a benchmark for the Ranking tests, see Keen (1991a, 1991b). This work then lead to the five results plotted in Figure 1. Result 1 was a set of real Boolean searches on a commercial service (but using the same queries and dataset as the main research) conducted by a novice searcher. Result 2 was a replica set of Boolean searches repeated by an experienced searcher. Result 3 was a set of non-interactive replica searches on a Quorum search engine in which the experienced searcher simulated real searches and so applied his own stopping decisions for each search. Results 4 and 5 were both obtained by applying stopping cutoff decisions equivalent to the experienced Boolean searches to two laboratory Ranking results: number 4 was the complete Quorum results and number 5 a term proximity Ranking method. Figure 1 gives six comparisons between Boolean and Ranked: experienced Boolean is better than the three Ranked, novice Boolean is worse than two of the Ranked and has a lower Recall but better Precision than the third. A deeper explanatory analysis of three of these results will be presented in the next section, and some other more laboratory-oriented ways of presenting these new Boolean versus Ranked comparisons have appeared in Keen (1992a Table 5 and 1992b).

The overall picture given by the 18 comparisons in Figure 1 is that 10 favour Boolean and 6 favour Ranked, with the remaining two favouring one method in Recall and one in Precision. The magnitudes of many of the differences are very small and can be judged to be of almost no practical significance - this would mean that other grounds of evaluation could be used to recommend one method or the other, such as search time, effort or user control. This is not the place to explore the reasons for the wide differences in absolute Recall and Precision values exhibited by the different projects, which will be due to subject area, record content exhaustivity, query type, strategy decisions, relevance judgments, collection size, concentration of relevant in the collection, and other IR variables - it is quite remarkable that none of the paired comparisons overlap with one another on the graph.

3 Further Comparisons Using the Aberystwyth Results

The use of just Recall and Precision ratios provides no diagnostic facility to explore further characteristics of performance differences, so some of the immediately obtainable summary data that provides such a deeper complementary picture is given in Tables 1 and 2 for two Boolean and one Ranked result. The first measure given in Table 1 is that of number of records retrieved, a kind of measure of search breadth. This is worth knowing because most research comparisons have been made using a fixed cutoff, whereas the use of a cutoff 'natural' to each method would seem to be the most representative of reality. In Table 1 the experienced non-interactive Quorum searcher retrieved around 50% more records than on his Boolean searches, thus were the two methods to have had equal Recall ability Quorum would have been better in Recall, whereas as Table 1 also shows it was worse by 12% (mean) or 17% (median). Table 2 complements this result by showing that in fact 31 of the 35 searches retrieved more on Quorum than Boolean, and this difference is statistically significant (using the sign test) at the .2% level. So, Quorum's lesser Recall was not due to the searcher stopping too early, though Quorum's worse Precision ratio was clearly influenced by the broader inspection strategy used. Table 2 shows that Quorum's worse Recall occurred on 18 of the queries only, and was not statistically significant; also, Quorum's worse Precision was in 29 of the queries and was significant. The final column of Table 1 shows another query count and gives a hint of Quorum's poorer Recall performance by revealing that 3 queries retrieved no relevant at all. One would expect any Ranked system to offer the chance to inspect more records than a Boolean one, and the ease of using a browsing engine which offers a sight of the next ranked record at the press of a key may generally cause searchers to inspect more.

	Records Retrieved		Recall Ratio		Relevant Retrieved		Precision Ratio		Non-relevant Retrieved		Queries Retrvng zero	
	Mean	Med	Mean	Med	Mean	Med	Mean	Med	Mean	Med	Docs	Reldocs
Quorum S	24.1	20	54%	50%	5.5	4	19%	15%	18.6	18	0	3
E Boolean	16.8	14	66%	67%	6.5	4	35%	33%	10.3	8	0	0
N Boolean	20.4	4	24%	17%	3.0	1	20%	5%	17.4	3	8	15

Table 1: Performance results of Quorum Searched, Experienced Boolean and Novice Boolean, showing means and medians of 35 searches using five measures and queries retrieving zero from the Aberystwyth tests.

	Records Retrieved		Recall Ratio		Relevant Retrieved		Precision Ratio		Non-relevant Retrieved	
	Qs	Sig	Qs	Sig	Qs	Sig	Qs	Sig	Qs	Sig
Quorum S	31	.2%	10		10		6		4	
E Boolean	4		18	(NS)	18	(NS)	29	.2%	30	.2%
equal	0		7		7		0		1	
Quorum S	28	.2%	23	.2%	23	.2%	23	(5%)	8	.2%
N Boolean	6		5		5		9		27	
equal	1		7		7		3		0	
E Boolean	25	1%	29	.2%	29	.2%	29	.2%	11	
N Boolean	9		2		2		5		23	(10%)
equal	1		4		4		1		1	

Table 2: Further performance data giving numbers of searches (Qs) and statistical significance using the Sign test.

In the natural cutoff used in the Cirt experiment (Robertson, S. E. 1987) the opposite result was found, with the weighted Ranking method retrieving fewer records, 35% fewer in citations viewed online and 30% fewer in records printed offline. This result was found to have been influenced by the longer search time per request for Ranked (mean 19.5 minutes) than Boolean (mean 24.5 minutes) and the fact that the intermediary searchers had a strong perception that the weighted searches were taking too long.

Tables 1 and 2 also offer insight into the performance of the novice Boolean searches where the records retrieved have a high arithmetic mean but a very low median because just a small number of queries retrieved very large amounts and eight queries retrieved no records at all. This is clearly a major reason why novice Recall was less than half the other methods, significantly worse, especially since 15 of the 35 queries retrieved no relevant records at all. Precision is also significantly worse than the experienced Boolean, but the other measure of irrelevant retrieval performance which is not contaminated by Recall is Non-relevant retrieved, in which the novice did rather well (but rather too often by retrieving nothing at all).

The need for natural cutoffs and a user-oriented picture is further illustrated by the non-ratio measures in Tables 1 and 2, the relevant retrieved and non-relevant retrieved. It is numbers that users would be concerned with, not the ratios used by researchers for comparing across projects. Relevant retrieved mostly follows Recall for the comparisons, though the median relevant retrieved of 4 is in fact achieved by both Quorum and experienced Boolean, casting some doubt on the practical importance of the difference shown by the means and ratio measure. A further user-oriented picture is given by the query counts already referred to in the two tables: it is interesting to observe that the number of queries performing equivalently is quite small, perhaps showing that the methods are somewhat different in nature, which may support the development of a hybrid Boolean/Ranked system to be proposed later in this paper.

4 The Implementation of Ranked Output

Two aspects of implementation have surfaced in this paper. One is the kinds of search tactic information a user sees and provides in either Boolean or Ranked. The other is to explain and assess the implementation of Ranked results using only Boolean operators. The typical search tactics of an interactive Boolean search are reasonably well known though they have not been evaluated much. The three initial components seem to be the supply of search terms, the assignment of Boolean operators to construct one or more Boolean expressions, and the postings information which gives the number of records that match each term and expression. For example, one of the test queries used is on "occupational health information services or libraries, including occupational nurses, doctors and medicine". A Boolean search could proceed as follows, with postings from the collection of 6004 records:

Subsearch 1:
occupational AND health AND information AND services. 3 records
Subsearch 2:
occupational AND health AND libraries. 2 new records, total 5
Subsearch 3:
health AND information AND services. 60 new records, total 65
Subsearch 4:
health AND libraries. 41 new records, total 106

This strategy does provide a weakly ordered output and inspected records could be confined to those matching subsearches 1 and 2, 5 records, plus say the first 5 from subsearch 3, to give 10 records.

The tactics of a Ranked search are less well known. It may not be enough simply to automatically process the search terms and leave the searcher ignorant of any concept of match levels and postings by which a sense of search direction and success may be judged. So, in the Quorum search engine used in the test reported here the same query prompted the following kind of displayed information:

Search terms: occupational, health, information, services, libraries, nurse, doctor, medicine.
Match level 8 terms: no records
Match level 7 terms: no records
Match level 6 terms: 1 record, Rank 1
Match level 5 terms: 21 new records, Ranks 2 to 22
Match level 4 terms: 93 new records, Ranks 23 to 115
Match level 3 terms: 1192 new records, Ranks 116 to 1307

Records could then be inspected in rank order or a jump could be made to records whose rank was in a particular match level perhaps to see how far down the list it was worth looking. For high recall the searcher tended to look at the first two matching levels, then look at the first few in the next level and terminate if more records that looked relevant were not found. In operational systems such as Status-IQ and Personal Librarian such match levels are presented graphically.

This kind of Quorum presents an ordering that looks as weak as that of the Boolean subsearch method, so Table 3 was drawn up to compare the number of subsearches and levels, just counting as a subsearch or level only those that retrieved new records. The averages show Quorum to have 3.2 per search, Boolean 2.8 (novice 1.2). The maximum numbers of subsearches/levels were 6 or 7, with novice only 3. This data shows that Boolean is, in one sense, a system that ranks the output; it also shows that simple unweighted Quorum does not rank much more strongly than Boolean. A further inference is that the novice Boolean searcher's deficiency was that not enough subsearch tactics were devised. It is perhaps worth noting that two additional laboratory-style comparisons of Boolean versus Quorum have been published using both match levels and rank positions in Keen (1992b Figures 2 and 3). Table 4 gives further information on the 35 Quorum searches showing the numbers of search terms and the levels used by the searcher in inspecting records. It can be seen that using these fairly long queries the median number of terms was 9, and there were 9 searches using between 15 and 20 terms thus rendering a search device capable of more than eight terms a necessity, as will be discussed shortly. Though queries with many terms do not establish matches on all these terms with these fairly short records (bibliographic with abstracts) there was one query which matched on ten terms.

Turning both to the matter of strengthening the ordering of Ranking and implementation by Boolean methods, the one public operational Quorum system is that offered by the European Space Agency described by Mulhauser (1985). Here is the way in which the ESA Questquorum search operates using a query with six terms as searched currently on the INSPEC database:

Search terms:

expert, 24028 records, set 1	system, 785539 records, set 2
front, 25066 records, set 3	end, 59206 records, set 4
information, 235993 records, set 5	retrieval, 24639 records, set 6

Quorum at level 6:
sets 1 AND 6 AND 3 AND 4 AND 5 AND 2, 5 records
Quorum at level 5:
sets 1 AND 6 AND 3 AND 4 AND 5, 11 new records
sets " " " " " " " " 2, 0 new records
sets " " " " " " 5 " ", 1 new record
sets " " " " 4 " " " ", 45 new records
sets " " 3 " " " " " ", 26 new records
sets 6 " " " " " " " ", 83 new records
total matches at level 5, 166 new records

The exact layout used involves the automatic use of Boolean NOT and OR, and is illustrated in Hartley, R. J. (1990 p. 346-350). The strengthening of Quorum Ranking is seen by the way the Boolean combinations are ordered at level 5: the term combinations with the least postings are combined first, thus giving the five groups of records of sizes 11, 1, 45, 26, and 83. Thus the idea of inverse collection frequency is invoked within Quorum levels to give a more refined ordering. Though the records are ordered by level and then by the sets as generated there is no reminder of these match parameters displayable during record inspection, unfortunately. No test is known of whether Quorum performance is enhanced by this sub-ordering: since inverse collection frequency without Quorum has been found to be superior in Ranking it may well have a beneficial effect.

A ranking strength measure is now proposed, with a maximum value of 1, meaning that all the inspected output has unique match values, down to a minimum of the number of documents inspected (reflecting no ranking at all). In this example the value would be 171 divided by 6 if all of levels 6 and 5 were inspected, giving a rank strength of around 28. This result could then be compared with a Boolean search of the same query: in this case a single compound Boolean expression of the kind:
set ((1 AND 2) OR (3 AND 4)) AND 5 AND 6
matches 656 records, and it is not clear that anything between this and the combination of all six terms ANDed (to match 5 items) is devisable for this query, so if two Boolean expressions were used as subsearches the ranking strength measure would be 656 divided by 2 to give a result of 328.

Turning to the implementation of Quorum by explicit multiple Boolean ANDs as just illustrated, and used by Cirt and by Day (1991), it must already be clear that an impossibly large number of expressions is often needed. It is perhaps worth, once for all, quantifying this. Table 4 has a column showing the number of AND expressions that would have been required had this technique been used in the Aberystwyth tests. Any search with more than eight terms requires several hundred, and the count rises through thousands to over one million for the 20 term search. The same data is exhaustively tabulated for search terms of between 2 and 20 in Table 5, the boxes showing the areas, on average, which the 35 Aberystwyth queries tested would require processing. These impossibly large values are due to the nature of the total combinations equation as given in Table 5, and the boxed areas show that something around 50% of the total combinations are needed for the shorter queries, rising to over 90% for the longer ones.

To be more accurate for the Cirt project, an ingenious algorithm was devised which processed short combinations first then avoided some of the long ones when null results were obtained as described in Bovey (1984). This helps but does not materially change the situation. Implementation of Quorum and other weighted Ranking methods needs either appropriate indexing or parallel scanning techniques in software or hardware or can

Number of subsearches or levels used	Numbers of searches Quorum Searched	Boolean Experienced	Boolean Novice
1	35	35	35
2	34	30	7
3	25	15	1
4	14	9	-
5	4	5	-
6	1	2	-
7	-	1	-
Means	levels 3.2	subsearches 2.8	subsearches 1.2

Table 3: Subsearches and levels used in the three methods in the Aberystwyth tests using 35 searches.

Search terms	1st level retrieving	Last level	Boolean ANDs per search	No. of queries
5	5	3	16	1
6	5	3	42	4
7	5	4	64	5
8	6	5	93	5
9	6	4	382	4
10	6	3	968	2
11	7	5	1486	1
12	8	6	2510	3
13	8	5	7099	1
15	9	5	30827	2
16	8	5	63019	3
18	10	5	258096	1
19	7	4	523128	1
20	9	6	1026876	2

Table 4: Search terms, levels used and number of ANDs theoretically required for the Quorum searches.

Match Level	Search Terms (n) 2	3	4	5	6	7	8	9	10	11	12	13	14	15	16	17	18	19	20	Match Level
20																			1	20
19																		1	20	19
18																	1	19	190	18
17																1	18	171	1140	17
16															1	17	153	969	4845	16
15														1	16	136	816	3876	15504	15
14													1	15	120	680	3060	11628	38760	14
13												1	14	105	560	2380	8568	27132	77520	13
12											1	13	91	455	1820	6188	18564	50388	125970	12
11										1	12	78	364	1365	4368	12376	31824	75582	167960	11
10									1	11	66	286	1001	3003	8008	19448	43758	92378	184756	10
9								1	10	55	220	715	2002	5005	11440	24310	48620	92378	167960	9
8							1	9	45	165	495	1287	3003	6435	12870	24310	43758	75582	125970	8
7						1	8	36	120	330	792	1716	3432	6435	11440	19448	31824	50388	77520	7
6					1	7	28	84	210	462	924	1716	3003	5005	8008	12376	18564	27132	38760	6
5				1	6	21	56	126	252	462	792	1287	2002	3003	4368	6188	8568	11628	15504	5
4			1	5	15	35	70	126	210	330	495	715	1001	1365	1820	2380	3060	3876	4845	4
3		1	4	10	20	35	56	84	120	165	220	286	384	455	560	680	816	969	1140	3
2	1	3	6	10	15	21	28	36	45	55	66	78	91	105	120	136	153	171	190	2
1	2	3	4	5	6	7	8	9	10	11	12	13	14	15	16	17	18	19	20	1
Total (2n-1)	3	7	15	31	63	127	255	511	1023	2047	4095	8191	16383	32767	65535	131071	262143	524287	1048575	

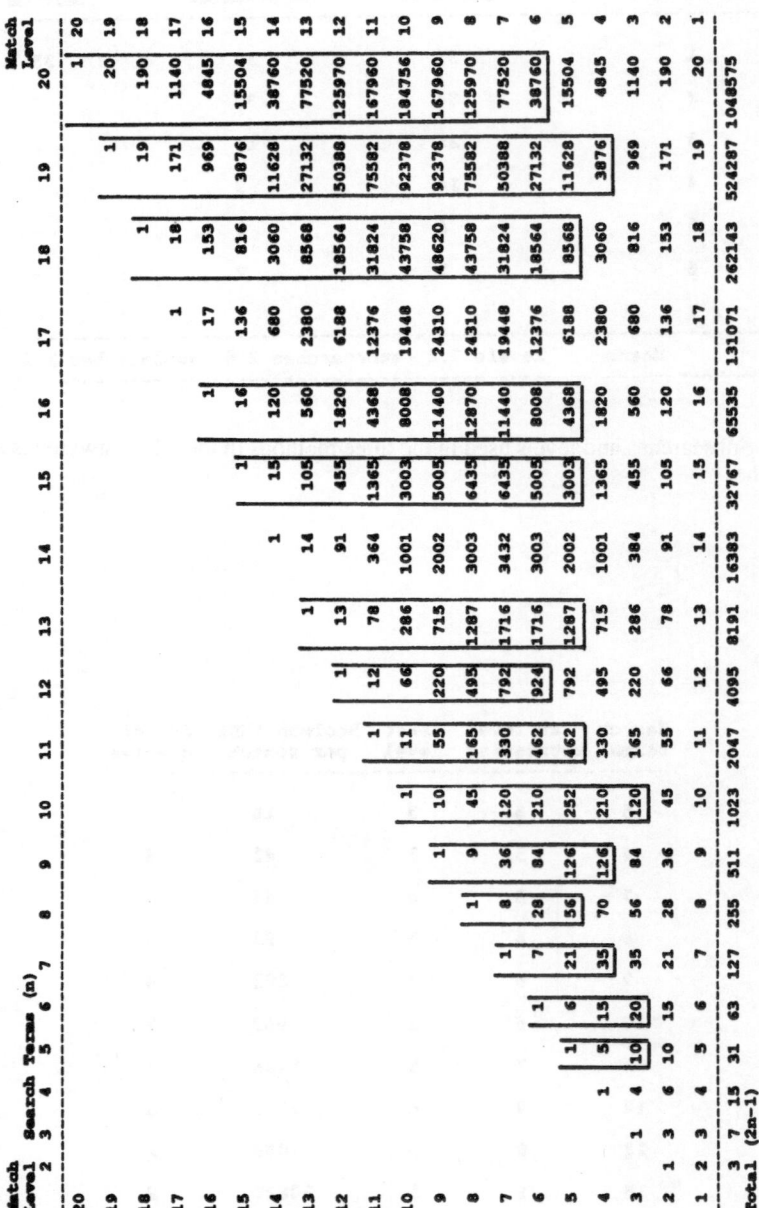

Table 5: Numbers of Boolean ANDs required for quorum with theoretical levels needed for the 35 searches

be implemented using conventional inverted files by the postings list addition method described by Perry (1983).

5 A Proposal for an Integrated Boolean/Ranked System

Current systems such as INSTRUCT, Status-IQ, Personal Librarian and ESA Questquorum offer the searcher either Boolean or Ranked, not a mixed mode. There is not even any easy to use facility to conduct a search in one method then have it automatically applied to the other. A system is proposed which allows a searcher in mid-search to change method and to have access to algorithms which will re-process the initial search in terms of the method not selected. Here is how it might work for the user assuming simple Quorum to illustrate Ranking.

An initial strategy could be conducted in Boolean. If too few items were retrieved, a switch to Quorum automatically using the same search terms would reveal whether some of the lower Quorum levels match more records, and to what level the search would have to descend to retrieve more than the Boolean did. If the Boolean outcome was too many items then a Quorum re-run would reveal whether a tighter AND strategy matched a smaller set of records so that those could be consulted first to get feedback strategies under way. This switch would also be a useful way of introducing the experience of Ranked output to professional Boolean searchers to evaluate.

The opposite strategy would be to start off with Quorum and ask for a report on what Boolean strategies could have been used to retrieve the same items. This might require some quite sophisticated analysis routines along the lines of those provided in Tome Searcher. It could allow a specific Boolean-within-Ranking search to counteract cases where too many terms in an OR relationship had allowed an important concept to escape being ANDed. This kind of strategy switch could provide an easy means of learning Boolean for novices because intermediaries are clearly going to be needed for the entrenched Boolean systems for some years to come.

The incorporation of relevance feedback could add the dimension that a method change could be linked just to match those items judged relevant. Of course, a more advanced Ranking method than Quorum could well be used. A further role for an integrated system would be as a researchers tool so that cases performing better by one method or by the other could be more readily identified and studied.

6 Some Claims for Ranked Systems

If this paper has narrowed the differences between Boolean and Ranked then one of its purposes will have been met. The literature of IR is replete with half-truths when it comes to comparing rival systems. For example, to claim that Boolean systems divide a collection into two, and non-Boolean provide a Ranked output is not the whole picture as this paper has shown. Not only can Boolean do some weak ordering but, at the end of a search on any system a user must make a binary decision as to which documents to examine and which not, thus dividing the collection into two. The labelling of Ranked systems as providing "relevance ranking" is a salesperson's unsubstantiated claim: in the comparative tests reported there are a few more Boolean systems performing better than Ranking ones, and in any case Ranking has only to do with query record match not relevance, which is a judgment of the utility of records to the query need. It really should be called variable match ranking. Both Boolean and Ranked equally endeavour to increase the probability of relevance of the records inspected.

The strengths of Boolean are in its specification and control power, mentioned by some users in Al-Hawamdeh (1988) and commented upon by Keen (1991b). It has yet to be demonstrated that a user's query, information need, or anomalous state of knowledge can be more successfully coped with by one method or the other. The weaknesses of Boolean lie more in its implementation, its difficult command syntax, necessity for learning, skill and effort required, error proneness, and difficulty of incorporating weighting algorithms. Cleverdon (1990) persuasively put this view and the novice Boolean results presented here do provide evidence of Boolean's problems. But it is simply too early to be sure either that these weaknesses cannot be overcome, for example, by better interface design or automated Boolean construction algorithms, or that Ranked systems will be universally better, liked by users and free from new problems of their own. The variable match principle, however implemented, does seem to have merit in the design of IR systems, and continued studies of both methods will be needed to make genuine and well-founded advances.

References

Al-Hawamdeh, S. and others. (1988) Best match document retrieval: development and use of INSTRUCT. In Proceedings of the Twelfth International Online Information Meeting, Learned Information, 761-777

Al-Hawamdeh, S. and Willett, P. (1989) Paragraph-based nearest neighbour searching in full-text documents. Electronic Publishing, 2(4), 179-192

Bovey, J. D. and Robertson, S. E. (1984) An algorithm for weighted searching on a Boolean system. Information Technology, 3(2), 84-87

Cleverdon, C. (1984) Optimizing convenient online access to bibliographic databases. Information Services & Use, 4(1/2), 37-47 (There is a typesetting error in Table 3 page 42 in the data used in Figure 1 here: Quorum total relevant level 4 should be 214 not 314)

Cleverdon, C. (1990) Letter to Online Review 14(1) 35-36

Day, S. R. (1991) (Unpublished Thesis)

Evans, L. (1981) An experiment: search strategy variations in SDI, in Sparck Jones, K. Ed. Information retrieval experiment, Butterworths, 285-315

Hartley, D. and Hallas, M. D. (1976) Search strategy variations in current awareness profiles in the field of chemistry. British Library Research and Development Department Report 5294, United Kingdom Chemical Information Service, Nottingham.

Hartley, R J, Keen, E M, Large, J A and Tedd, L A (1990) Online searching: principles and practice. London, Bowker-Saur, 387p.

Keen, E. M. (1981) Laboratory tests of manual systems, in Sparck Jones, K. Ed. Information retrieval experiment, Butterworths, 136-155

Keen, E. M. (1991a) The use of term position devices in ranked output experiments. Journal of Documentation, 47(1), 1-22

Keen, E. M. (1991b) Query term weighting schemes for effective ranked output retrieval. In Online Information 91, Proceedings of the 15th International Online Information Meeting, Learned Information, 135-142

Keen, E. M. (1992a) Proximity searching in text retrieval systems. Journal of Information Science, 18(2), 89-98

Keen, E. M. (1992b) Presenting results of experimental retrieval comparisons. Information Processing and Management, Special issue on evaluation issues in information retrieval, 28(4), 1992 (In press)

Keen, E. M. and Digger, J. A. (1972) Report of an information science index languages test. 2 Parts, College of Librarianship Wales, Aberystwyth (also OSTI Report 5120)

Mohan, K. C. see Al-Hawamdeh, S. and others. (1988)

Mulhauser, G. (1985) Dawn of next generation information retrieval. In Proceedings of the 9th International Online Information Meeting, Learned Information, 365-371

Perry, S. A. and Willett, P. (1983) A review of the use of inverted files for best match searching in information retrieval systems. Journal of Information Science, 6, (2/3), 59-66

Robertson, A. M., Thompson, W., Vickery, A. and Willett, P. (1990) Effectiveness of retrieval in statistically-based retrieval systems. Report to British Library Research and Development Department. Department of Information Studies, University of Sheffield.

Robertson, S. E. and Thompson, C. L. (1987). An operational evaluation of weighting, ranking and relevance feedback via a front-end system. Department of Information Science, The City University. Report to the British Library Research & Development Department.

Robertson, S E and Thompson, C L. (1990) Weighted searching: the Cirt experiment, in Informatics 10, Aslib, 153-165

Salton, G. (1972) A new comparison between conventional indexing (Medlars) and automatic text processing (Smart). Journal of the American Society for Information Science, 23(2), 75-84

Salton, G. (1975) Dynamic information and library processing. Prentice-Hall.

Sparck Jones, K. and Bates, R. G. (1977) Research on automatic indexing 1974-1976, 2 Vols., British Library Research and Development Report 5464, Computer Laboratory, University of Cambridge.

Pictorial information systems - prospects and problems

J P Eakins,
Department of Computing,
Newcastle Polytechnic,
Newcastle upon Tyne,
NE1 8ST.

Abstract

While text retrieval systems are now commonplace, picture retrieval systems - particularly those capable of direct retrieval by shape feature or object position - are still a comparative rarity, perhaps surprisingly so in view of the growth of interest in multimedia databases. Has the development of sophisticated retrieval capabilities for pictorial information systems lagged behind because of inherent problems in providing them, or are they simply not needed?

This paper aims to answer the above question by reviewing some recent work on pictorial information retrieval, including Chang's IIDS (intelligent image database system), Rabitti & Stanchev's GRIM_DBMS retrieval system, and the author's own SAFARI system for engineering drawings. It discusses some of the lessons which can be drawn from these experimental systems in key areas such as image description and indexing, interface design, and the measurement of retrieval effectiveness. It proposes a taxonomy of such systems, and examines some of the features that the next generation of such systems should aim to provide.

1 Introduction

Graphics are an important communication medium in many areas of human activity. Engineers and architects use drawings (and, increasingly, 3-D computer models) to specify their designs, geographers communicate via maps, and medical practitioners use X-rays and other scanning techniques in diagnosis. More and more of such communication in these areas is now mediated by the computer, as processing power increases and storage costs fall. Numerous examples of specialist applications can be found in areas as diverse as CAD/CAM, satellite image processing, and computerized tomography.

Research into the storage and retrieval of pictorial information has been gathering pace over the last few years - driven partly by the availability of new technology such as optical discs and broad-band communication networks, but mainly, one suspects, by the realization that the next generation of information systems will need to handle a whole range of media, including text, graphics and even sound. A key research area here lies in the area of image content analysis. It is important to remember that the ability to store digitized pictures on optical disc is only a partial solution to the image retrieval problem. Digitized images consist purely of arrays of pixel intensities. Any semantic content (such as the presence, extent and location of forests, rivers or towns in LANDSAT images) has to be inferred from the picture by the person viewing it. The key to effective picture retrieval lies in the identification of suitable image indexing features - either by a human indexer, or through the application of automatic pattern recognition techniques.

The image database field was reviewed on three occasions in the mid-eighties - by Tamura & Yokoya (1984), Nagy (1985) and Chang (1985). Their comments are worth repeating, even though the situation has changed in many ways in the intervening years.

Tamura & Yokoya defined an *image database* (IDB) as a system in which a large amount of image data and "related information" are stored in an "integrated" fashion. They commented that "it does not seem that the significant concepts of IDB have been established yet, because there exist too few systems that we can call a true IDB". Their paper went on to describe examples of systems that might be characterized as IDBs, including GRAIN and REDI, referred to in section 2.1 below. Among the key design issues they identified were (i) what entities to include - images, features, and/or ancillary data? (ii) how data should be represented at the logical and physical level, (iii) levels of retrieval - by identifier alone, Boolean combinations of features, or similarity to example query image? and (iv) query languages - based on existing command languages such as SQL, or designed from scratch?

Nagy shared many of Tamura & Yokoya's reservations about the maturity of the field, stating that "our own impression is that much of the work appearing under the heading 'image database' describes either image nondatabase systems ... or nonimage database systems". He felt that concepts such as logical and physical data independence had been ignored in image database design, and that effort needed to be put into problems such as the discrete representation of continuous variables like image intensity distribution, and developing efficient search algorithms for image elements ordered in two or more dimensions. Relational database technology, he suggested, could overcome many of these difficulties.

Chang defined an *image database* as a collection of shareable image data encoded in various format, and an *image information system* as the software to manage input, output, storage and communications providing access to a collection of image data for a large number of users. He saw the main needs for such systems arising in areas such as office automation, computer-aided design and manufacturing, image understanding, and "fifth-generation systems", and went on to describe a number of developmental and commercial systems. The main research trends he identified were (i) image database design: extension of the relational model of data to capture spatial relationships, and to formulate pictorial queries, (ii) spatial data structures: development and exploitation of hierarchical data structures such as the *quadtree* for the efficient representation of image data, (iii) user interface design: the development of flexible picture query languages, and (iv) image communications: development of a conceptual framework for multimedia messages which may consist of text, image elements, attributes or annotations. He also introduced the important concept of the *generalized icon*, a visual representation of an abstract object present in an image, which can be used in image description and indexing as well as in interface design.

Section 2 of this paper reviews some of the more recent systems described in the literature, highlighting trends which may prove significant in the development of future systems. It groups these systems into three main classes in order to highlight differences in approach. Section 3 attempts to summarize current research trends, and section 4 points at possible ways forward. No attempt has been made to provide an exhaustive coverage of the literature. In particular, hardware developments are ignored, though it is hoped that most current strands of software development are represented.

2 Some Current Systems

Current image databases show substantial differences from the examples reviewed by Tamura & Yokoya, Nagy and Chang. Significant advances have been made in areas such as data representation, database support and interface design. Perhaps more importantly, new types of image database and new search techniques are becoming available. Virtually all the databases reviewed by Tamura & Yokoya, Nagy and Chang fell into one of two categories: spatial databases where the main focus for retrieval was the relative position of known elements in the image, or image stores offering retrieval based on manually-assigned keywords. Several of the more recent systems reviewed below can be characterized as *image content retrieval* systems, performing automatic shape analysis or object matching on every image added to the database, allowing image retrieval on the basis of shape feature or object type present.

The working definition of an image database which will be adopted for the rest of this paper (Eakins, 1990) is "a collection of images, together with descriptive data derived directly from those images, maintained in applications-independent form, and organized for efficient storage and retrieval". It should be noted that this definition is intended to exclude drawing archives where retrieval is purely by externally-assigned keyword or other identifier - ruling out several of the systems reviewed by the authors quoted above.

Such systems can be characterized in several ways. Firstly (a distinction not always drawn by earlier authors), are the images entities in their own right, such as design drawings or CT scans, or merely graphic representations derived from underlying non-graphic data, such as bar charts of monthly sales? It is seldom worth creating an image database for derived data, as simpler mechanisms are generally available to retrieve the underlying data. (One could perhaps still envisage some circumstances where retrieval of a report containing a specified bar chart was needed). Secondly, is the image database intended to stand alone, or to form part of a multimedia database in which output has to be integrated with numeric data, text or recorded sound? This will have profound effects on the type of user interface provided, and could affect the underlying data structure as well. Thirdly, how specialized is the database - has it been designed purely to handle a single type of application (such as architect's plans of domestic housing), or with general image retrieval in mind? Specialist systems can often exploit natural constraints, such as the fact that floor plans of domestic houses are drawn from a restricted domain of shape elements, to improve search efficiency.

Of greater importance than any of these, however, is the nature of the image retrieval provided by the system. Is the prime focus on retrieval of images containing objects conforming to a given paradigm (e.g. all images containing an object recognizable as a chair)? Are shape characteristics paramount (e.g. all cylindrical parts with a length/diameter ratio more than 3.0)? Or are absolute or relative positions of image elements of the greatest importance (e.g. all forested areas up to 50 miles south-west of New York)? As can be seen from the examples below, these three types of retrieval impose very different constraints on the database designer. They are not, of course, mutually exclusive - indeed it will be argued later that the next generation of image retrieval systems should be capable of answering all three types of query - but do provide a useful framework for distinguishing between present systems, all of which emphasize different aspects of image retrieval.

2.1 Spatial Information Systems

Some of the earliest examples of pictorial information systems were those developed for geographical applications in the early 1970s. Such geographical information systems developed naturally from automation of the map-making process; as well as drawing maps, they could calculate distances and areas, and allow different kinds of spatially referenced data (such as rainfall and land use) to be related to each other. Typical queries put to such a system could include:

What cities with populations over 100 000 border Lake Michigan?

What rivers cross highway N65?

What districts with population density over 100 km^{-2} had SO_2 levels over the permitted limit last week?

What length of interstate highway passes through Cook county?

In some ways it is misleading to describe such systems as *image* databases, since the underlying data are not necessarily derived from image scanning, and the true answer to many of the questions above is not a retrieved image, but numeric or textual data derived by querying such an image. The crucial point is that all data items are spatially referenced to some standard coordinate system, allowing the system to deduce answers in the appropriate format.

Two main methods have been used to represent data in such systems, the *grid* and *point-set*. Grid-based systems such as PICDMS (Chock et al, 1984) divide the image or region of interest into a 2-D grid, and store values of data items such as land use, rainfall, population density, and intensity of corresponding point on each LANDSAT image for every grid element. Point-based systems such as REDI (Chang and Fu, 1980) and PROBE (Orenstein et al, 1988) store sets of coordinates representing the location or extent of each object of interest. A river, for example, would be represented by a set of (x,y) coordinates tracing its path as a series of straight-line approximations. Both types of system suffer from performance limitations. A pure gridded system is very wasteful of space when representing regions where values change little from one element to the next. Point representations often involve inordinate amounts of calculation when relating data stored against (say) political entities like electoral districts with data stored against natural features like river valleys. More recent systems have attempted to overcome this by using more elaborate data structures such as the *kd*-tree, *R*-tree or quadtree (Roussopoulos et al, 1988, Orenstein et al, 1988) - effectively a form of 2-D indexing. A form of 2-D indexing which promises to have widespread applicability, *iconic indexing*, proposed by Chang et al (1988), is discussed in more detail below.

Most systems described in the literature have been based on an underlying relational database. However, this database model has limited ability to represent spatial relationships, and to formulate spatial queries. Hence several authors (e.g. Chang et al, 1980, Roussopoulos et al, 1988) have proposed extended relational query languages including superimposition operators and length and area calculations. Other authors have rejected the relational model altogether in favour of application-dependent data structures (Chock et al, 1984) or object-oriented database (Orenstein et al, 1988). Because of the complexity and specialized nature of many of the queries handled by such systems, their user interfaces have frequently been based on command languages such as relational algebra or SQL rather than using graphics for query formulation. Systems such as REDI (Chang and Fu, 1980) and IIDS (Chang et al, 1988) are notable exceptions to this trend.

The degree to which incoming data - particularly image data - is processed automatically to identify objects or features of interest has varied considerably; more recent systems are not necessarily more advanced in this respect. Automatic pattern recognition techniques have been successfully used in systems such as REDI to identify and characterize image features as towns, road, or rivers. But some manual content analysis is always required. Recognizing and tracing the path of a river or road can be performed automatically; naming the river as the Mississippi or the road as the M4 requires some human intervention.

Early examples of such systems include:

- GRAIN (Chang et al, 1977), also known as DIMAP. This was developed at the University of Illinois, to demonstrate the feasibility of an integrated pictorial database with both retrieval and browsing capabilities. It comprised two separate but linked subsystems; an image store of digitized aerial photographs, and a relational database of *picture object tables*, describing objects such as towns, rivers and railways identified on the photographs. Users could access the database via an interface based on extended relational algebra, to obtain answers to specific questions such as those illustrated above. Alternatively, they could browse either the physical image store or the picture object tables, using generalized pan and zoom facilities to display images or picture objects at different levels of detail. The degree of automated content analysis (if any) involved in generating the picture object tables was not specified.

- REDI (Chang and Fu, 1980), later know as IMAID. This was developed at Purdue University, to manage data from LANDSAT images. Like GRAIN, it used a linked digitized image store and relational database of extracted image features such as roads and rivers. Unlike GRAIN, the authors described the feature extraction process; the technique of syntactic pattern recognition was used to identify the presence and location of roads, rivers and cities, with names added by human operators. The user was able to put textual or spatial queries to the database via a *query-by-pictorial-example* interface in which skeleton tables were displayed on the screen so that the user could specify examples of the type of output required; results could then be displayed either as text, a sketch or the original image.

- PICDMS (Chock et al, 1984). This system, developed at the University of California, was perhaps more specifically a geographical information system than GRAIN or REDI. It aimed to provide the storage and correlation of different kinds of data relating to same geographical region. The user command language included functions to compute spatial or statistical data for regions meeting specified criteria, such as identifying the numbers and locations of residents in areas with below-average rainfall and certain types of vegetation, so that they could be warned of fire risks. Data were represented logically as a multidimensional grid, physically implemented as a set of sequential files.

More recent systems, aiming to extend functionality or improve performance, have included:

- PROBE (Orenstein and Manola, 1988). This system, developed at the Computer Corporation of America, was aimed specifically at extending database functionality for spatial applications. The project was therefore primarily concerned with database operations rather than interfacing or content analysis. It provided users with a comprehensive set of spatial functions such as *location*, *altitude*, *components*, and *overlaps*, expressible either in PDM (Probe Data Model) algebra or via a graphical interface. The underlying object-oriented database stored two basic types of picture entity, *objects* and *point sets*. In order to improve the efficiency of computationally-expensive operations such as overlap calculation, PROBE used a *geometry filter* to screen out obviously unsuitable candidate objects.

- IIDS (Chang et al, 1988) This prototype system, developed at the University of Pittsburgh, aimed to test methods of enhancing the spatial reasoning capability of image databases. Like many of its predecessors, it consisted of several linked modules - an image store, a relational database of picture indexes, and a spatial reasoning module.

  The picture index database was perhaps the most noteworthy aspect of IIDS. It used two-dimensional *iconic indexing* to provide information on the relative positions of picture objects. Individual objects in the image were identified either by a human indexer or automatic pattern analysis, and allocated a code letter. Each picture was divided into a grid of arbitrary resolution. The code letter for each picture object was then allocated to each grid element it covered. Two character strings were then derived from these grid entries, one indicating the relative ordering of picture objects along the *x*-axis, and one along the *y*-axis. These two strings formed the iconic index to the picture. Queries were translated into the same type of index string, and matched with stored picture indexes. Quite complex spatial reasoning was possible, e.g. "find pictures containing a lake surrounded by a forest on three sides".

  Users of the system could search simple pictures by keyword or desired spatial relationship. A sophisticated windowing environment was provided, allowing queries to be submitted from the keyboard or built up on the screen by choosing suitable icons from a menu and positioning them to give an example of the type of picture required. Pictures containing a car to the left of a house could thus be retrieved by placing a "car" icon somewhere to the left of a "house" icon on the query screen.

The concept of iconic indexing has generated a significant number of publications in its own right. Its theoretical underpinning has been discussed by Chang (1987); its further exploitation to provide the capability for generalized similarity retrieval by Chang and Lee (1991); and an extension to the concept, allowing representation of additional spatial relationships such as adjacency and overlap by Chang and Jungert (1991).

2.2 Image Paradigm Retrieval Systems

By contrast with the wealth of spatial information systems described in the literature, there are as yet comparatively few retrieval systems concentrating on image content analysis - the automatic recognition and characterization of picture objects and their attributes. As indicated above, the difference between these two types of system is one of degree rather than of kind, the emphasis being on the nature and type of object being sought rather than its relative position in the image. Queries such as:

Which report contained that pie chart of last October's market shares?
Which culture plates contain cells with abnormal chromosomes?
What plans do we have of dining rooms with oval tables and at least six dining chairs?

are all concerned with retrieval of images containing objects conforming to (or failing to conform to) specified paradigms rather than images showing specified spatial relationships. The search criteria relate primarily to image objects themselves - and are frequently less clear-cut than for spatial retrieval systems. How does one judge precisely when a chromosome is deemed abnormal, for example?

Too few systems of this kind have yet been described in literature for any common approach towards design issues like data structuring or user interface design to be discernible. Examples of systems that have been described in the literature include:

- CUPID (Yokoya and Tamura, 1982). One of the earliest such systems described in the literature. A linked store of cytopathology images and relational database of ancillary data was used in the development of image-processing software for automated diagnosis. SEARCH and DISPLAY commands were provided for the retrieval of text and image data respectively. An analogous system for retrieving and interpreting chest X-ray data was described by Toriwaki et al (1980). This used pattern recognition techniques to generate and store sketches of abnormal features in chest X-rays, which could then be searched to establish similarities between individual cases.

- GRIM_DBMS (Rabitti and Stanchev, 1987; Rabitti and Stanchev, 1989). Developed at the National Research Council, Pisa, as part of the MULTOS multimedia database project, it aimed to derive a general technique for retrieval of images from large collections. It provided automatic analysis and indexing of images input in some standard format such as CGM (Computer Graphics Metafile), augmenting image data with automatically-generated index descriptions.

  Image analysis followed a four-stage process: (i) recognition of the type and position of individual picture elements such as lines, curves and filled areas, (ii) recognition of predefined picture objects such as tables and chairs, and assignment of scores reflecting the certainty of recognition, (iii) computation of the *belief interval* (upper and lower probability bounds) of each likely interpretation of each object, and (iv) classifying the entire image on basis of the above content interpretations. Finally, an index entry was created for each image and each of its constituent objects.

Images were retrieved on basis of the objects they contained - a text-based command language was used to formulate queries. The system has been tested on two prototype databases, one of architectural plans, one of diagrams drawn with a business graphics package, apparently with successful results. A further refinement of the system (Rabitti and Savino, 1991) has been the addition of multi-level signatures (bit patterns indicating the presence or absence of specified image or object features) to improve system performance by screening out obviously unsuitable images.

This system is of particular importance because it has been developed to a much greater state of completeness than any other in this group, and because it appears capable of generalization to a wide range of applications. It is also of interest through its use of belief functions to generate and maintain alternative picture interpretations, and information retrieval techniques such as clustering and multi-level signatures. As one might expect from a system that is designed to recognize object paradigms, however, it needs to be "primed" with application-specific descriptions of all object types likely to be present in the image database - significantly limiting its generalizability in practice. The choice of a text-based command language for retrieval also seems odd, given the variety of graphical interface tools now available.

2.3 Shape Retrieval Systems

A further range of queries one might reasonably expect to put to an image database relate to the shape of objects represented in those images. One might wish to retrieve objects either on the basis of their overall similarity to some reference shape, or the presence of a common set of shape features, e.g:

What fingerprints match the partial print on the murder weapon?
What parts do we have similar to the one illustrated in drawing no XYZ1000?
What plans of four-bedroomed houses with L-shaped dining-rooms do we have?

Here, we are less concerned with retrieving examples of objects conforming to specified paradigms (it may be that the entire database consists of different examples of the same type of object) than with identifying local or global shape similarities between a query and database objects. Retrieval systems of this kind share similarities with both types of system described above. Like spatial information systems, they need to take account of both the nature and relative position of features extracted from the image; like image paradigm systems, they need to analyse image objects at different levels of detail, and may have to cope with uncertain or conflicting interpretations.

There are important differences, too. Spatial retrieval systems depend on a fixed coordinate system to provide a viewpoint for deducing relationships such as "left of" or "above". Shape retrieval systems have no such fixed frame of reference. The image paradigm systems described so far in the literature can recognize only a relatively small number of predefined object types. Shape retrieval systems can extract, store and match elements from a much wider domain of images.

The most widespread examples of shape retrieval systems, even though they operate in a very restricted domain) are the fingerprint matching systems used by many police forces (e.g IEEE, 1985). Examples of shape retrieval systems in other areas include:

- Multimedia architectural database (Maeda et al, 1988). Developed at the Mitsubishi Electric Corporation, this project was aimed at developing methods of similarity retrieval in multimedia databases. It stored images of architectural plans on optical disc, linked to indexing information on magnetic disc, and was capable of retrieving and displaying drawings similar to an input sketch. It offered semi-automatic content analysis: the overall layout of an architectural plan could be inferred automatically from a digitised drawing, but details such as window layout or room usage had to be added manually. Room layout was represented as a connectivity matrix, which was transformed into standard form for ease of matching.

- SAFARI (Eakins, 1989; Eakins, 1990). This system is part of an ongoing project at Newcastle Polytechnic, aimed at investigating the problems of providing image retrieval by shape feature in one applications area - engineering drawings. At present, it caters only for a restricted domain of 2-D shapes, though plans for a full 3-D version are well developed. It provides facilities both for example-based similarity retrieval and partial shape matching. Drawings are input as transfer files in standard IGES (Initial Graphics Exchange Specification) format, and an automatic content analysis process performed as detailed below.

  A multi-level canonical representation of shape boundary segments is created (Eakins, 1989), and three types of shape feature extracted and stored to characterize each level of boundary description. Firstly, global boundary features (length/width and perimeter^2/area ratios, mean and variance of segment length, etc) are derived from the entire set of segments making up a boundary, to give a measure of its overall shape and complexity.

  Secondly, local boundary features are derived from individual line segments, angles, or sets of contiguous segments. These include simple fragments such as line length or arc angle frequency distributions, and more complex fragments such as *discontinuity angle triplets* consisting of two neighbouring lines and the discontinuity angle linking them, and *parent feature* fragments based on a connected set of segments forming a protrusion, depression or corner feature (Fig 1).

  Finally, inner boundary pattern features, indicating the presence or absence of regular patterns of holes or other machined features (collinear, concyclic, rectangular, etc) are extracted and stored as attributes of the shape as a whole. For full details of the feature extraction process, and a justification of the feature set chosen, see Eakins (1990).

  At present, all drawing elements and derived features are stored together in a CODASYL database, though the possible advantages of using a relational database, or more object-oriented alternatives such as the NF^2 data model (Kemper and Wallrath, 1987), are being investigated.

  A graphical query formulation module allows users to build up complete or incomplete query shapes on the screen, one segment at a time (Fig 2). This is then submitted to the same canonicalization and feature extraction process as for stored shapes, and matched against the shape database. Retrieved drawings can be displayed directly on the screen or written to a file for laser printer output.

  Three basic types of search are offered - global feature matching, local feature matching, and segment matching, as defined below. Each can be used for matching of outer boundaries only, or for matching inner boundary positions or shapes as well. Global feature matching relies on computing a distance measure between query and stored shape boundaries based on normalized differences between global feature values.

  Local feature matching uses local features, plus inner boundary pattern features if appropriate. Two alternative means of calculating difference measures are used. The first, referred to as *local matching*, is basically analogous to global matching, aiming to assess overall similarity between query and stored shapes. It computes a difference measure on the basis of differences in frequency of each feature present in either query or stored shape, and would therefore tend to exclude shapes containing large numbers of features not present in the query. The second, *existence matching*, works on the principle that a shape containing specified features should be retrieved however many additional features it contains. In this case, a tally is kept of the number of query features present in the stored shape, and used to compute a difference measure.

Segment matching aims to compute a difference measure between query and stored shape boundaries by expressing both in intrinsic coordinates, as plots of q, the cumulative angle traversed, against s, cumulative length. If both query and stored boundaries are traversed at comparable boundary levels, it is possible to compute a difference measure by integrating $(q_q - q_s)^2$ (where q_q and q_s are the angles traversed around the query and stored shape boundaries respectively) over the complete length of the boundaries. Note that matching requires only a single traversal of each boundary.

Finally, combined matching may be specified. This uses one of the feature-based methods (global, local, or existence matching) as a preliminary screening search (the user can specify a maximum number of shapes, a maximum difference threshold, or both), followed by segment matching on the subset of shapes retrieved by the preliminary search.

An evaluation of the SAFARI's retrieval effectiveness was attempted by comparing its output with relevance judgements made by independent human observers. Students from the Engineering Faculty at Newcastle Polytechnic were given drawings of a set of "query" shapes, and asked to match them under controlled conditions with illustrations of all shapes in the test database, identifying those they considered to match the "query" shape most closely. For the great majority of query shapes presented to test subjects, results from different subjects were remarkably consistent (Fig 3). This permitted the identification of a set of stored shapes "relevant" to each query, to provide a benchmark against which results from SAFARI could be compared. The same query shapes were then matched against the test database using SAFARI (see Figs 4-6), employing a variety of different matching paradigms as defined above. A somewhat surprising finding from the evaluation experiments (reported in detail in Eakins, 1990) was that all three feature-matching methods (particularly global matching) performed well on their own - it was originally expected that both feature matching and segment matching would have to be combined to yield acceptable results.

The significance of the SAFARI system (in the author's not totally impartial view) is that it has demonstrated that an image retrieval system based on the extraction of relatively simple invariant shape features can deliver acceptable retrieval performance. The extent to which these results can be generalized remains to be established. Many of the global features used by SAFARI, such as length/width and perimeter^2/area ratios, are standard measures which have been applied to shape characterization in several contexts (e.g. Ireton and Xydeas, 1991). Many of the local and inner boundary position features, however, were derived by exploiting the special nature of machined parts (their high degree of symmetry, the fact that machined shape features form a natural hierarchy, and so on). It would be surprising if these proved as widely applicable as the global features.

- While not a complete system, the 3-D shape indexing language proposed by Horikoshi and Kasahara (1990) could well have a profound effect on the development of future systems in this area. The authors show how a wide variety of regular shapes can be represented parametrically when their surfaces are defined as *superquadrics* (Barr, 1981), and how machine representations of such shapes can readily be modified by verbal or pointer-driven commands. Such objects can thus be represented in a shape database purely by their superquadric parameters. Users can build up 3-D query shapes on a screen with relative ease, and then match parameters with those of stored shapes. Irregular objects are more of a problem - while they can easily be built up from regular superquadric primitives, there is no guarantee that the resulting shape has a unique representation. Hence shapes which are actually very similar could have widely different sets of superquadric parameters. Nevertheless, the idea shows considerable promise.

2.4 General Image Retrieval Systems

Each of the three types of system described above has emphasized one aspect of image retrieval. This is an entirely reasonable approach for research purposes - but when designing systems for general applicability, a broader view is necessary. It is unreasonable to expect future users of such systems to classify their queries into one of the three classes listed above. The next generation of such systems should aim to handle any of these types of query.

One project is already attempting to develop this next generation. The Manchester University Multimedia Information Systems Project (O'Docherty et al, 1990) aims to investigate the problems involved in building a genuinely usable multimedia system, capable of handling text, graphics, voice and computable data. Their system is still under development, but aims to allow users a wide range of functions, including browsing, direct content retrieval of images by query sketch and editing of output images. It will make extensive use of object-oriented concepts, particularly in interface and database design.

Image content retrieval is stated to be a key element in their research. This is to be achieved by enhancing image databases with a semantic representation of their content, using general rather than application-specific methods of content analysis where possible. Some results from this research have already been published (Ireton and Xydeas, 1991) - confirming that invariant shape features such as length/width and perimeter^2/area ratios do indeed have wide applicability in image analysis.

3 Current Research Issues

A number of general issues can be identified as a result of examining the systems described above. These can be grouped under the following headings:

3.1 Functionality

Are such systems needed at all? This is always a hard question for a system designer to answer. The rapid growth in the literature over the last few years suggests that research workers consider the field a fruitful one, though this is not necessarily an indication of genuine need. The existence of picture libraries and drawing archives, and of parts classification schemes such as the Opitz code (Opitz et al, 1969) provides more objective evidence of a long-standing need, likely to become more acute as computer-based graphical communication grows in importance.

But this does not in itself mean that image retrieval systems are needed. In the engineering field, there is a present a lively debate between researchers attempting to process geometric CAD models to extract feature information for process planning, and those who claim that this effort is misguided, since engineers should specify such information at the design stage (see e.g. Dixon et al, 1990). Were feature-based design universally used, it can be argued, systems such as SAFARI would be unnecessary, as designers could retrieve objects with desired features simply by specifying these features by name.

Such a position is tenable only if all designers specify features in the same way - a position that can perhaps be achieved within a single organization where procedures can be laid down and enforced, but which becomes less feasible as the range of contributors to the drawing archive widens. For any database which aims to handle a range of different types of image from a variety of sources, pre-specification of input format becomes impossible, and one has to rely on the database to perform any necessary content analysis on stored images - though for specialized image collections used only by a small group of individuals, such techniques may not be necessary (see e.g. Willis and Hunter, 1991).

If the answer to the first question is "yes", what features should this type of system offer? Again, this question should ideally be answered by potential system users rather than designers. However, there does seem to be some consensus on this issue from system designers, judging by the features designed into those systems reviewed above. On this basis, an image database system should certainly provide:

(a) a means of storing raw image data at a resolution sufficient to meet users' needs;
(b) a linked store of semantic information enabling images to be retrieved in a variety of ways;
(c) software to generate this semantic information with the minimum of human intervention;
(d) a means of formulating user queries and matching them efficiently with stored data;
(e) a means of displaying results in a variety of formats.

Additional features have been mentioned by some authors, including:

(f) the ability to direct queries to an individual image;
(g) the ability to edit or otherwise modify retrieved images;
(h) the ability to mix retrieved images with other types of data.

The difficulty, as always, lies not in enumerating these needs, but in analysing and then meeting them. Some of the main unresolved issues are discussed below.

3.2 Image Description and Indexing

Content analysis has been identified as one of the prime areas for further research by several authors. Existing spatial and image paradigm systems use pattern recognition techniques developed for computer vision applications such as identifying "unknown" objects in noisy images. In the majority of cases, these techniques have been developed using ten or fewer reference shapes for matching. There is little evidence that such techniques work effectively in discriminating between the much larger number of image types likely to be encountered in a general environment. Image database systems of this type which attempt to cover more than the very restricted domain of the prototype systems described here are thus based on unproven technology. This implies an urgent need for research into shape discrimination methods which do work effectively with large numbers of different types of image.

Another issue is the integration of spatial and shape descriptions in a complex picture. Present-day systems either assume (like IIDS) that identification of object type in a picture is no problem, and that spatial relationships between picture objects are the main focus for retrieval - or (like SAFARI) that each picture contains only a single object, whose shape is of paramount interest. Both viewpoints are entirely tenable in a research environment - but in a database of real images, neither set of assumptions is going to hold. Reconciling the demands of these two types of image description may not prove easy.

A more fundamental issue, barely touched on by most authors, is that of defining the wider aspects of picture meaning in a way that makes sense to database users. The experimental systems described above have concentrated on deliberately simplified situations such as idealized floor plans, where the semantic information conveyed by the stored images is limited in extent. The techniques they employ may well prove useful for specialized applications such as engineering design or medical diagnosis, where images are used for specific, limited purposes. They are unlikely to be able to cope with general collections of images such as newspaper photographs, most of which are incapable of any but the most trivial interpretation without the aid of external cues. Studies on picture comprehension performed over 20 years ago (Firschein and Fischler, 1971; Firschein and Fischler, 1972), contrasting the way in which different subjects attempted to interpret identical scenes in the light of their own personal experience, illustrate the significance of this problem admirably.

A non-issue is the question of when feature extraction should be performed. Some earlier authors tried to suggest that there could be advantages in delaying the generation of image features until the query was run, rather than when it was first added to the database. The theory was that run-time feature generation was more flexible, and could therefore allow the database to handle a wider range of queries. The performance overhead of this option would be considerable - and its advantages largely illusory, since no body of expertise yet exists to judge which types of feature are likely to be most useful in answering any given type of query.

3.3 Feature Matching

In his review, Nagy (1985) made the point that improved algorithms and data structures were necessary to improve the computational efficiency of spatial information retrieval. Significant strides have been made in this direction, particularly in terms of improved 2-D indexing and filtering techniques (e.g. Chang, 1988; Orenstein, 1988; Rabitti and Savino, 1991). There is almost certainly scope for further development along these lines.

3.4 Database Support

It is no coincidence that most of the experimental systems described here have used some form of database management system to handle the mechanics of data storage and retrieval. A DBMS provides applications-independent data definition, logical and physical independence, and integrity and security features, as well as providing access paths to individual items of data. It would be an unwarranted waste of effort for systems designers to write their own routines for these purposes.

Most of the earlier systems described here are based on relational databases; many of them (such as GRAIN and REDI) have used query languages which are direct extensions of standard relational languages. More recently, there has been a trend towards the adoption of object-oriented data models to underpin graphical database - though debate continues about what constitutes a true object-oriented database (Kim, 1990). The reasons normally given for favouring object-oriented models (e.g. Orenstein, 1988, O'Docherty et al, 1990) are flexibility, extensibility, and ease of design. It is hard to take exception to this, though experience from the SAFARI project would suggest that the choice of underlying data model is far from crucial. Replacing its present underlying CODASYL database with a relational or object-oriented DBMS, though not difficult, would bring only minor advantages to the system designer, and none at all to users. (It could however be argued that the advantages of the object-oriented approach would become more apparent as the system grew in size and complexity). In the long run, it may well be that image information systems should follow bibliographic database systems in developing their own specialist file structures.

3.5 User Interface Design

Interfacing is, in the author's opinion, another crucial research area for image database systems. Such systems will never gain wide acceptance until end-users can formulate queries quickly and easily without having to learn a complex command language or take a six-week course in technical drawing. The difficulty of providing this level of user interface should not be underestimated. In many ways, the most natural way to formulate a query to an image database system is to submit a sketch of the type of picture required. Not all users will have the artistic ability to make their needs known in this way. Alternative methods of query formulation are therefore needed.

Several types of query interface have been proposed for image database systems, including text-based command languages (Chang et al, 1977; Rabitti and Stanchev, 1987), menu-driven systems (Frasson and Er-Radi, 1986), and example-based systems (Chang and Fu, 1980; Chang et al, 1988). Some of the novel graphics-based interfaces developed for conventional databases (e.g. Herot, 1980; Kim et al, 1988) could also prove suitable for graphics databases. Four alternative types of interface were proposed for SAFARI (Eakins, 1990):

- an example-based interface where the user builds up a query structure on the screen, and then submits it for feature extraction and shape matching;
- a sketch-based interface where the user submits a query sketch which is scanned, digitized and "cleaned up" before matching as proposed by Kato (1982);
- a menu-based interface allowing users to select and combine query features (represented as text or icons) in Boolean fashion;
- a browsing interface similar to that proposed by Herot (1980),

though only the first of these has yet been implemented.

There is clearly no shortage of ideas in this field, though considerable work will be needed to test them out in practice. Significant gaps still remain; few of the techniques outlined above are suitable for interrogating individual pictures (e.g. to find the length or area of a given picture object); few of them (with the exception of Horikoshi and Kasahara's (1990) shape indexing system) can handle 3-D queries; and there has been very little systematic analysis of users' real needs.

3.6 Measurement of Effectiveness

One surprising feature of the image database field is the reluctance of many systems designers to submit their prototypes to any systematic evaluation. All too often, prototype systems are designed, tested by members of the design team, and the new system's features reported with no more than an indication of the type of output expected. Objective evidence on system effectiveness is sadly lacking - despite the fact that evaluation techniques adapted from the bibliographic retrieval field (e.g. Salton, 1971) are readily available.

This situation is not entirely the designers' fault. In order to evaluate the effectiveness of SAFARI, the author had to build up a collection of test drawings from a variety of sources. There was no way of knowing how representative this test collection was of drawing archives in general, and hence how widely applicable were the results of the evaluation experiments. This problem - the lack of any effective benchmark for judging system effectiveness - could significantly hamper future research. Its solution is the same as the one adopted by the bibliographic retrieval community when faced with a similar situation 25 years ago - to build up standard test collections that different research groups can access to test the comparative effectiveness of their approach.

4. Conclusions

4.1 The Present State of the Art

The above discussion should have given the reader an indication of the range of current image database research. The three different types of system highlighted illustrate three of the most important strands in current research - object recognition, spatial analysis and shape analysis. As indicated in the previous section, however, major research issues common to all three types of system also need to be resolved. It is unlikely that any image database systems reaching the marketplace will fall neatly into any one of these three classes.

4.2 Prospects for Future Systems

The volume of image database research can be expected to grow over the next few years, and an increasing variety of image management software will reach the marketplace - a reflection of the growing influence of multimedia applications in office environments. Most are likely to offer a set of features similar to those listed in section 3.1. Unless there are rapid breakthroughs on the unresolved research issues listed above, however, it is unlikely that many of them will offer any meaningful degree of automatic content analysis. Experience of using these systems should enable the next generation of multimedia systems to be better tailored to users' real needs.

4.3 Unresolved Problems

The major short-term obstacle to effective image information system design probably lies in the need to provide users with high-quality interfaces for query formulation. Without this, it will be difficult to encourage sufficient usage of such systems to gain a reliable indication of users' real requirements. Another short-term obstacle is the lack of suitable collections of images to act as benchmarks for evaluating retrieval performance.

In the long term, however, the problems of automatic content analysis are likely to prove the main factor limiting development. The best analogy here may be with the artificial intelligence field. Successful expert systems have been developed within narrow areas of specialization, but efforts to build general problem-solving machines have so far proved fruitless. In a similar way, the present generation of image retrieval systems operate only within a specialized domain. One suspects that some fundamental conceptual breakthroughs will be needed before any real progress is made in developing a general-purpose image retrieval system. Hopefully, the research community will rise to the challenge.

5. References

Barr, A (1981) "Superquadrics and angle-preserving transformations" *IEEE Computer Graphics and Applications* **1**(1), 1-20

Chang, C C and Lee, S Y (1991) "Retrieval of similar pictures on pictorial databases" *Pattern Recognition* **24**(7), 675-680

Chang, N S and Fu, K S (1980) "A relational database system for images" pp 288-321 in *Pictorial Information Systems*, (ed Chang, S K and Fu, K S), Springer-Verlag, Berlin

Chang, S K et al (1977) "A relational database system for pictures" pp 142-149 in *Proceedings of the IEEE Workshop on Picture Data Description and Management*, Chicago, April 1977

Chang, S K (1985) "Image information systems" *Proceedings of the IEEE* **73**(4), 754-764

Chang, S K (1987) "Iconic semantics - towards a formal theory of icons" *International Journal of Pattern Recognition and Artificial Intelligence* **1**(1), 103-120

Chang, S K et al (1988) "An intelligent image database system" *IEEE Transactions on Software Engineering* **14**(5), 681-688

Chang, S K and Jungert, E (1991) "Pictorial data management based upon the theory of symbolic projections" *Journal of Visual Languages and Computing* **2**, 195-215

Chock, M et al (1984) "Database structure and manipulation capabilities of a picture database management system (PICDMS)" *IEEE Transactions on Pattern Analysis and Machine Intelligence* **6**(4), 484-492

Dixon, J R et al (1990) "Unresolved research issues in development of design-with-features systems" pp 183-196 in *Geometric Modelling for Product Engineering* (ed Wozny, M J et al) Elsevier, Amsterdam

Eakins, J P (1989) "SAFARI - a shape retrieval system for engineering drawings" pp 50-71 in *Proceedings of 11th BCS Information Retrieval Specialist Group Research Group Colloquium on Information Retrieval* (ed Pollitt, A S)

Eakins, J P (1990) "Design and evaluation of a shape retrieval system" PhD thesis, University of Newcastle upon Tyne

Firschein, O and Fischler, M A (1971) "Describing and abstracting pictorial structures" *Pattern Recognition* **3**, 421-443

Firschein, O and Fischler, M A (1972) "A study in descriptive representation of pictorial data" *Pattern Recognition* **4**, 361- 377

Frasson, C and Er-Radi, M (1986) "Principles of an icons-based command language" *SIGMOD Record* **15**(2), 144-152

Herot, C F (1980) "Spatial management of data" *ACM Transactions on Database Systems* **5**(4), 493-514

Horikoshi, T and Kasahara, H (1990) "A 3-D shape indexing language" pp 493-499 in *Proceedings of 9th Annual Phoenix Conference on Computers and Communications*, Los Alomitos, California

IEEE (1985) "Computer graphics in the detective business" *IEEE Computer Graphics and Applications* **5**(4), 14-17

Ireton, M A and Xydeas, C S (1991) "Classification of shape for content retrieval of images in a multimedia database" pp 111-116 in *Proceedings of 6th International Conference on Digital Processing of Signals in Communications*

Kato, O et al (1982) "Interactive hand-drawn input system" pp 544-549 in *Proceedings of IEEE Computer Society Conference on Pattern Recognition and Image Processing (PRIP 82)*, Las Vegas, June 1982

Kemper, A and Wallrath M (1987) "An object-oriented database system for engineering applications" *SIGMOD Record* **16**(3), 299-310

Kim, H J et al (1988) "PICASSO: a graphical query language" *Software Practice and Experience* **18**(3), 169-203

Kim, W (1990) "Object-oriented databases: definition and research directions" *IEEE Transactions on Knowledge and Data Engineering* **2**(3), 327-341

Maeda, A et al (1988) "A multimedia database system featuring similarity retrieval" pp 239-244 in *Proceedings of the 2nd International Symposium on Interoperable Information Systems*, Tokyo

Nagy, G (1985) "Image database" *Image and Vision Computing* **3**(3), 111-117

O'Docherty, M H et al (1990) "Advances in the processing and management of multimedia information" *ICL Technical Journal* **7**, 271-287

Opitz, H et al (1969) "Workpiece classification and its industrial application" *International Journal of Machine Tool Design Research* **9**, 39-50

Orenstein, J A and Manola, F A (1988) "PROBE spatial data modelling and query processing in an image database application" *IEEE Transactions on Software Engineering* **14**(5), 611-629

Rabitti, F and Stanchev, P (1987) "Graphical Image Retrieval from Large Image Databases" vol 2, pp 69-89 of *Proceedings of AICA conference*, Trento

Rabitti, F and Stanchev, P (1989) "GRIM_DBMS: a GRaphical IMage DataBase Management System" pp 415-430 in *Visual Database Systems* (ed Kunii, T L) Elsevier, Amsterdam

Rabitti, F and Savino, P (1991) "Image query processing based on multi-level signatures" pp 305-314 in *Proceedings of 14th International ACM/SIGIR Conference on R & D in Information Retrieval*, Chicago

Roussopoulos, N et al (1988) "An efficient pictorial database system for PSQL" *IEEE Transactions of Software Engineering* **14**(5) 639-650

Salton, G (1971) "The SMART retrieval system - experiments in automatic document processing" Prentice-Hall, Englewood Cliffs, New Jersey

Tamura, H and Yokoya, N (1984) "Image database systems: a survey" *Pattern Recognition* **17**(1), 29-43

Toriwaki, J et al (1980) "Pictorial information retrieval of chest X-ray image database using pattern recognition techniques", pp 1116-1119 in *Proceedings of the Third World Conference on Medical Informatics*, Tokyo, October 1980 (ed Lindberg, D A B and Kaihara, S), North-Holland, Amsterdam

Willis, P and Hunter, A (1991) "A picture archive browser" *Computer Graphics Forum* **10**, 49-59

Yokoya, N and Tamura, H (1982) "A database system of microscopic cell images", pp 471-476 in *Proceedings of ISM III '82, the first IEEE Computer Society International Symposium on Medical Imaging*, Berlin

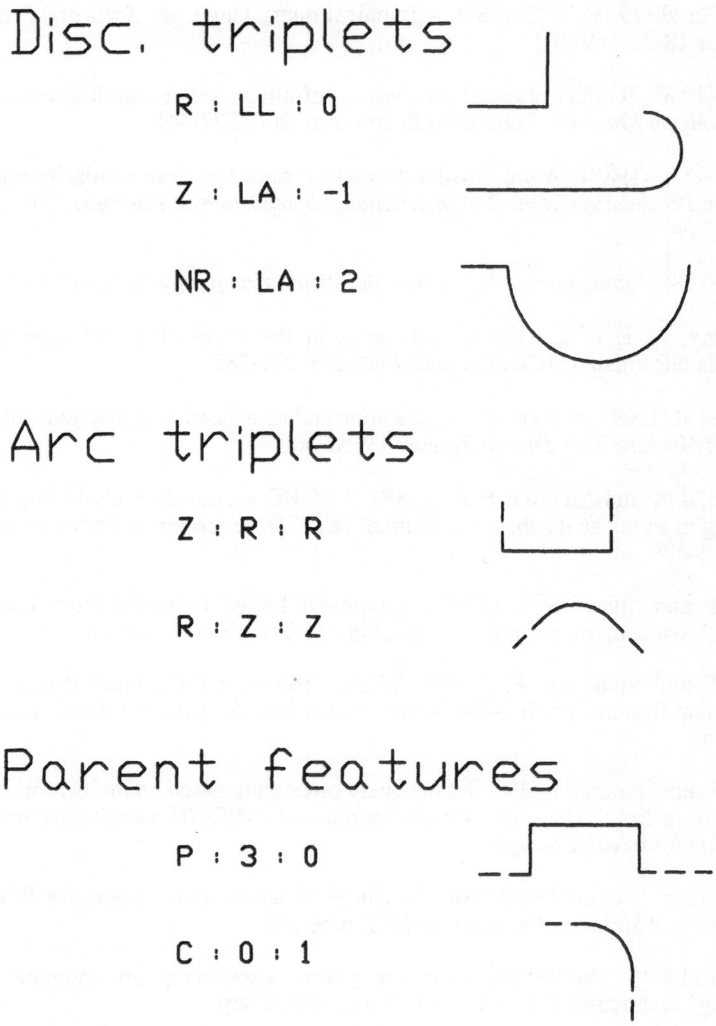

Figure 1: Illustrations of some of the "local" boundary features incorporated into SAFARI. Discontinuity angle triplet features indicate the environment of each boundary angle, showing successively the angle type (right-angle, acute, obtuse, etc), the types of line enclosing the angle (line-line, line-arc, etc) and the relative lengths of the two lines (expressed as round ($\log_2(l_1/l_2)$)). Arc angle triplets illustrate the angular environment of each line (arc angle class plus discontinuity angle with each adjoining line). Parent features indicate the presence of local shape features (protrusions, depressions, corner features, etc), together with their composition in terms of numbers of straight lines and circular arcs.

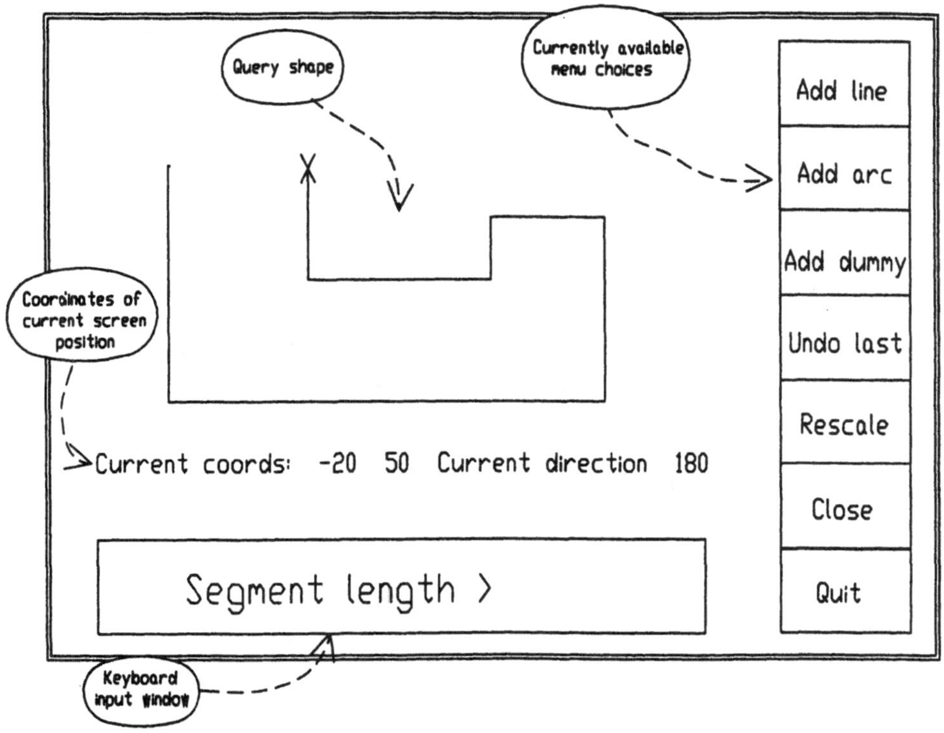

Figure 2: A typical query input screen for SAFARI in keyboard input mode. The user can build up a query shape consisting of one or more boundaries on the screen by indicating start coordinates and direction for each boundary, then specifying length, arc angle and discontinuity angle for each boundary segment. Facilities are provided for UNDOing the last segment created, and rescaling the drawing if it becomes too large to fit on the screen. Segments may be specified as "real" or "dummy", thus allowing incomplete queries to be defined for Type C matching. Note that the coordinate system used when drawing a query is purely arbitrary and has no effect on its final representation - query shapes are canonicalized in the same way as stored shapes before matching takes place.

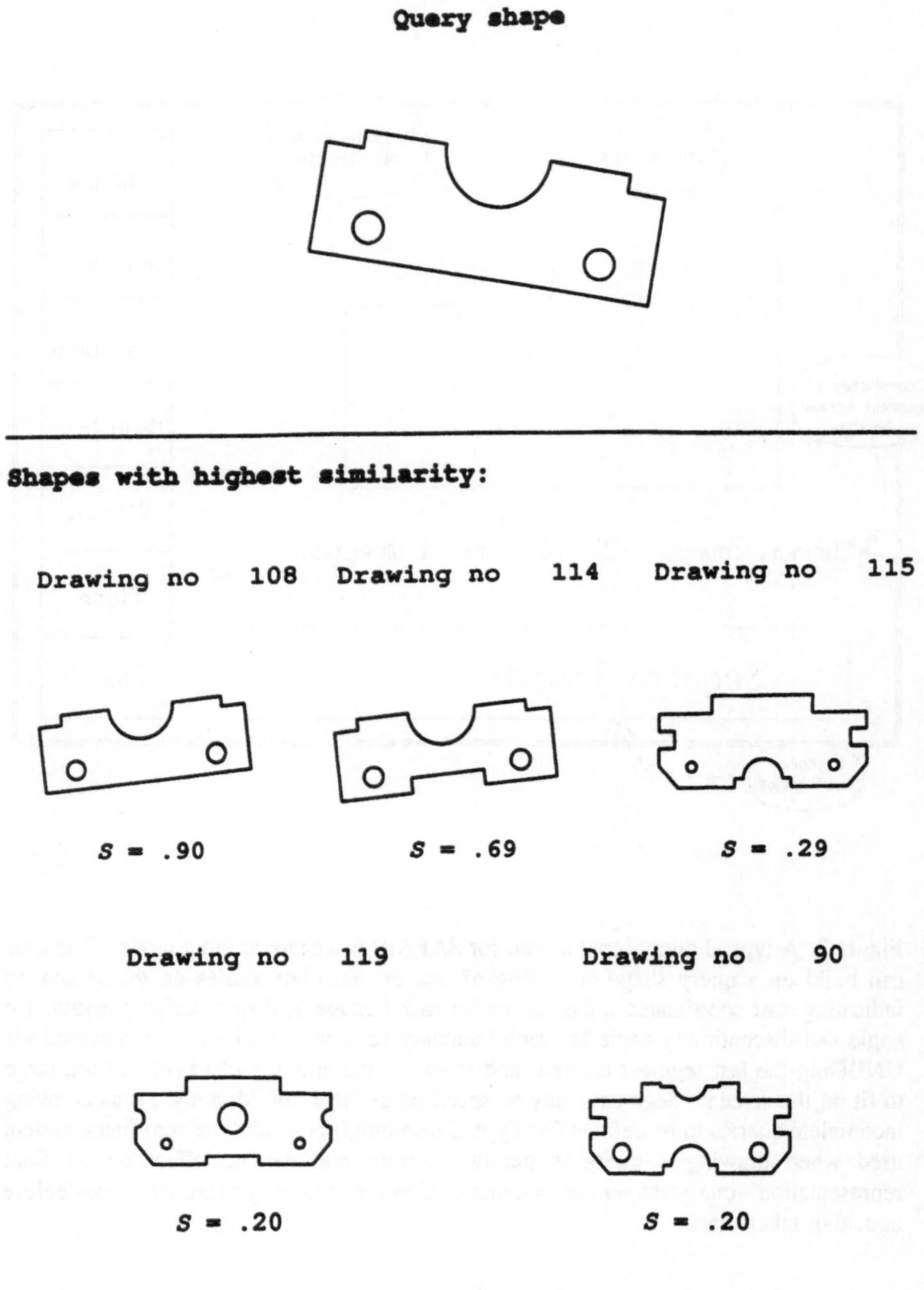

Figure 3: Results from a typical experiment on human shape retrieval judgements. Students were asked to rank up to 5 shapes from the test database in order of similarity to the test query (counting an exact match as position zero). Shapes were then ranked in order of similarity index

$$s = (10*f_0+7*f_1+5*f_2+3*f_3+2*f_4+f_5)\ /n,$$

wher f_i is the number of rankings for each drawing at position i, and n is the total number of subjects performing the test. (Other similarity measures give almost identical rankings).

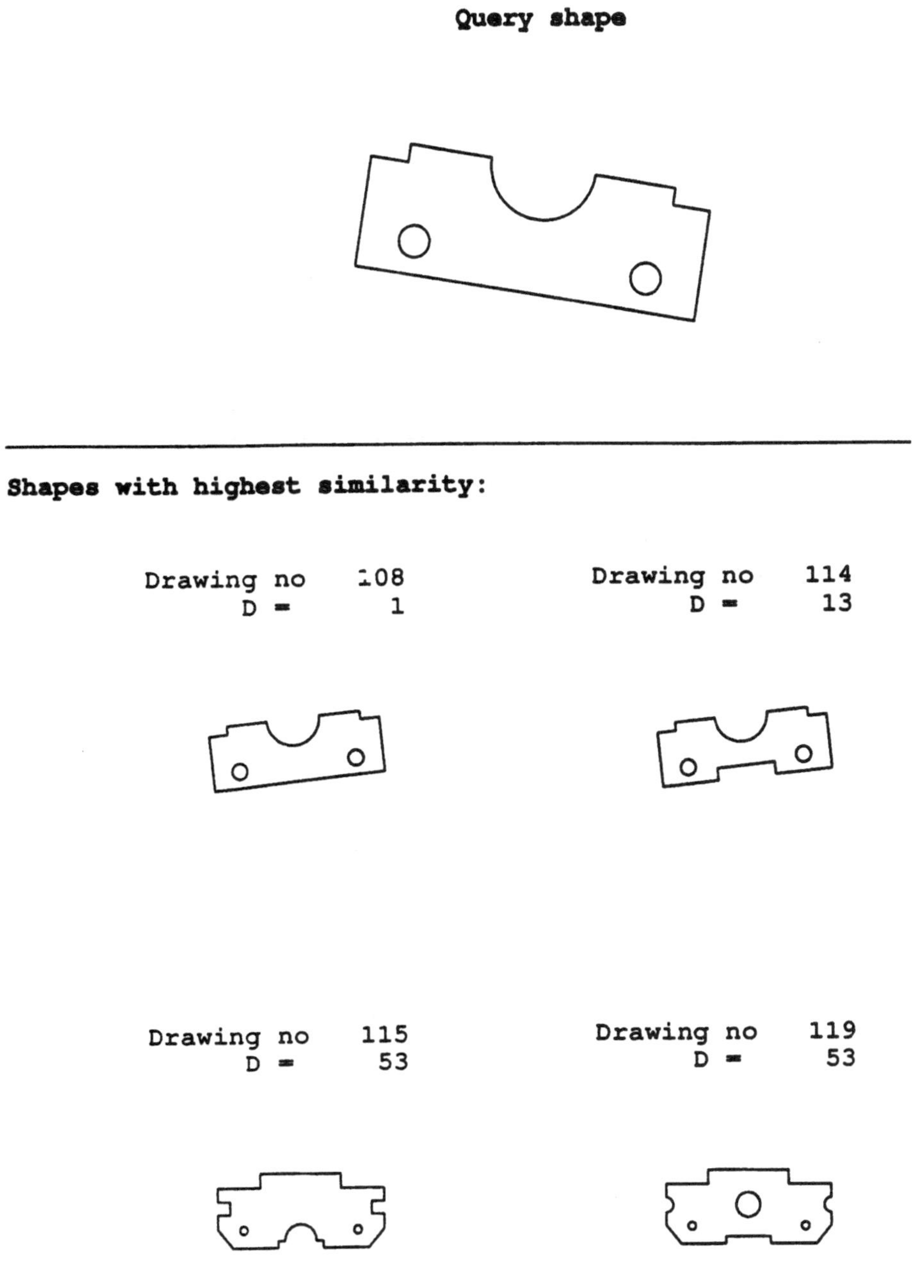

Figure 4: Results from the prototype version of SAFARI, using the same query as in Figure 3. In this case, a multi-stage matching process was used: firstly, feature matching using "arc triplet" and "parent feature" fragments; secondly, outer boundary segment matching; finally, inner boundary position (and shape class) matching. Here, the measure $D = F^*(S+k^*B)$, where F, S and B are measures of distance between query and stored shapes on the basis of fragments, outer-boundary segments and inner-boundary positions respectively, and k is a weighting parameter.

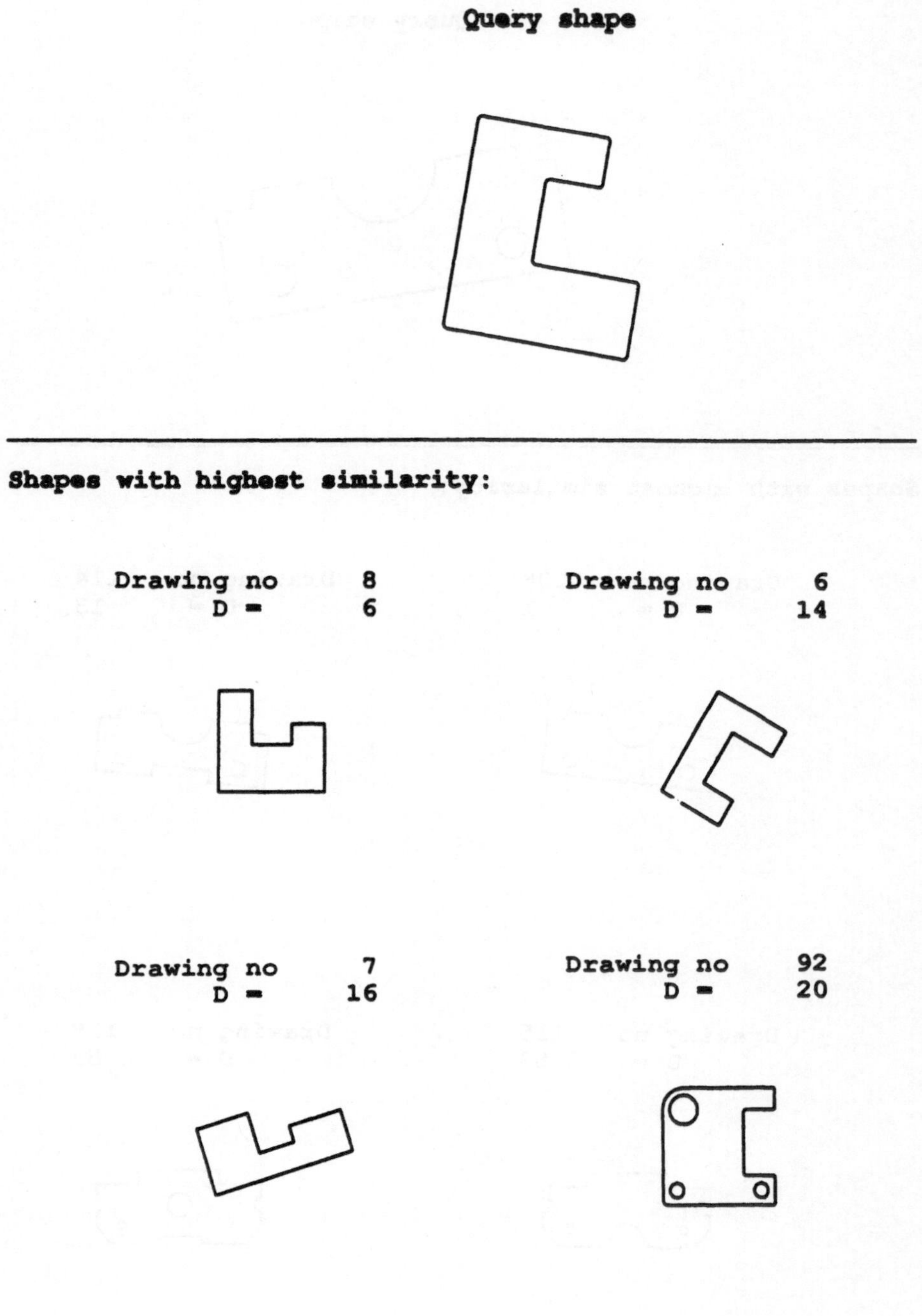

Figure 5: A query requiring only the outer boundary shape to be searched. The results shown were obtained by a combination of "arc triplet" and "parent feature" fragment matching, followed by outer-boundary segment matching.

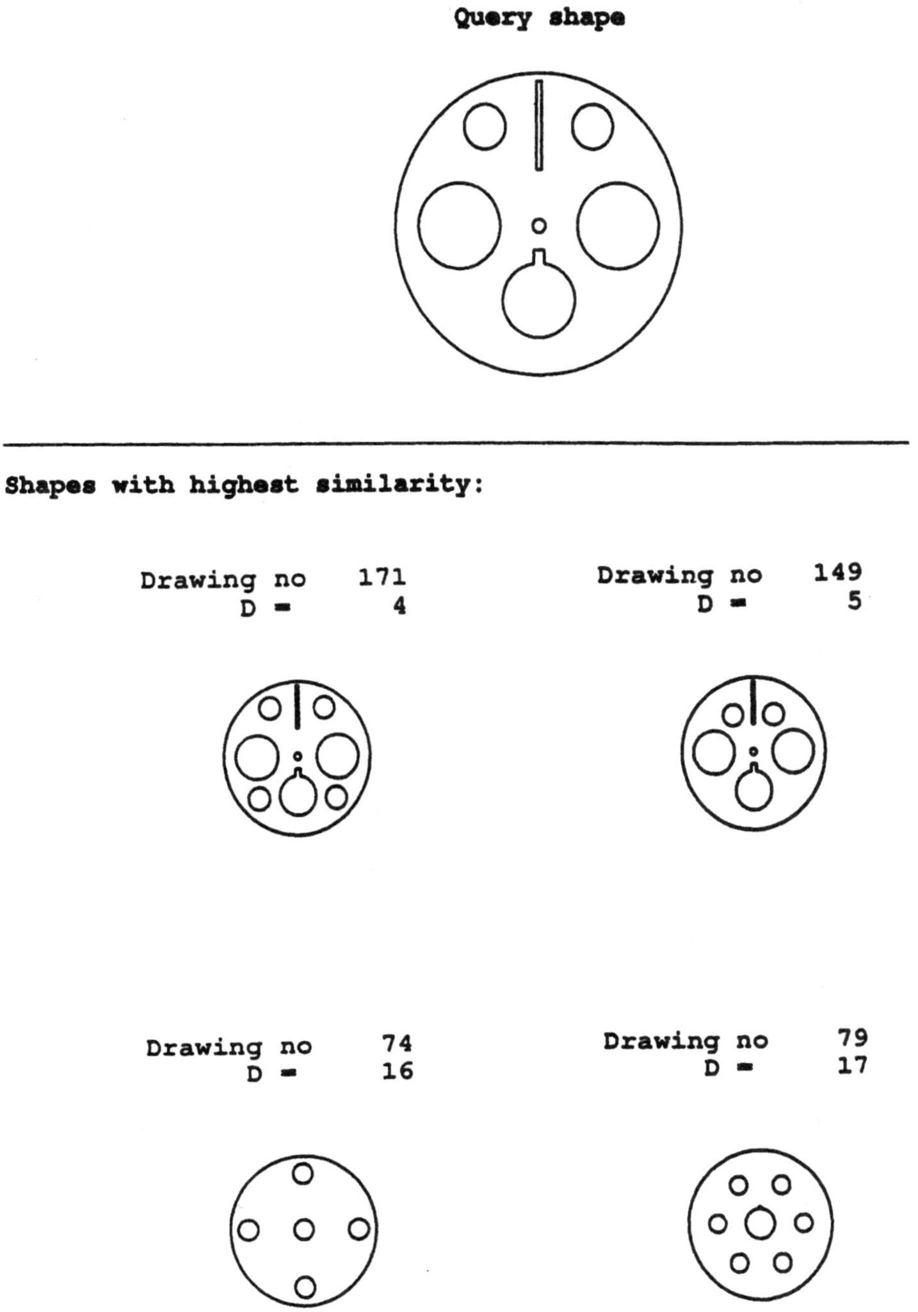

Figure 6: A query showing SAFARI's ability to search on inner boundary position and shape.

Modelling Online Database Systems in an Intelligent Interface

Bruce Robinson
Information Technology Institute,
University of Salford, Salford M5 4WT
UK

Abstract

Intelligent interfaces to online databases employ metadata, which describes the host systems to be accessed and the structure and content of the databases stored on them. As the range of information available through an interface grows, this metadata increasingly reflects the complexity, heterogeneity and inconsistencies of the online systems themselves. If intelligent interfaces are to be easily maintained and extensible, data modelling methods which take account of the specific characteristics of online systems must be developed.

This paper outlines a set of requirements for such models, drawing on practical experience in the design of a data dictionary for an intelligent interface. Some existing approaches are assessed for their applicability to online systems, in particular:
- models of federated or multi-database systems, which consist of many distributed, heterogeneous and autonomous databases;
- object-oriented data models.

1 Introduction

To a non-expert user the online world appears like a Tower of Babel of differing databases, hosts, command languages and field structures. Tools to aid the end user must tame the diversity, complexity and inconsistency of more than 3,000 databases scattered over a large number of hosts with the goal of providing powerful but easy to use methods of accessing this information. As the scope and power of interfaces grow, and more and more information becomes available, the question of how to do this is likely to become more acute, as it, at least partly, reflects a real diversity in the types of information on offer. It is unlikely therefore that standardisation would totally solve the problem and, in any case, little activity of this kind can be expected from the database producers or the hosts.

If intelligent interfaces or gateways are to be of real use to the user, they must be able to provide transparent access to a large number of information sources, and make use of the full facilities offered by the databases and the hosts. This requires methods for handling the mapping from a query expressed in terms of the user's information needs and independently of the target database and host to a query aimed at a particular database in a particular host language. If the interface is to be easy to extend to new information sources and to maintain, this function should be driven by data describing the hosts and databases, rather than hard-wired program code translators, which are too inflexible to exploit the facilities provided by the host.

This paper examines the structure of this metadatabase and what is necessary to model online databases adequately. The author has been involved in the early stages of development of a Source Data Dictionary, which aimed to fulfil this function in an intelligent natural language interface. This experience indicates that it is not sufficient to build a database and populate it with data. The structure and complexity of the metadata reflects that of the online systems and requires more sophisticated modelling. This paper will therefore look at recent research in related areas, which may be applicable to modelling online information retrieval systems.

2 Database Autonomy, Heterogeneity and Distribution

A DBMS1 implementation is typically assumed to consist of a single database (and therefore a single schema and data model), located in one place and with a single authority deciding on its content and structure. As the quantity of information available to a user grows, each of these assumptions begins to break down. Increasingly the database environment open to a user will be:

- distributed i.e. located at a number of sites internal or external to the user's organisation;
- heterogeneous in a number of respects;
- and autonomous, where the existence of multiple schemas combines with a lack of central control.

Federated [Heimbigner and McLeod 1985, Sheth and Larson 1990] and multidatabase [Litwin 1986, 1990] architectures have been developed to provide a framework for modelling data sharing between information sources in a loosely connected environment where each database maintains its autonomy and heterogeneity. They are distinguished from distributed databases because the components possess the property of autonomy and there is no single, central controlling definition of the data or schema.

Online information retrieval has been proposed as an area to which these architectures can be applied [Litwin, Mark and Roussopoulos 1990, McLeod 1991]. All databases within an online system are remote and distributed from the user's point of view. To satisfy a given query a user may need to access databases at more than one remote location. Online databases are more highly heterogeneous than the record-based models which are typically used to describe the purpose of these architectures. The less highly formatted structure of much of the data in online IR increases the range of retrieval methods used and the scope of the metadata required to model them (compare, for example, the methods used in full text searching and in searching statistical databanks). While online databases may sometimes contain attributes that can serve as unique keys (e.g. ISBNs or database accession numbers), they are rarely used in user searching, which is usually based on less precise indicators of record content and often involves the retrieval of some unwanted information. In the online world autonomy is total, with control of content and structure lying completely outside the user's organisation with the hosts and database producers.

As the goal of federated and multidatabase architectures is to present diverse databases as if they were a single system, their function clearly overlaps with that of an intelligent interface for online or a gateway. These architectures also share a focus on the addition of a homogenising layer on top of the component databases to give users the illusion of a single system [Kim and Seo 1990]. Models differ on the degree of integration of the schemas and transparency presented to the user, but, as a minimum, aim for multidatabase interoperability , where the user is aware of the heterogeneity, but is able to manipulate all the databases through a common language [Litwin, Mark and Roussopoulos 1986]. These architectures often assume a Canonical or Common Data Model (CDM), the use of which provides a level of abstraction able to overcome the underlying heterogeneity. (A taxonomy of types and models is provided in [Sheth and Larson 1990].)

As distributed locations and total autonomy can be taken for granted in online information retrieval, we shall concentrate on the extent and types of heterogeneity found in online systems. The types of heterogeneity found will then be used to assess the applicability of the reference architecture for federated database systems given by Sheth and Larson [Sheth and Larson 1990].

3 Heterogeneity in Online Information Retrieval Systems

Heterogeneity of database content and structure is inherent to the purposes and organisation of online information retrieval systems. Databases come from a large number of producers, who in some cases use structures taken from previously available hard copy information, such as abstracting journals. Hosts put databases onto different software platforms and may also make different subsets of an individual database available to searchers. The searcher has to deal with the information in the formats and through the command languages made available by the hosts. Most importantly, however, information types may differ radically in size and structure from full text documents to individual numeric data items. This diversity may require different types of retrieval or use of different command language features despite the information sources being used covering the same subject area. This might even occur for fields within the same database.

If the databases are to be exploited to the full, it is not sufficient just to provide a common command language. This may enable access to a number of hosts, but at the expense of 'losing the advanced features of the command language and the special capabilities of certain databases.' [Efthimiadis 1990]. Nor is it practical to implement ad hoc translation programs from a common language aimed at making use of many of the advanced or database-specific features as the number and complexity of the translation programs grow in proportion to the number of databases and hosts. Equally, the ability to search across several databases at once, now common on hosts, may also not deal adequately with heterogeneity - when one tries to use, for example, field searching across databases.

An intelligent interface must therefore be capable of capturing the heterogeneity of the systems and the databases and using its knowledge of databases and hosts to exploit the features available fully. It must as far as possible be driven by metadata, which is easy to change and can reflect different structures at a much more detailed level. This can then be supplemented by limited but general procedures that can exploit as many of the common features as possible while taking account of exceptions, advanced features and database or field specific features. To do this it is necessary to understand the different levels at which heterogeneity occurs.

3.1 Semantic Heterogeneity

Sheth and Larson [1990] refer to semantic heterogeneity in a federated database system as "a disagreement about the meaning, interpretation or intended use of the same or related data". In the DBMS world this typically refers to definitions given in the schema of the data contained in certain fields of, say, a relational database.

In the online IR world, these concerns are too limited as relatively few online databases contain merely atomic values and are more likely to use inherently ambiguous and fuzzy methods of representing information such as un- or semi-structured text. As consistency here depends on the content of documents and the way in which they are indexed, semantic heterogeneity often occurs within databases as well as between them. Techniques to reduce the semantic heterogeneity in information retrieval include well known methods such as the use of thesauri, use of controlled vocabulary, and truncation of search terms.

There is even less guarantee of consistency between databases as different terminology, thesauri and indexing rules may be used and their subject scope may differ. To overcome differences between or within databases, the contents must be mapped on to common codification of knowledge of the subject area. Where more than one thesaurus exists, this task consists of mapping between thesauri. This would enable semantic descriptions of the content of databases and of the contents of fields to be used to map query content on to the different linguistic descriptions in the databases.

3.2 Data Model Heterogeneity

A data model can be defined as a method for structuring collections of data and defining operations and constraints on them. With structured data it is generally assumed that a single data model will be used for each database which will be under the control of a given DBMS. In this context, data model heterogeneity therefore occurs between groups of databases running under different DBMSs.

In online systems the situation is more complex. A single host using a single command language may allow the use of many different data models and accordingly support different methods of retrieval (for example, text retrieval and retrieval by specifying one or a range of values for a field). Data models may not be consciously defined and may just emerge from the properties of the host software. As Staud [Staud 1988] states:

"Online databases usually arise directly from practice, where there is no underlying data model (as for example the relational model) which determined the structure of the database. The basis is the programming language, by which the organisation is achieved."

This pragmatic approach arises from the organic development of online systems, which is also reflected in the fact that, while information retrieval has developed methods for the structuring and representing knowledge, relatively little work has been done on data modelling.

One cannot therefore deduce the data model being used for the database management software and often need to look at individual databases in some detail. The boundaries between data models are less distinct and a single database may be a hybrid of several data models.

To take one particularly complex example, the 'Disclosure' database on Dialog contains US Company information as disclosed annually to the SEC. It can be searched on fields with a wide range of properties:

- on company name (three text fields, including one on subsidiaries);

- on specific subfields within the corporate resume (e.g. TS = ticker symbol, CS = current outstanding shares, CY = city. City and ticker symbol fields use coded values);
- on numeric fields representing financial data (e.g. SA= for sales, CA = 0:3000 for cash values between 0 and 3000);
- on different types of bibliographic data (e.g document type and period);
- on text (e.g /DE for a description of the business, /PL for the full text of the President's letter);
- on officers (mixed text and numeric).

In this case, fields range from those based on a highly unstructured full text data model to others based on individual values, which can be searched in the same way as a DBMS based system. Thus data model heterogeneity may exist within as well as between databases. Secondly, the distinction between databases or fields containing document descriptions and those containing actual documents or structured data means that in the former cases another level of indirectness is added between the document structure and its content. Staud [Staud 1988] describes this distinction as being between source and reference databases in his categorisation of online data models.

3.3 Structural Heterogeneity

Two databases may share a data model and still differ in structure. For example, while bibliographic databases will always need author and title fields, the content of the other fields may vary considerably (e.g. the use of abstracts or citations). Structural heterogeneity may also exist between versions of the same database implemented on different hosts (See Fig.1 for an example). This type of heterogeneity may requires some way of indicating equivalence between differently named fields.

3.4 Retrieval Language Heterogeneity

Two otherwise identical databases may be heterogeneous because they require to be searched with different command languages. Host command languages vary both in their syntax and in the range of features they supply. This means that different data must drive the translation and a description of the syntax must be stored in the dictionary so that a translation can be made.

3.5 Data Format Heterogeneity

Individual fields may contain the same information but use different representations or formats. For example, in one database an industry classification may be a text field, in another it may use a UK or US SIC code. This type of heterogeneity requires a translation mechanism such as a lookup table to be able to map from one set of values to another.

Online databases therefore fall in an extreme part of the spectrum as far as all three characteristics - autonomy, heterogeneity and distribution - are concerned. This suggests that federating online information sources may be more difficult than federating structured business databases.

4 Online the Federated Database Model

The goal of the federated database model is to allow the sharing of data between a number of heterogeneous, distributed and autonomous database systems. To analyse this we shall look at the reference model for this architecture developed in [Sheth and Larson 1990]. It consists of five interacting schemas (or data descriptions) and a description of the mappings between them. (See fig 2.)

The lowest level is the local schema, which contains a logical description of a component database (i.e. one participating in the federation) in terms of its own data model. This is identical to the schema that would exist if the database was standing on its own outside the federation. This can be translated into a component schema, which represents the same individual database in the canonical or common data model. This enables integration into the federated schema and allows the addition of more complex semantics.

In a DBMS model, the owner of a federated database may wish to specify which parts of the component database participate in the federation, thus retaining access control over the data. The schema that implements this - the export schema - is therefore particularly concerned with security and the interfaces between the component database and the federation. It is a subset of the component schema.

The federated schema is an integrated collection of export schemas. Though they are all already in the CDM, there remains the issue of how they should be integrated in the federated schema, which also contains information on the location of each database. The federated schema may also function as a federation dictionary, indicating what information sources are available across the federation. Mapping to or from the export schemas of the individual databases occurs by means of one or more constructing processors, which are responsible for decomposing commands on an integrated schema into commands for components databases as well as integrating the multiple imported export schemas into one federated schema.

Finally, on top of the federated schemas, there may be one or more external schemas, which define a subset of the federated schema available to a particular set of users. This may be necessary in order to enforce access control at the level of the federation (in interfaces to online this will be necessary to control costs) or to provide customised subsets of the federated schema to meet particular information needs.

4.1 The Federated Model and Online Information Retrieval

This federated architecture was originally oriented towards the typical structures provided by DBMSs for structured data. For online IR some of these components are redundant and others need to be supplemented. The reasons can be summed up as: the total autonomy and goals of the database hosts; no user updating of the database; the extent and importance of semantic heterogeneity; and the multiple levels at which heterogeneity occurs.

Once a user has registered with a host, the host has no interest in control of access to the databases. It is in the host's interest to maximise the usage of as wide a range of information as possible. It can therefore be assumed that the whole of the component schema is made available to the federation and no separate export schema is required. Access control from the host's point of view is implemented by registration and passwords. The administrator of the federation may wish however to restrict access to the component databases on grounds of cost and users may wish to be restricted to certain information sources, which they have found match their information needs The external schema, which defines the access of individual users to the federated databases, thus retains its function.

In online IR a database schema is rarely available to the users outside the pages of the manuals containing detailed descriptions of the database structures or online help systems. They are not available for importing into or manipulation by an interface or federation. Nor is there likely to be an explicit common data model. There is however a common descriptive language (the host command language), but it has been developed to suit the databases rather than the other way round. The builder of the federated system therefore has much more work to create the federated schema as there is no ready-made schema to provide the target for integration. The creator of the federation has also to create notional component schemas themselves (which implies that they have correctly interpreted the descriptions in the host manuals). We will examine below how the federated schema can be structured so as to make this task as easy as possible.

The user of online is unable to change anything on the host, as autonomy is total. This means that many of the functions which have to be provided for in a DBMS environment can be forgotten as they are simply functions of the host software and are hidden from the user. These include methods for updating the database, most performance considerations, integrity and concurrency. While it may be useful for the user choosing a database to know how often it is updated and what order the records are stored in, these functions do not affect the mechanisms for translating a query to exploit a particular database and can therefore be ignored in discussing the modelling of databases in an interface.

The nature of the data models found in online IR and the traditional tools used in information retrieval point to the need for an additional layer, which we shall call the semantic schema [Ruspini and Fraley 1984, Rasmus 1991]. This provides a common reference point for the resolution of semantic issues such as ambiguity, the use of synonyms, the relationships between terms and the identification of the names and content of fields. (It could serve a similar role with federated DBMSs but is less crucial.) The knowledge bases required here are an extended dictionary covering the vocabulary in use in a particular subject area with semantic categorisation of terms and cross-references to an extended thesaurus with named relationships. [Vickery et al 1987, Vickery et al 1988, Tome Associates 1991]

The semantic schema would serve a number of functions. The first, independent of the hosts and databases, is to provide a basis for the interface to understand a user's natural language query in terms of the concepts underlying terms used in a particular subject area.2 The second is to provide a basis for a description of the content of a database independently of the data model used. This can both provide a means to identify the content of individual fields and to relate them across databases, even if they are named differently. The semantic schema therefore plays a part in overcoming semantic heterogeneity between databases and can also be used in translation from a linguistic representation of the query into a database / host specific representation.

A modified version of the federated database architecture suitable for online IR is shown in Fig 3. The modelling method and structure of the federated schema will now be assessed in the light of work on the Source Data Dictionary project and suggestions made for how it should be implemented.

DATA-STAR	DIALOG	ESA	ORBIT
ABSTRACT (AB)	AB	AB	AB
DESCRIPTORS (DE)	DE	DESCRIPTORS(CT)	DESCRIPTORS(IT)
TITLE (TI)	TI	TI	TI
AUTHOR (AU)	AU	LA	AU
LANGUAGE (LG)	LA	AU	LA
PUB. YEAR (YR)	PY		PY
PUB. MONTH (YM)			ENTRY YEAR (EY)
PUB. DATE (YD)			

Figure 1: Structural and naming heterogeneity: The Materials Business database
Each column shows the fields on the given host in the order in which they appear.

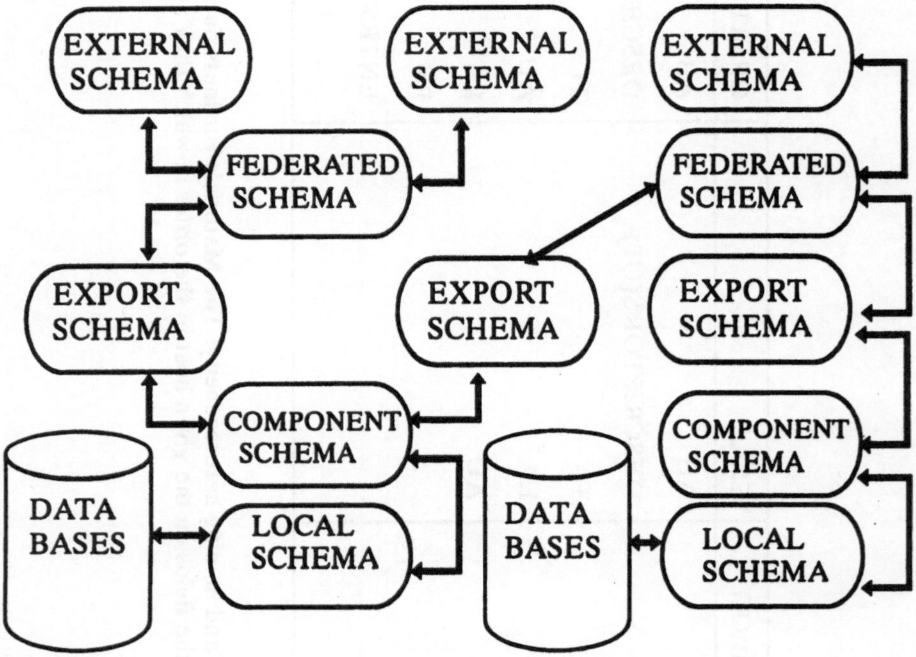

Figure 2: Federated database architecture

.5 The Source Data Dictionary

The Source Data Dictionary3 (SDD) was designed to resolve the problem of accessing a number of databases in one subject area through a common intelligent interface. The aim was to make the interface itself into a shell, which could be driven by the collection of metadata stored in a database, so that programming to deal with the specificities of databases and hosts could be kept to a minimum and ideally done without altogether. The SDD was seen as growing to contain all the data and processes, which were specific to a database or host.

Two subject areas were initially chosen to test this: pollution and environmental health and business. The initial focus was on command language syntax and translation from a common internal representation to a query in a host command language, which would retrieve information from a given host / database pairing. This process went from initial connection and logging on to the host, through an ordered search strategy, in which different types of commands followed in a particular order to display and downloading of the information and logging off from the host.

The metadata was gathered from host documentation, codified into a consistent representation (Backus Normal Form), modelled and stored in a CODASYL database, which was interfaced to the other parts of the system through a series of function calls built on top of the DBMS, which provided the metadata specified by the interface programs as required.

The initial work on environmental health focussed on a single data model - bibliographic databases - which might be expected to have the least heterogeneous features. Five databases, located across five hosts, were chosen, some databases being available on more than one of the hosts.

To derive a correct syntax definition it is necessary to take up to four factors into account: the host, database, field and command (e.g. whether a search or display command). The highest level was that of the host, which contained data describing features global to all databases operating under a given host. The second level was that of a database. As structural heterogeneity may occur between versions of the same database on different hosts, there must be one set of data for each database / host combination. The lowest and most specific level was that of the individual field.

Many of the attributes of the command language can be assigned directly to one of these levels, which can be seen as a hierarchy of one-to-many relationships with the host containing many databases and each database containing many fields. The field level, (which can itself have more than one level reflecting the nesting of subfields) can be assumed to be the most specific and thus to override more global definitions. There are a number of types of data for which more than one definition can occur at different levels; in particular command syntax where there is most often a conflict between the global host level and the individual field level.

The syntax definitions are classified according to their field type, which shows the type of syntax required for a particular field or set of fields, and the variable type, which indicates the format required for any variable data within the syntax definition. Thus, for example, an author search on Dialog has the field type <prefix> and the variable type <author_di> and the syntax definition is 'SS <prefix>=<author_di>'. This would be translated into

'SS AU=ROBINSON, B'. Other fields would share the same <prefix> field type, which would give a similar 'SS <prefix>=' syntax for the first part of the command.

The variable type is used to indicate to the calling program whether any transformation of the search variable will be required. For example, in the BIS Infomat database, country, events and product codes are used, so that the Source Data Dictionary will return one of the variable types <BIS_country>, <BIS_event>, <BIS_product>. This indicates to the calling program that a natural language term must be transformed to another data type - in this case, by consulting a lookup table. A pair of input and output variable types can be used to select the procedure for translation.

The organisation of the metadata - even for the single task of command language translation - comes to adopt the complexity of the ad hoc methods employed in the databases themselves. While the SDD enables some definitions to be shared between different pieces of data, it can only be maintained by someone who knows in some detail how information should be classified. If a common data model is to be used in the federated schema to integrate the underlying database structures, this model must be able to:

- support a number of different levels of granularity and complexity so that exceptions to rules may be implemented easily;
- enable the association of pieces of code with classes of data (e.g. code to perform translation using lookup tables);
- be easy to extend and maintain;
- deal easily with heterogeneity in a number of different dimensions and at a number of different levels.

The main candidate for this role is currently object-oriented databases, which we shall now examine in more detail.

6 Object-orientation as a Model for the Federated Schema

The object-oriented database [Brown 1991, Garvey 1989, Jackson 1991, Mariani 1991, McLeod 1991b, Smith and Zdonik 1987] is increasingly being seen as a way of providing a data model for non-traditional (i.e. non-record based) applications of information storage and retrieval such as CAD databases, multimedia and office information systems. In all these cases, the information is characterised by a range of differing and complex structures, each requiring a degree of specific processing and requiring a richer set of semantic constructs than is available in the record-based models. For similar reasons, object-oriented databases have also been identified as a means of linking and enabling access to heterogeneous applications and information sources. [Bertini 1988, Connors and Lyngbaek 1988, McFadden 1991]. After a brief examination of the properties of object-oriented databases that make them particularly useful for this class of applications, we shall show how they could support a metadatabase for retrieval from online databases.

6.1 The Object-oriented Model

All data stored in an Object-oriented DBMS consists of objects. An object can be defined as a set of data or attributes, together with a set of methods (or procedures) for operations on that object. The set of methods can be taken to define the behaviour of the object. The attributes can themselves be objects, which permits the representation of objects of arbitrary complexity as well as performing the operation of aggregating many objects into one, a basic construct of semantic data models. Access to the data in an object can only be through the interface provided by the methods and the rest of the data is hidden from the application using the object. As data and process are stored together, objects may be considered active and can communicate with other objects by way of message-passing (which effectively means invoking one of its methods).

Objects belong to classes, which contain a definition of the data and methods of objects of that type. Classes may have any number of instances of objects. They are organised in hierarchy, which permits the inheritance of data and methods by lower levels from higher ones. This enables the easy definition of sub-classes that only differ slightly from their parents. In some systems, multiple inheritance where the properties of more than one parent class can be inherited and where the database designer has to specify which are taken from each class.

Finally, objects in an Object-oriented DBMS have the property of object identity, which means that objects have an identity apart from the values of their attributes, which is given by the DBMS and does not change. This means that problems such as referential integrity (the interdependence of key values in a database), which cause particular problems for relational systems, are avoided in object-oriented systems.

6.2 Object-orientation and the Federated Schema for Online

If the object-oriented database model is to play the role of a common data model in a federated schema for online, it must deal with the characteristics of online identified in the earlier parts of this paper. These are:

- the variety of information types to be found and the different operations required;
- ease of structuring information provided by hosts into a common format;
- the ability to produce reproduce complex relations between different levels and aspects of the same object (e.g. a database)
- the need for an inheritance mechanism, probably involving multiple parent classes;
- translation mechanisms tied to individual classes of data;
- ease of maintenance and extension.

Object orientation has a number of clear advantages for most of these purposes. In particular, object-orientation does not force data into a strait-jacketed format and allows different sizes and granularities of information to be represented in the same database without taking on a single highly structured format. Thus it would be possible to have an object representing the highly varied structure of a database such as Disclosure, with different fields inheriting the properties of the different data models and types to which they belong. These properties would not merely be data structures, but also the operations required, for example, to translate from the system's internal representation to the host command language.

The independence of individual objects from others means that the federated schema can be extended easily, though changes to the pre-existing class hierarchy are more difficult to implement. It also means that it is easy to provide different groups of objects to different groups of users and that users can add their own information sources in order to personalise the information management capabilities of their PC. However this would at present, given the interfaces to Object-oriented DBMSs, presuppose a high level of technical ability on the part of the user.

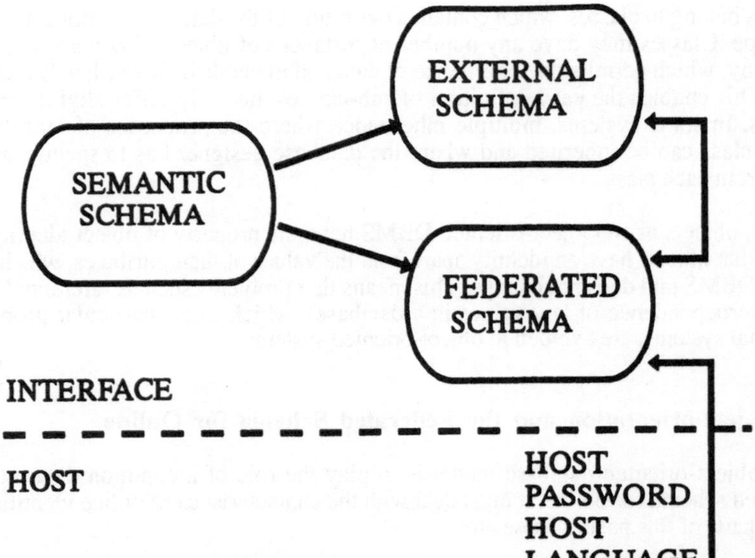

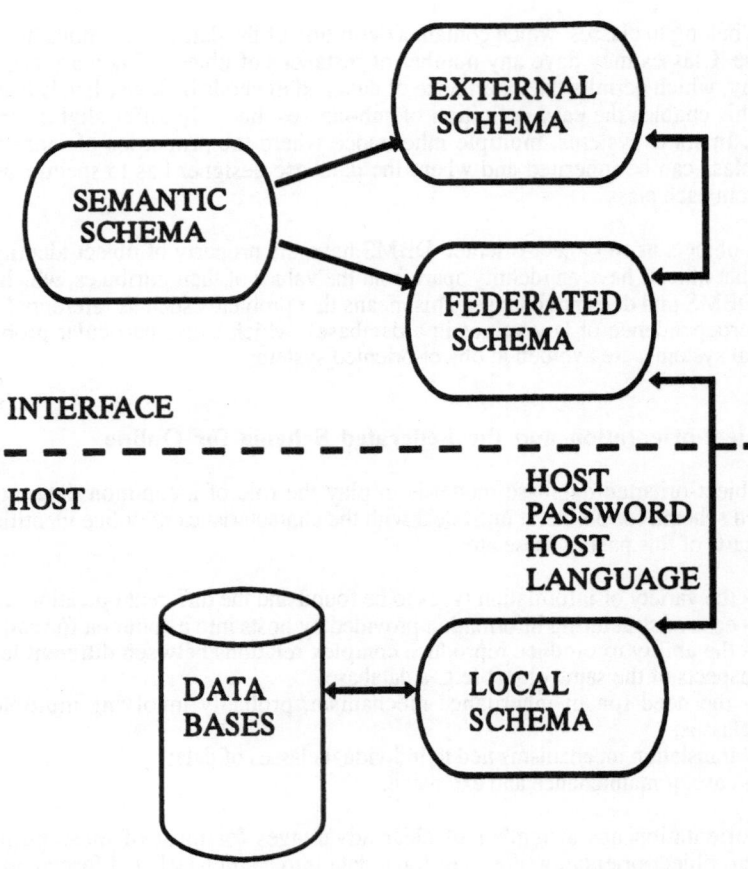

Figure 3: An intelligent interface architecture for online

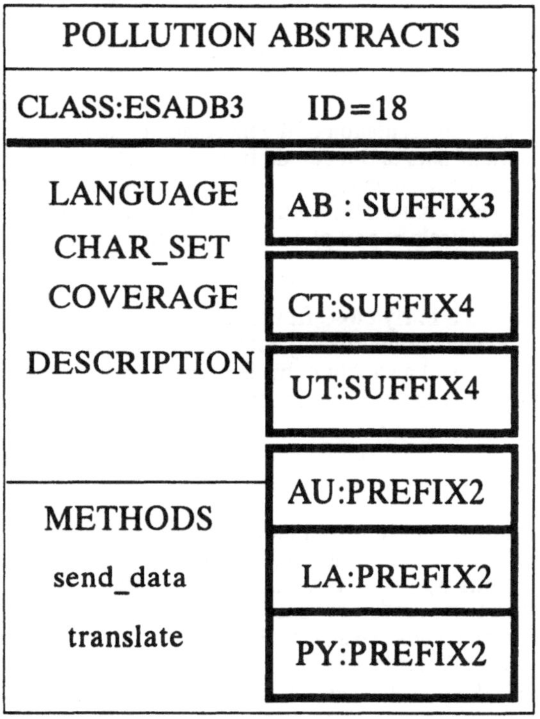

Figure 4: An example of a database object

The relatively high level semantics of the object oriented model allow a closer modelling of the complexity of the real world. This is not just an added extra, but is central to the process of schema integration. As Sheth and Larson [Sheth and Larson 1990] put it:

"The choice of CDM is critical. The CDM should be semantically rich; that is, it should provide abstraction and constraints so that the semantics relevant to schema integration can be presented. Thus semantic data models are much preferred over traditional data models.. the concept of generalisation is important for schema integration. One reason is that similar or related concepts are represented at different levels of abstractions in different schemas."

This is even more clearly the case with online than with DBMSs as the degree of heterogeneity is much higher.

Fig. 4 shows a possible representation of the metadata for an individual database. Its class 'ESADB3' would inherit data and methods from the host for general purposes. Its own data and methods are illustrated with the boxes on the right indicating the fields, which are themselves objects, which inherit the data and methods from their field type (e.g. suffix 3). The field type would itself be part of a class hierarchy similar to that used in the Source Data Dictionary.

This shows that there is a fairly close fit between the object oriented way of seeing the world and the requirements of interfacing online databases. However more work needs to be done to see how practical a structure this is. It is also not clear how successful object-orientation would be for representation of semantic information, such as dictionaries and thesauri.

7 Conclusions

Online systems share the defining characteristics of autonomy, heterogeneity and distribution which have spurred the development of federated and multidatabase systems. However because online possesses these qualities in rather extreme forms, some of the assumptions on which these models are based must take a different form. In particular, the total autonomy of online means that schema integration becomes entirely the responsibility of the creator of the federation and the federation does not provide schemas to be integrated. The high degree of heterogeneity also requires extension of the model to provide a common knowledge of the domain which can be used to deal with semantic heterogeneity. However research in this area does show the types and structures of the information needed to support multiple, heterogeneous information sources.

The experience of building the Source Data Dictionary indicates some of the difficulties of building a federated schema based around existing record-based models and confirms the need for a higher-level data model to serve as the basis for a store for so complex and diverse set of data. Object orientation seems to be a prime candidate for the role of common data model. Subsequent work will focus on developing the structure for a federated schema for online in an object-oriented database and also seeing how metadata and domain knowledge can be closely integrated.

References

Bertino E., Gagliardi R., Plagatti G., Sbatella L. The COMANDOS integration system: an object-oriented approach to the interconnection of heterogeneous applications. In Advances in Object-Oriented Database Systems, Lecture Notes in Computer Science 334, Berlin, Springer Verlag, 1988.

Brown, A. Object-Oriented Databases: Applications in Software Engineering. London, McGraw Hill, 1991.

Connors, T. and Lyngbaek P. Providing uniform access to information bases. In Advances in Object-Oriented Database Systems, Lecture Notes in Computer Science 334, Berlin, Springer Verlag, 1988.

Efthimiadis, E. Online searching aids: a review of front ends, gateways and other interfaces. Journal of Documentation, Sept. 1990, pp 218-262

Garvey M.A. and Jackson M.S. Introduction to object-oriented databases. Information and Software Technology, December 1989, pp 512-528.

Heimbigner D. and McLeod, D. A federated architecture for information management. ACM Transactions on Office Information Systems. Vol 3., No.3, July 1985, pp 253-278.

Jackson, M.S. A tutorial on object-oriented databases. Information and Software Technology, Jan/Feb 1991, pp 4-12.

Kim, W. and Seo, J. Classifying Schematic and Data Heterogeneity in a Multidatabase System. IEEE Computer, December 1991, pp 12-17.

Litwin, W. and Abdellatif, A. Multidatabase interoperability. IEEE Computer, Vol. 19 No. 12, pp 10-18.

Litwin, W., Mark L. and Roussopoulos, N. Interoperability of Multiple Autonomous Databases. ACM Computing Surveys, Vol. 22 No. 3, Sept. 1990, pp 267-293.

Mariani, J.A. Object-Oriented database systems. In Blair, Gordon (ed). Object-oriented languages, systems and applications, London, Pitman, 1991.

Mark, L. and Roussopoulos, N. Metadata management. IEEE Computer, December 1986, pp 26-36.

McFadden, F.R. Conceptual design of object-oriented databases. Journal of Object-Oriented Programming, Sept.1991, pp 29-33.

McLeod, D. Interbase: An approach to controlled sharing among autonomous, heterogeneous, database systems. IEEE Transactions on Data Engineering: Database Engineering, Vol. 9, 1990, pp 70-74.

McLeod, D. Pespective on object databases. Information and Software Technology, Vol. 33, No.1, Jan / Feb 1991, pp 13-21.

Rasmus, D.W. Integrating distributed information. Byte, November 1991, pp 247-253.

Rusinkiewicz, M. and Czejdo B. An approach to query processing in federated database systems. Proceedings of the 20th International Conference on System Sciences, Hawaii, 1987, pp 430-438.

Ruspini, E.H. and Fraley, R. ID: an Intelligent Information Dictionary System. Journal of Systems and Software, 4, 1984, pp 187-205.

Sheth, A.P. and Larson, J.H. Federated Database Systems for managing distributed, heterogeneous and autonomous databases. ACM Computing Surveys Vol. 22 No. 3, Sept 1990, pp 183-235.

Smith, K. and Zdonik, S. Intermedia: a case study of the differences between relational and object-oriented database systems. In OOPSLA 87 Proceedings, Sigplan Notices, Vol. 23 No.5 pp 452-465. New York, ACM, 1988.

Staud, J.L. The Universe of online databases: Reality and model(s). Journal of Information Science, Vol. 14, pp 141-158.

Tome Associates. Project SAINT 2: Intelligent Intermediary System - Reference functional model. Report to the CEC. March 1991. Luxemburg, CEC DG XIII.

Vickery A., Robinson B., Brooks H., Vickery B. 'A reference and referral system using expert system techniques', Journal of Documentation, Vol 43, no.1, March 1987, pp 1-23.

Vickery A., Brooks H., Robinson B., Stephens J., Vickery B. 'Expert System for Referral', British Library Library and Information Research Report 66, London, British Library, 1988.

1 We distinguish between typical business databases using models for structured data (e.g. relational, network, hierarchical), which we refer to as DBMS methods or applications, and the less structured data models used in online, which will be put under the heading of Online Information Retrieval applications.

2. We are here assuming that the user inputs a query to the interface in natural language.

3. The Source Data Dictionary was developed at Tome Associates as part of two projects: EUROSAGE, an intelligent tutoring system and interface to databases concerning information relevant to the Single European Market funded by the Training Agency; MITI a multi-lingual interface for information in the fields of environmental health and pollution funded by the EC.

A 'Select and Generate' Approach to Automatic Abstracting

P. A. Jones & C. D. Paice
Computing Dept., Lancaster University, Lancaster, LA1 4YR,
United Kingdom

Abstract

This paper describes on-going work on a new method of automatic abstracting which uses general domain knowledge in association with extracting techniques. A representation of the main concepts of a paper are stored in an abstract-frame. Each section of the abstract-frame has a group of phrases associated with it, and the occurrence of these phrases are used to extract relevant portions of text from source documents. The completed abstract-frame is then run through a program which uses an abstract-template to produce a coherent, cohesive abstract.

The system is being developed with papers in the area of agriculture, specifically papers dealing with experiments, trials or observations on crops. One aim of the project however is to produce a system which may be easily transferred to other domain areas.

1. Introduction

1.1 Automating the Abstracting Process

Abstracting technical literature is one area of information processing which has not exploited the increase in electronic-data-processing techniques. This is despite the fact that the raw material for abstracting (documents) are, through the increased use of desk-top publishing systems and networks, becoming more available in machine readable form.

Automatic abstracting may not be attracting the research it deserves for exactly the reasons that make it more viable. As full documents are increasingly available in machine readable form, many assume that the production of abstracts is unnecessary. It is true that the use of abstracts has changed, from mainly appearing in secondary journals to appearing more in on-line retrieval systems, but abstracts are still required as they have definite advantages over full texts. Abstracts are easier to scan when deciding if the article is worth reading, and they are cheaper to transmit (i.e. they use less bandwidth in an electronic environment or less paper using traditional communication methods). Also, despite what may be imagined, there is no real evidence that retrieval is more successful with full texts, since a full text tends to contain a lot of 'noise', whereas an abstract contains just the central content of a document.

Maybe automatic abstracting has not received widespread research interest because there is no need for it ? Yet all abstracting companies are overloaded with work, and, because of this abstracts are taking longer to appear in abstracting journals and on-line systems. It seems sensible to try to improve the time it takes, from an article being published to its abstract being included in a system. This would provide benefits to the entire scientific community, allowing work to be shared sooner and avoiding work being repeated unnecessarily.

Many publications insist that abstracts are provided by the author, apparently removing the need for automatic abstraction of that document. However, author abstracts may be unreliable and biased. Evans and Pollock [4] evaluated 45 articles on antibiotic prophylaxis in surgery and reported that 20% of the author abstracts had either omitted important numerical results or had made unjustified conclusions. Similar findings in other studies are summarised in Narine et. al. [10]. The bias contained in the author abstracts would not occur if the abstracts could be produced automatically.

Although it may be some time before it is feasible automatically to abstract all work to a sufficient quality level to be accepted by users, we hope to show that simple methods utilising traditional extracting techniques along with the recent knowledge acquired about the rhetorical structure of texts may provide a way forward.

1.2 The Domain Area

The work described in this paper is partially sponsored by CAB International (abbreviated to 'CABI' below), who are a company who produce more than 50 abstract journals in the area of agriculture. This is a vast area, so we have decided, in the first instance, to concentrate on papers in a specific area of agriculture, namely those papers which are about experiments, trials or observations on crops.

The source documents that are produced in this field have various characteristics which are of interest to an automatic abstractor. The titles of the papers are often long and descriptive, e.g.,

> "The effect of date of planting on field establishment of serotinous cape Proteaceae"

The papers themselves are usually fairly short and concise, and tend to follow the same stylised structure, containing the following sections :-

Introduction (inc. previous work)
Materials and Methods
Results
Discussion
Conclusion

1.3 The Present Paper

There are two major types of abstracts: indicative and informative. *Indicative abstracts* are statements of subject matter, whereas *informative abstracts* also give details of results and conclusions. Previous work on automatic abstracting has concentrated on the production of the simpler indicative abstracts. Our work described below is also aimed at the generation of this simpler style of abstracts, though at a later stage in our research we plan to address the problem of generating informative abstracts.

In Part 2 of this paper we summarise existing techniques and highlight their unsuitability in a 'real world' environment. A brief discussion of rhetorical structure and its importance for the problem of automatic abstracting is then presented in Part 3. We then describe in Part 4 the methodology 'select & generate' (subtitled 'a frame-based approach'), which uses the rhetorical structure of texts to overcome some of the limitations of existing approaches. Examples of abstracts produced in this way are included in Part 5 to highlight its effectiveness. In Part 6 on-going extensions to the method are outlined.

2. Existing Approaches

There are two broad approaches which have been used in the production of automatic abstracts and summaries. We will describe these approaches and give a brief outline of their relative advantages and disadvantages, before detailing how our methodology promises to improve on the previous work.

2.1 The "Extract & Rearrange" Approach

Attempts at automatically summarising texts began in the 1950s [8]. All the early work was on the production of *extracts*. An extract consists of a number of sentences selected from the source text. Typically, sentences are assigned weights which are supposed to reflect their usefulness in revealing the central ideas in the text. Weights may be assigned on the basis of a sentence's statistical properties, surface level features or textual position, or by a combination of such methods [3]. For instance a sentence may be assigned a positive weight if any of a number of clues are present, e.g.,

1) It contains an occurrence of a content word which also occurs in the title [3].

2) It contains an Indicator phrase (e.g. "This paper shows ....") [11].

3) It is the first sentence in a paragraph [1]

Similarly, a sentence may be assigned a negative weighting if it contains a literature citation or a stigma term, e.g. 'doubtful', 'unlikely'. After weights have been decided and combined then the top scoring sentences are selected. This, it was hoped, would provide the reader with the pertinent details of the text.

Unfortunately, these early attempts at summarisation produced, as might be expected, very disjointed pieces of text, which suffered from the problem of dangling references caused by *anaphors* (e.g. pronouns, demonstratives etc.) as in the example :

"**This** shows that the use of triadimenol seed dressing improves the yield of winter wheat."

Leaving the reader to ask "What does '**This**' refer to ?".

In 1971 Rush, in his ADAM system, took account of the dangling reference problem [17]. If ADAM detected an anaphor in the first clause of a selected sentence, then it would be resolved by either adding preceding sentences or, if more than three sentences were required, by deleting the selected sentence. However ADAM did not treat anaphors in a very 'intelligent' manner. It did not take into account that most potential anaphors can be non-anaphoric depending on their context and on their particular grammatical usage. Therefore, before an attempt is made at resolving an anaphoric reference, it must be correctly identified. In two papers Paice has described rules to recognise whether a potentially anaphoric word is anaphoric or not [12, 14]. If an external reference is identified (i.e. one whose antecedent is in a different sentence), it may be neutralised by any of the following methods :

1) Reject the sentence.
2) Delete the referential word or expression.
3) Rephrase the referential expression
   (e.g. "the system" Æ "a certain system").
4) Add the sentence referred to (if you can decide which it is).
5) Add the antecedent concept expression (if you can decide which it is).

The only practical attempt to deal automatically with anaphors, since Rush [17], was undertaken by Paice who developed the process of *aggregation* [11]. The aggregation process works by testing each sentence for external references. If only short-range references are present then preceding sentences are added one by one; if a definite reference (starting with "the") is found then several preceding sentences may be added at once. This process continues until the resulting passage may be considered 'tidy' (i.e. contains no unresolved anaphor or other referential device).

Once sentences have been selected and tidied they may then be arranged into what is hoped to be a readable form. Finally, pairs of sentences may be combined to give the text a more flowing style, and hence increase readability [9], e.g.,

Given two extracted sentences :
a) "The Primary tillers were measured."
b) "The Secondary tillers were measured."

We could generate the single sentence
"The Primary and Secondary tillers were measured."

Although all these methodologies work up to a point, neither the extraction nor the rearrangement process can, at present, be made to perform very accurately. We believe that this is due to a lack of understanding of text structure rather than to an inherent weakness in the methodologies. Hopefully a greater understanding of rhetorical structure (see section 3) will allow researchers to improve the performance of these techniques.

2.2 The "Understand & Generate" Approach

This method approaches the problem of abstracting using techniques from Artificial Intelligence and Expert Systems. It extracts semantic data from the text and holds it in some intermediate form. This representation is then used as the input to a natural language generator, which produces the abstract.

As an example, DeJong's FRUMP system operates using what may be called an expert system approach [2]. FRUMP works on news stories and has operated successfully when confronted with original news stories from United Press International's news wire. At its heart is a group of *sketchy scripts*, each containing a list of expected events. Thus the following is part of a sketchy script called $DEMONSTRATION :-

Predicted Event 1:
The demonstrators arrive at the demonstration location.
Predicted Event 2:
The demonstrators march.
Predicted Event 3:
Police arrive on the scene.
Predicted Event 4:
The demonstrators communicate with the the target of the demonstration.
Predicted Event 5:
The demonstrators attack the target of the demonstration.

As can be seen, the sketchy script is a detailed list of various activities and incidents which are likely to occur during a particular type of event. DeJong developed 60 scripts to cope with the variety of news stories that FRUMP was likely to encounter. The decision on which script to use, and how to instantiate it, was decided by detailed semantic analysis of the text. During the processing of the news story the sketchy script is used to allow the predictor part of the system to make inferences which are then 'fleshed out' by the substantiator part of the system.

There are a number of limitations to FRUMP-type approaches. These kinds of approaches require considerable world-knowledge and due to this can only work in a very restricted domain. This means that any FRUMP-type system will not be domain portable. These systems also require that the input text has to undergo detailed semantic analysis; this is a very time consuming process and as such any programs which require it tend to run slowly.

2.3 Comparison of Existing Approaches

To compare the existing approaches we need some criteria for judging the quality and effectiveness of each abstract. Judging any piece of text on these criteria is largely a subjective matter, and it is important to examine a text from a specific viewpoint. The correct viewpoint in the present case is that of a CABI journal reader. Such a reader would have a scientific background and would consider the following essential :

1) Abstracts must be coherent and readable
2) Major concepts of the paper must be covered
3) The setting of the study should be included, i.e., duration of study, cultivars used, soil types, etc.

A further viewpoint is that of the company producing the abstracts. In addition to (1), (2) and (3) they are likely to require that any abstract system is not restricted too tightly to its domain and, for CABI, the methods must work with texts on empirical work.

A summary of the main results and conclusion of the paper are usually included in a CABI abstract. Nobody seems to have attempted to solve the many problems encountered when trying to automatically abstract results (e.g., extracting data from tables, graphs etc.). We believe that the frame-based methodology, to be described in this paper, may prove useful in producing result summaries; however those ideas will not be included here as they have not yet been adequately investigated.

Table 1 : Comparison of existing approaches

Criteria	Simple Extracting System	Extract and Rearrange	FRUMP
Produced text is coherent and readable	no	perhaps	yes
Includes the major concepts	perhaps	perhaps	yes
Includes the setting of the study	perhaps	perhaps	no
Suitable for empirical work	yes	yes	no
Large domain or easily portable	yes	yes	no

Table 1 shows a comparison of the methods that have been mentioned. It is obvious that none of these methods provides a satisfactory solution to the problem of producing abstracts for a company like CABI. It seems likely that one reason for the poor performance of the above approaches is their failure to take account of the overall structure of the source texts. The method we will now describe uses information about *rhetorical structure* to aid in both the final output of abstracts and also in selecting information from the document to be used in the produced abstract.

3. Abstracts and Rhetorical Structure

Studies of the rhetorical structure of text have tried to uncover an underlying framework to written work. As early as 1958 researchers were becoming aware that different authors writing texts of the same general type tend to structure their texts in the same way [15]. Any piece of written work may be viewed as a collection of *meaning elements* (abbreviated to 'ME' below), where each ME is related to other MEs in hierarchical and syntagmatic ways [13], e.g.,

Hierarchical Paragraph
Ø
Sentence

Syntagmatic Situation ´ Result

Recently work has been conducted on defining how the MEs are used in the building up of the rhetorical structure of texts.

Liddy has suggested a template which can represent the majority of abstracts on empirical work in psychology and education research [7]. Kircz has suggested 'A Template for an Argumentational Syntax' of full papers, dealing with research in physics [6]. Kircz developed his template with the idea of improving retrieval systems by allowing a searcher to retrieve only specific sections of a document , e.g. 'experimental conditions' or 'mathematical approximations'. Although Liddy's and Kircz's work concentrated on different domain areas (Psychology & Education and Physics respectively), it is noticeable how similar their definitions are. Liddy has seven prototypical sections, and of Kircz's eleven major sections, eight of them are represented in Liddy's definition (Kircz has two reference sections compared to Liddy's one).

Another relevant piece of work is that of Rama and Srinivasan, who have defined a text grammar which fits the majority of abstracts in the field of Diabetes research [16]. This, together with Liddy's and Kircz's work, shows that empirical texts (both full texts and abstracts) share a common superstructure† .

Figure 1 shows Liddy's outline of the structure of empirical abstracts, slightly modified by us to suit papers on crop studies.

4. A New Method "Select & Generate"

The aim of Liddy's work was to clarify the way in which abstracts of empirical papers are structured [7]. We use the derived frame-structure in our new system to ensure that our automatic abstracts cover the concepts which are required for a well balanced abstract.

Liddy showed that abstracts in empirical disciplines may be divided into a number of sections (Figure 1). Paice has suggested that, as this frame-style structure is intrinsically present in abstracts, a system to mimic this stylisation may be possible [12]. If each important section of Liddy's frame-structure can be instantiated with an appropriate excerpt from the source text, we would have an abstract which covered the important details of the paper. It seems possible that frames will provide a more adaptable approach than semantic schemas, since they are much less tied to the semantic details of the domain.

4.1 Abstract-Frames

Sometime ago, Kent suggested a 'stylised ' arrangement for abstracts where a *pro forma* with headings such as Purpose, Procedures, Findings, etc. was generated and then filled in for each paper [5]; this could then, Kent said, act as an abstract. Our belief is that these stylised abstracts will never be fully accepted either by abstract users or abstract producers. However, the stylised abstracts could be used as an intermediate form from which a conventional textual abstract might be generated.

Liddy's [7] and Kircz's [6] templates are at the superstructure level of 'Introduction', 'Method' and 'Results' etc. Our approach uses *abstract-frames* which are more specifically adapted to the domain in question, though they still require far less domain detail than the semantically-based 'understand & generate' approach. The abstract-frame is in fact a data structure into which any details required for constructing an abstract may be stored. It may be considered as an 'abstract of an abstract' for the domain. Thus the abstract-frame serves as an intermediate form, which is then used by a simple language generator to produce abstracts of the type favoured by users.

Figure 3 shows an abstract-frame for papers on crop agriculture. The slots of the frame may be filled either by individual items (e.g.for the cultivar section , individual cultivar names would be included) or by whole sentences from the selected paper (e.g. for the cultivar section

† The term superstructure was in fact coined by van Dijk, who constructed a superstructure for newspaper articles [18].

Figure 1 : Structure of an abstract

The section headings and sub-section headings are based on those from Liddy's paper, but extra sections, which are specific to the area of crop agriculture, have been added to the Methods section. Possible sentence styles are inserted from the domain of crop agriculture by the author.

Portions of text (from source document.)	Sub Sections		Section
This paper studies			Purpose
the effect of		Research Question	Purpose
various seed dressings	Independent Variables	Research Question	Purpose
on		Research Question	Purpose
the vegetative growth of Winter Wheat.	Dependent Variables	Research Question	Purpose
Rapier, Norman, Galahad, Avalon and Armada Cultivars were used	Subjects		Methodology
The experiment took place over 9 months	Location & Soil etc		Methodology
Seeds were sown 5cm x 7.5cm apart and at 4cm depth. A routine fungicide and herbicide program was adopted. The layout was a randomized-block design.	Management		Methodology
Data was collected at two to three day intervals	Data Collection		Methodology
	Data Analysis		Methodology
Triadimenol seed dressing delayed seedling emergence by 2 days. Triadimenol seed dressing caused a reduction in stem length. etc	Results		Outcome
In inhibiting tillering during the period of main production, triadimenol seed dressing is likely to increase harvestable yields more than where a conventional mercury dressing is used.	Conclusions		Outcome

To examine this approach we are developing a frame-based abstracting technique for papers in the restricted domain of crop agriculture. When this system is proved effective we will begin investigating its portability and domain independence.

Figure 2 : Overview of the new system

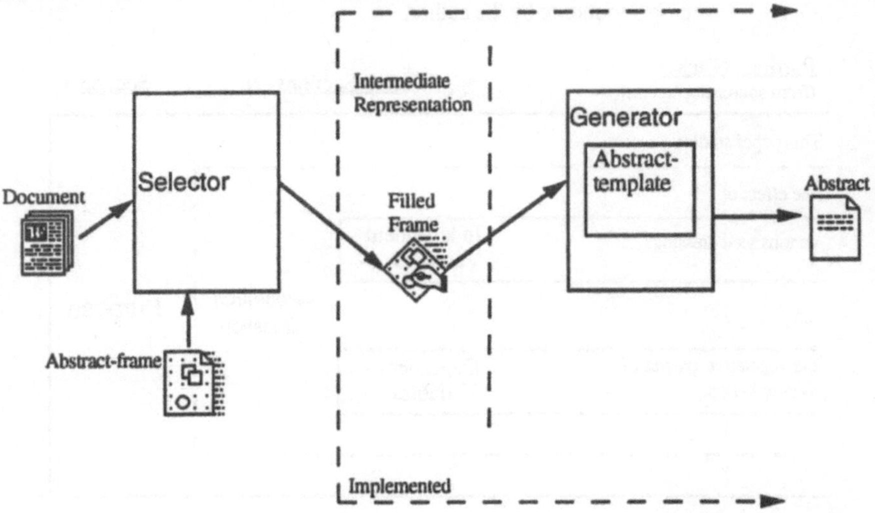

"17,16,17 and 18 cultivars were planted in 1983,1984,1985 and 1986 respectively.").

We are still at an early stage in the evolution of this methodology and we are hoping to move towards a more generic platform as our understanding of the necessities of this method increases.

4.2 The Selector

The function of the Selector is to scan the document and to fill in as many slots as possible in the abstract-frame. This is at present performed by hand, but will be automated at a later date; see section 6.1.

4.3 The Abstract Generator

This component produces the finished abstracts. The heart of this component is an *abstract-template* containing a collection of portions of text, with gaps where key concepts are missing. The missing concepts are inserted into the abstract-template if they are present in the instantiated abstract-frame. An abstract is then generated by outputting any portions of the abstract-template in which all gaps have been filled.

Figure 4 shows a portion of an abstract-template. The text in normal style will be generated literally as shown, the text which is 'shadowed' shows gaps which refer to locations in the abstract-frame. Where a location is referred to then the contents of that location in the abstract-frame would be displayed in the produced abstract.

The portions of text are not output *ad hoc*, since there are two mechanisms to control which of the portions of text are output. The first control is that a portion of text may not be output unless all its missing concepts are present in the abstract-frame. The second control is used to decide which portion of text to output when a choice is required. Thus, in Figure 4 a choice is required so that the correct phrase on location is output (Numbers 5 and 6); this decision depends on whether there is one, or more than one location known.

Figure 3 : A filled abstract-frame for papers dealing with crop agriculture

This abstract-frame is used to produce Abstract A in the 'Early Results' Section

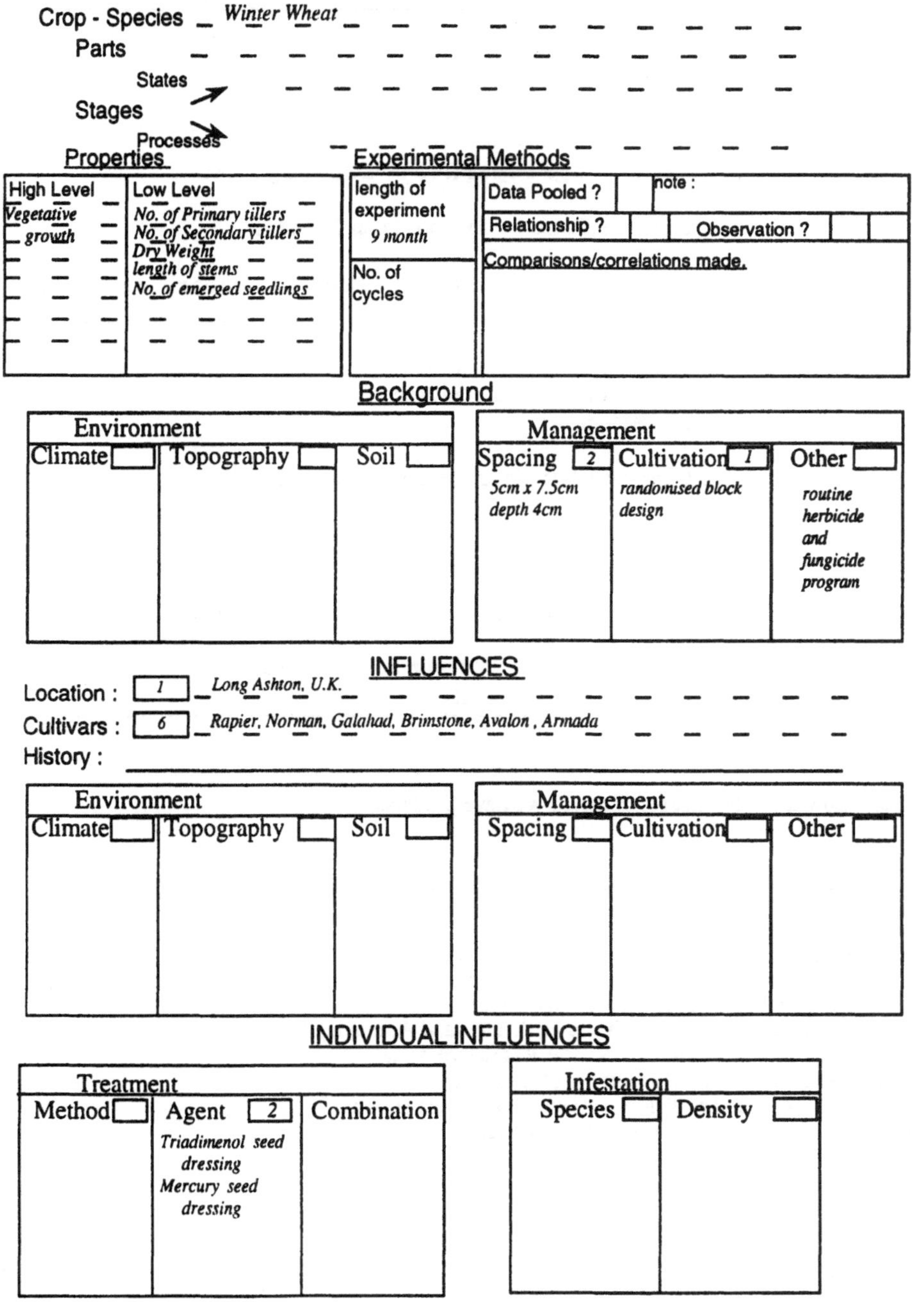
Crop - Species
Winter Wheat
Parts
Stages
States
Processes
Properties
High Level
Vegetative growth
Low Level
No. of Primary tillers
No. of Secondary tillers
Dry Weight
length of stems
No. of emerged seedlings
Experimental Methods
length of experiment
9 month
No. of cycles
Data Pooled ?
note :
Relationship ?
Observation ?
Comparisons/correlations made.
Background
Environment
Climate
Topography
Soil
Management
Spacing
2
5cm x 7.5cm depth 4cm
Cultivation
1
randomised block design
Other
routine herbicide and fungicide program
INFLUENCES
Location :
1
Long Ashton, U.K.
Cultivars :
6
Rapier, Norman, Galahad, Brimstone, Avalon, Armada
History :
Environment
Climate
Topography
Soil
Management
Spacing
Cultivation
Other
INDIVIDUAL INFLUENCES
Treatment
Method
Agent
2
Triadimenol seed dressing
Mercury seed dressing
Combination
Infestation
Species
Density

Figure 4 : A Partial abstract-template

No.	Control	Text Portion
1		This paper studies the effect of **Treatment.Agent** on the **High_Level_Properties** of **Crop_Species**
	OR	
2		This paper studies the effect of **Treatment.Method** on the **High_Level_Properties** of **Crop_Species**
3		when it is infested by **Infestation.Species**
4		A **Length_of_experiment** experiment using **Cultivars.Number** cultivars (**Cultivars**) was undertaken
		{Additional option here to handle case where number of cultivars is known, but the individual cultivars are not }
5		in **Location**
	OR	
6		at **Location.Number** locations (**Location**)
		{Additional options here for cases where alone is known, and also where only location and duration is known, but no cultivar details}
7		The results contain details on the relationships between **Correlations**.
	OR	
8		The **High_Level_Properties** are measured by analysing the **Low_Level_Properties**.

5. Early Results

The following is the first set of results we have produced :

Abstract A.
Title :-Effect of triadimenol seed dressing on vegetative growth in winter wheat.
Citation :- Crop Research , 1989, 29(1), pp29-36

This paper studies the effect of Mercury seed dressing and Triadimenol seed dressing on the Vegetative growth of Winter Wheat. A 9 month experiment using 6 cultivars (Rapier, Norman, Galahad, Brimstone, Avalon and Aramada) was undertaken in Long Ashton, UK. The Vegetative growth is measured by analysing the Number of Secondary Tillers , the Number of Primary Tillers, the dry weight, the length of stems and the Number of emerged seedlings.

Abstract B.
Title :- The assessment of the tolerance of partially resistant potato clones to damage by the potato cyst nematode *Globodera pallida* at different sites and in different years.
Citation :- Ann. Appl. Biol, 1988, 113, pp79-88

This paper studies the effect of nematicide on the Tolerance of Potato when it is infested by Globodera Pallida. A 4 year experiment using 17,16,17 and 18 cultivars in 1983,1984,1985 and 1986 respectively, was undertaken at 3 locations (Lincoln, Peterborough and York). The results contain details on the relationships between year x clone, year x site and site x genotype.

Abstract C.
Title :- The effect of date of planting on field establishment of serotinous cape Proteaceae
Citation :- Vegetatio 79 , 1989, pp 185-192

This paper studies the effect of date of planting and season of burn on the field establishment of Proteaceae. The investigation, using 4 cultivars (Leucadendron rubrum, Protea repens, Protea lorifolia and Protea punctata), was undertaken at 4 locations in S. Africa. The field establishment is measured by analysing the plant mortality and the percentage germination.

Abstract D.
Title :- No-tillage and dry ploughing compared with puddling for wet-season rice on an alluvial sandy clay-loam in eastern India.
Citation :- Journal of Agricultural Science, 1990, 114(1), pp 79-86

This paper studies the effect of puddling,no tillage and dry ploughing on the Yield and Growth of Wet Season Rice. The 5 year experiment took place in E. India. The Yield and Growth is measured by analysing the root weight, the root diameter and the root length.

Abstract E.
Title :- The effect of mildew seed treatment and foliar sprays used alone or in combination in 'early' and 'late' sown Golden Promise spring barley, Aberdeen, 1976 to 1982.
Citation :- Research and Development in Agriculture, 1986, 3(3), pp 165-174

This paper studies the effect of tridemorph and ethirimol on the Mildew assessment, grain moisture, straw characteristics, Fertile tiller number and Plant establishment of Golden Promise Spring Barley. The 6 year experiment took place in Aberdeen.

5.1 Discussion

The titles of agricultural papers, as mentioned earlier, are usually very informative. In comparison to their titles, abstracts A, B and C provide a large increase in the amount of information available to a reader. Abstract D is slightly more informative than abstract E but neither provide any really important details which are not apparent from the title.

The fact that abstracts D and E provide no more information than their respective titles does not detract from the success of the system. The aim of this work was (and is) to produce a system which generates indicative abstracts, and this it appears to do. The fact that some titles of papers are very descriptive is not really relevant when viewed in that context.

6. On-going Developments

6.1 Instantiation

There is an important question which we have not covered in any detail above: how to fill the abstract-frame from a source paper ? We wish if possible to avoid any need for sophisticated syntactic and semantic analysis during the instantiation process. The aim will be to use simple clues to identify portions of the text to fill the abstract-frame. We will be looking for clues of two kinds :

a) Presentational
b) Lexical

Presentational clues rely on the idea that certain stock words and expressions are used to present important ideas and facts, and thus indicate a particular slot. Thus the word "Cultivars" is often used early in the Methods section of agricultural papers, to lead into a list of the names of the cultivars being used. Similarly the construction "the effect on .... of" is often used in the title and contains the species being investigated between "on" and "of".

The characteristic expressions will be discovered by analysis of the papers which have had abstract-frames manually filled for them. Use will also be made of the generic clues discovered by Liddy [7], and we hope that it may be possible to produce a set of phrases which perform well in our system and are also as general as those Liddy discovered. It is unlikely we will be able to achieve this totally, but we are hoping that the discovered phrases and constructions will not be too domain specific.

Finally in instantiating a frame we will make use of *lexical clues*, which can be verified by reference to the CABI Thesaurus or some other convenient lexicon. Thus if a source text contains the word 'lucerne' it is very probable that this belongs in the 'Crop_Species' slot, whereas 'tobacco mosaic virus' almost certainly belongs in the 'Infestation_Species' slot.

6.2 Future Work

One drawback of our abstracts is that they are all noticeably similar in style. However, it is possible to develop groups of text portions, with the same meaning but expressed in different words, which could be used randomly. Thus abstracts which are printed together on a page should appear not to have been written by the same system , e.g.,

Instead of always starting :- "This paper studies ...."
we could use :- "Here we investigate ...."
or sometimes :- "The effect of .... is studied"
etc..,

Other tasks to be tackled in future include :

1) Using the frame-based system to produce summaries of the Conclusions section of a source document.

2) Using the frame-based system to produce summaries of the Results section of a source document.

3) Testing the degree of domain independence of the frame-based methodology.

7. Summary

We have shown that where source texts have a stereotyped structure, a frame-based method of automatic abstracting can produce texts which are coherent, easy to read, and mention all the main concepts plus a small amount of background. We believe that our results so far show that the method deserves more investigation, and that within a restricted domain, automatic abstracting has a definite economic future.

References

1. Baxendale, P. B. Man-made Index for Technical Literature - An Experiment. *I.B.M. Journal of Research and Development.* **2**(4): 354 - 361, 1958.

2. DeJong, G. "An Overview of the FRUMP System." In *Strategies for Natural Language Processing*, Lehnert and Ringle (eds.) 1982. Hillsdale, NJ: Lawrence Earlbaum Associates.

3. Edmundson, H. P. New Methods in Automatic Extracting. *Journal of the Association for Computing Machinery.* **16**(2): 264 - 285, 1969.

4. Evans, M. and A. V. Pollock. Trials on trial : a review of trials of antibiotic prophylaxis. *Archives of Surgery.* **119**: 109-113, 1984.

5. Kent, A. *Textbook on Mechanized Information Retrieval.* second edition, New York:1966. Wiley Interscience.

6. Kircz, J. G. Rhetorical Structure of Scientific Articles: The Case for Argumentational Analysis in Information Retrieval. *Journal of Documentation.* **47**(4): 354-372, 1991.

7. Liddy, E. D. The Discourse Level Structure of Empirical Abstracts : An Exploratory Study. *Information Processing and Management.* **27**(1): 55 - 81, 1991.

8. Luhn, H. P. The automatic creation of literature abstracts. *I.B.M. Journal of Research and Development.* **2**(2): 159 - 165, 1958.

9. Mathis, B. A., J. E. Rush and C. E. Young. Improvement of automatic abstracts by the use of structural analysis. *Journal of the American Society for Information Science.* **24**(2): 101 - 109, 1973.

10. Narine, L., S. Y. Deanna, T. R. Einarson and A. L. Ilersich. Quality of abstracts of original research articles in CMAJ in 1989. *Canadian Medical Association Journal.* **144**(4): 449 - 453, 1991.

11. Paice, C. D. "The Automatic Generation of Literature Abstracts : an approach based on self indicating phrases." In *Information Retrieval Research.* Oddy, Robertson, Rijsbergen and Williams (eds.) 1981. London: Butterworths. 172-191.

12. Paice, C. D. Constructing Literature Abstracts by Computer : Techniques and Prospects. *Information Processing and Management.* **26**(1): 171 - 186, 1990.

13. Paice, C. D. The Rhetorical Structure of Expository Texts. In *The Structuring of Information*, K. Jones (ed.), Proceedings of Informatics 11. London: ASLIB 1991. 1-25.

14. Paice, C. D. and G. D. Husk. Towards the automatic recognition of anaphoric features in English text : the impersonal pronoun *it*. *Computer Speech and Language*. 2: 109 - 132, 1987.

15. Propp, V. *Morphology of the folk-tale*. 1958. Bloomington: Indiana University Press.

16. Rama, D. V. and P. Srinivasan. An investigation of content representation using text grammars. *ACM Transactions on Information Systems*. in press: 1992.

17. Rush, J. E., R. Salvador and A. Zamora. Automatic Abstracting and Indexing. II. Production of indicative abstracts by application of contextual inference and syntactic coherence criteria. *Journal of the American Society for Information Science*. 22(3): 260 - 274, 1971.

18. van Dijk, T. A. *Macrostructures: An interdisciplinary study of global structures in discourse, interaction, and cognition*. 1980. Hillsdale, NJ: Lawrence Earlbaum Associates.

Evaluation Of Techniques For The Conflation Of Modern And Seventeenth Century English Spelling

Alexander M. Robertson and Peter Willett*

Department of Information Studies, University of Sheffield,
Western Bank, Sheffield, UK, S10 2TN.

Abstract.

This paper discusses a range of techniques for the identification of those words in a database of 17th-century English text that are most similar to a query word in modern English. The experiments have used n-gram matching, non-phonetic coding and dynamic-programming methods for spelling correction, and have demonstrated that high-recall searches can be carried out, although some of the searches are very demanding of computational resources. It is also shown that neural networks, which seem to be well-suited to use in this context, cannot, in fact, be employed for this application.

1 Introduction

Large amounts of text are created, stored and searched by computer. Most of this text has been created in recent years, but growing amounts of historical material is becoming available in machine-readable form. The resulting databases contain texts employing the spellings of the time, which are often very different from those used today owing to the changes that have taken place over the centuries. In addition, modern English spelling is relatively standardi~ed, but the concept of 'correct' spelling is quite a recent one, and thus a given word might well appear in several equally valid forms in a historical database that contains documents from the same time period.

Before the invention of printing, there were wide local variations and inconsistencies in spelling in Britain. Since there was no agreed correct spellings of words, phonetic spellings and variant word forms were representative of the local dialects, and this was only acceptable when an individual copy of a manuscript had a geographically-limited circulation. The development that stabilised spelling was the invention of printing [23], since the typesetting of a book would lead to the dissemination of the spelling used in that book throughout the country. However, authors had as little influence over the way that words were spelled in their works when they were typeset, as they had had when the words were copied by scribes. No proofs were supplied, and spelling was according to the house-style of the compositors. It was not until the 18th century that individual compositors began to adhere to a single spelling for a word and the spelling system became fixed with the introduction of dictionaries such as that of Samuel Johnson. Before spellings became fixed, letters would be added or omitted to ease the justification of a line [3], or a compositor might simply copy over another spelling from the source that was being used. Variant spellings within a single work were therefore common.

These factors present a serious problem to users who wish to carry out searches of databases of historical text. Even those familiar with older spelling conventions are

---

* To whom all correspondence should be addressed.

unlikely to be familiar with the complete range of possible variants, while a non-specialist or casual user would be likely to submit a query using modern spelling. In either case, documents will be retrieved only if they contain words spelt in exactly the same way as the query terms. This problem could be alleviated by the development of computational techniques that could transform the users' search terms into the forms of the language that is used in the database.

In this paper, we discuss the application of spelling-correction algorithms to this task. Such algorithms are designed, and normally used, to identify the single correct version of a mis-spelled word. Here, conversely, we seek the old-fashioned variants, called old forms, of a correctly-spelt modern word, called the modern-form, where neither the number nor the form of these variants is known, a priori. The particular context in which our work has been carried out is the Hartlib Papers Project, which has been under way in Sheffleld since 1987 [13] and which is transcribing and editing the surviving working papers of Samuel Hartlib, a polymath who was in correspondence with many of the leading intellectual figures of Europe during the first half of the 17th century. The Hartlib papers are held in Sheffield University Library and will all have been converted to machine-readable form by March 1993, to give a text database containing ca. 50 Mbytes. Some examples of old-forms identified in this database, together with the associated modern-forms, are shown in Table 1.

2 Types Of Spelling Error

An effective correction method must take account of the types of error occurring in the texts, and a correction strategy must take account of the nature and source of the text [16]. All errors can be traced to one or more of the following:

The input device used for text entry;
The content of the text;
The spelling ability of the text author.

When the only input device was a quill pen, the pen did not introduce errors by itself and mistakes, and\or variant forms, would have been largely due to the preferred spelling of the author (as discussed in Section 1). Nonetheless, 80% of errors fall into one of four categories, as demonstrated by Damerau [5]. These errors occur in text that has been keyed and transmitted over electrical circuits, and comprise:

Insertion errors: one extra character inserted, e.g., CRAOB for CRAB;

Deletion (or omission) errors: one character deleted, e.g., CONTNT for CONTENT;

Substitution errors: an incorrect character substituted for a correct one, e.g., INPIT for INPUT;

Transposition errors: two adjacent characters transposed, e.g., KYEED for KEYED.

A substitution can be regarded as one deletion and one insertion, and a transposition as two deletions and two insertions. Transpositions are very rare in historical text, accounting for only 2.1% of the errors in the Hartlib data, as these errors are normally a product of keyboarding and as the source texts studied here were hand-written.

This paper discusses the use of three types of spelling-correction method: n-gram matching [1], the SPEEDCOP non-phonetic coding method [14,15], and the dynamic-programming method [12,24].

3 Matching Methods

3.1 N-grams

An n-gram is a substring of length n characters that is derived from a word of length not less than n. Although it is possible to derive n-grams whose letters are not adjacent, we have considered only those where the letters are adjacent. Two different lengths of n-gram were used in the tests: digrams with a length of 2, and trigrams with a length of 3. One padding space was added to the ends of each word before the generation of digrams, and two before the generation of trigrams. Thus, the word SUBSTRING results in the generation of the digrams

S, SU, UB, BS, ST, TR, RI, IN, NG, G

and the trigrams

S, *SU, SUB, UBS, BST, STR, TRI, RIN, ING, NG*, G

where '*' denotes a padding space. There are $n + 1$ such digrams and $n + 2$ such trigrams in a word containing n characters.

The method assumes that the more similar two words are, the greater the number of n-grams that they have in common. Old-forms having the largest numbers of n-grams in common with a given modern-form are thus expected to be associated with it, and should thus be retrieved when that modern-form is used as a query term during a search of a text database.

Detailed results for this approach have been reported previously [17].

3.2 SPEEDCOP

SPEEDCOP is a non-phonetic coding method that is in operation on a day-to-day basis for the identification of spelling errors in the many scientific databases produced by Chemical Abstracts Service. Like all coding methods, it is based on the idea that a code captures the essence of a word, so that the codes of a misspelling and the corresponding correct word resemble each other more closely than do the originals; ideally, the codes should be identical [15]. If a code is generated for each word and the set of such codes sorted into alphabetical order, then the distance that entries sort apart is a measure of the similarity of the words from which the codes were generated.

The SPEEDCOP workers investigated two types of code, which they referred to as keys: the skeleton key and the omission key. Three principles underlie both of these keys:

The key must retain the fundamental features of a word or its misspelling;

The key must be similar to the word, but not too similar;

The key must be insensitive to typical spelling-error operations.

Thus, the key must blur the identity of the string, but not obliterate it. The SPEEDCOP project aimed at a key which would be more stringent than one which retained the letters of the original string in an arbitrary order, but less stringent than one which preserved all of the original inter-character relationships.

The first key, the skeleton key, consists of the string's unique letters in their original order and comprises:

The first letter;

The unique consonants in their order of occurrence in the word;

The unique vowels in their order of occurrence in the word.

'Unique' has a slightly different meaning for vowels and consonants in that if the first letter is a vowel, then this will reappear in the key if it occurs later in the string, whereas a consonant never appears more than once in the key. The skeleton key relies on the early consonants being correct, so that the nearer a wrong consonant is to the start of the word, the further apart will be the word and its misspelling in a list sorted by the key. This vulnerability to early consonant damage led to the development of the second method, the omission key. Analysis of the results of earlier spelling-correction experiments [14] showed that consonants tend to be omitted from modern words in the frequency order

RSTNLCHDPGMFBYWVZXQKJ

and thus the omission key for a string is constructed by ordering its unique consonants according to the reverse of this sequence, i.e.,

JKQXZVWYBFMGPDHCLNTSR

and then appending the unique vowels in their original order. Letter content, rather than letter order, is thus the basis of this key. Consider the modern-form ABBREVIATIONS: then the skeleton and omission keys are ABRVTNSEIAO and VBNTSRAEIO, respectively; the corresponding keys for the modern-form BREASTWORK are BRSTWKEAO and KWBTSREAO, respectively.

Two files were created for each of the words in the Hartlib test collection, one consisting of the skeleton key and its matching word, and the other of the omission key and its matching word. Each of these files was sorted alphabetically according to the respective key. Each key and its matching word can be considered as the centre of a window, since the assumption of this, as for other coding methods, is that the keys for a correct word and its misspelling will sort within a manageable distance of each other. In our experiments, as discussed in Section 4, those old-forms were retrieved whose keys occurred in a window centred on the key corresponding to the query modern-form.

3.3 Dynamic Programming

Dynamic programming is a method for the characterization of the homology, i.e., the degree of correspondence between two or more related sequences. The method is widely used in database systems that compare the nucleotide sequences of nucleic acids and the amino acid sequences of proteins in molecular biology [12]. In the same way that each protein molecule is a sequence whose elements are drawn from an 'alphabet' of 20 types of amino acids, so words can be considered as sequences whose elements are drawn from an alphabet of 26 letters. Thus, a dynamic-programming algorithm can be simply adapted to the comparison of old-forms with modern-forms. The basic dynamic-programming algorithm represents all possible pair combinations in a two-dimensional array, D, in which the element D(i, j) is set equal to one (or zero) if the i-th character of one sequence, A, is the same as (is not the same as) the j-th character of the second sequence, B. Weights other than zero and unity may also be used.

Our experiments used the algorithm due to Wagner and Fischer [24], which calculates the editcost. The editcost is a measure of the number of changes, i.e., insertions, deletions, or substitutions, required to convert one sequence into another. This involves a recursive summation through the array; three cells are employed at each stage, which involves calculating the the minimum of:

the cost of transforming A(i--1) to B(j -1), plus the cost of changing A(i) to B(j);

the cost of transforming A(i--1) to B(j) plus the cost of deleting A(i);

the cost of transforming A(i) to B(j -1), plus the cost of inserting B(j).

More formally, let:

$$\gamma(A(\iota) \rightarrow B(j))$$
$$\gamma(A(\iota) \rightarrow [])$$
$$\gamma([] \rightarrow B(j))$$

be the cost function for a substitution, a deletion and an insertion, respectively, where [] is the null character. Each element of:

D
D(i,j)
($1 \leq i \leq m$, $1 \leq j \leq n$, where m and n are the lengths
of the old and modern forms, respectively)

where m and n are the lengths of the old and modern-forms, respectively), is then calculated using the following recurrence formula:

$$D(i,j) = \min \begin{array}{l} D(i-1, j-1) + \gamma(A(i) \rightarrow B(j)), \\ D(i-1, j) + \gamma(A(i) \rightarrow []), \\ D(i, j-1) + \gamma([] \rightarrow B(j)) \end{array}$$

The editcost value is the value in cell *D(m,n)*. The editcost is zero when the words that are being compared are identical, and has an upperbound equal to the length of the longer sequence when unit-valued weights are employed.

The initial values of the elements of D can be varied. Note that when

$$\gamma(A(i) \rightarrow B(j)) \geq \gamma(A(i) \rightarrow []) + \gamma([] \rightarrow B(j))$$

i.e., when the cost of a substitution is greater than or equal to the sum of the costs of a deletion and an insertion, then the longest common subsequence, LCS, can be identified by a simple backtracking through the array. If A and C are strings of length m and n ($n \leq m$ 1), respectively, such that C could be obtained by deleting zero or more elements from A, then C is a subsequence of A: thus, COURSE, e.g., is a subsequence of COMPUTER SCIENCE. String C is a common subsequence of the strings A and B if it is a subsequence of both: it is the longest common subsequence, or LCS, if it is a common subsequence and if it is as long as any other common subsequence of A and B. In our experiments, this part of the algorithm was modified to identify the length of the LCS, rather than the LCS itself. This value is bounded by the length of the shorter word. Note that the length of the LCS is generally different from the editcost value that is obtained when the inequality above is satisfied.

3.4 Neural Networks

All of the above techniques require that the method be explicitly encoded in a program; accordingly, the upper bound on the performance of the method cannot exceed that implicit in the coding. Neural networks make it possible to present the data first, and then to let the network 'discover' a method for itself. In principle, the ability of networks to handle incomplete and conflicting data, and to allow the simultaneous consideration of competing hypotheses about solutions to problems and matching patterns [7], appeared to offer a potentially useful technique for historical text searching. Moreover, Jagota and Hung [9] have applied neural networks to the reverse problem, viz finding a correct word corresponding to a number of misspellings. They had limited success, since the network failed to retrieve any word about half the time; however, when it did retrieve a word, it was always the correct.

Spelling depends on the sequence of characters in a word, and it is known that 'dealing with sequence (whether spatial or temporal) has been one of the more difficult problems in connectionist modelling' [2]. This is because of the nature of neural networks. Theypermit graceful degradation i.e., faced with too many demands, the system ignores some extraneous data and begins to to perform sub-optimally [2]. The more overloaded it is, the less well it functions. In order to allow this, the input is distributed over many processing elements, and this generally results in the original order of presentation being lost. This does not matter in many cases, but is clearly of crucial importance for the present application.

The solution which appeared promising and practical was that used by Servan-Schreiber et al. [21], as first suggested by Jordan [10,11] and since refined by Elman [6]. This was the recurrent network, which is a variation on the back-propagation network, with the addition of a special subset of input units, called context units. Back-propagation networks consist of layers of units, an input layer, one or more hidden layers, and an output layer. In a three layer network, each hidden unit sends its activation to one context unit as well as sending activation forward to the output units. The result is that the hidden layers's output at time t is available to it at time t + 1. In turn, the context units feed their output back to the hidden units. Because the context units provide part of the input, and do so recursively, information about the entire preceding context, i.e., the preceding string of characters, is potentially available.

However, an additional and intractable problem was encountered. Neural networks are classifiers; they converge on a solution, and cannot provide multiple solutions. They are, in principle at least, candidate tools for the correction of modern spelling where the objective is to find the single correct form which corresponds to a number of misspellings. They cannot perform the task required here, because they cannot handle the fine distinctions between a number of putative old-forms as can be done by the spelling-correction methods using the Dice coefficient. In view of this factor, and the limited time available for this project, neural networks were rejected as a possible answer.

4 Experimental Details

4.1 Test Data

The experiments used a test collection consisting of old spellings extracted from a sample of the Hartlib Papers, together with their modern equivalents. Two dictionaries were used, these being the pairs dictionary and the master dictionary:

> The pairs dictionary was created by taking a sample of 88 Hartlib letters, and noting all words that did not conform to modern-day spelling, as represented by the Oxford English Dictionary. These old-forms were then matched with the corresponding modern-forms, and the resulting file of word-pairs, i.e., one modern-form and one old-form, sorted so as to bring together all variants of a modern-form. There was a total of 2620 unique word pairs, representing 2195 modern-forms and 2620 associated old-forms, i.e., some of the modern-forms had more than one associated old-form. The old-forms associated with a given modern-form are referred to subsequently as the appropriate old-forms.
>
> The master dictionary contained all the distinct old-forms in a larger sample of Hartlib letters. This contained 12191 old-forms, these including all of the 2620 old-forms in the pairs dictionary.

4.2 Calculation of Similarity

With the exception of SPEEDCOP, all of the matching methods discussed here produced a numerical score for the similarity between modern and old-forms: the value of this score is bounded by the length of, or the number of n-grams in, the shorter word, except for the editcost value. In order to rank putative matching words, the Dice coefficient was used. If the two words have lengths A and B, with the numerical score being C, then the Dice coefficient is defined to be:

$$\frac{2 \times C}{A + B}$$

In these experiments, old-forms were considered only if they exceeded a certain Dice co-efficient value. In the results reported here, this was set at greater than or equal to 0.4. An exception was the editcost score of Wagner and Fischer [24]: here a perfect match would produce a score of 0.0, and the Dice coefficient value was thus set, symmetrically, at less than or equal to 0.6. Note that this is not an exact symmetry; as the editcost value has an upper bound equal to the length of the longer sequence, the Dice coefficient value can exceed unity.

Each of the modern-forms in the pairs dictionary was used as a query for a search of the master dictionary to find the 20 old-forms that were most similar to it. The search procedure was as follows, each of the methods being implemented in Pascal on an IBM 3083 mainframe computer operating under VM/CMS at the University of Sheffield Academic Computing Services:

> In the case of the digram and trigram experiments, the modern-form was broken up into its constituent n-grams, the number of n-grams in common with each of the words in the master dictionary identified, and the Dice coefficient value calculated.
>
> In the case of the SPEEDCOP experiments, the appropriate key was generated for the modern-form. The most-similar old-forms were then obtained by retrieving the old-forms for which the corresponding keys occurred in the 20-key window centred on the key for the query modern-form.
>
> In the case of the dynamic-programming methods, the matrix operations were carried out as detailed in Section 3.3 to calculate the editcost or LCS values, and these were then used for the calculation of the Dice coefficient.

Once the 20 most-similar old-forms had been identified, they were then compared with the sets of appropriate old-forms from the pairs dictionary that corresponded to the query modern-form.

4.3 Use of Substitutions

In a previous study of the Hartlib data [18], Rogers and Willett improved the performance of the Phonix phonetic-coding method by the use of phonetic substitutions, i.e., the replacement of certain character strings by others in the old and modern-forms before generating the code itself. It was decided to test the same method in order to see if this could improve the performance of non-phonetic, sequence-comparison methods. Each substitution in Table 2 details a search string, a replacement string and the necessary location of the search string. Location is indicated by S, M or E (for start, middle and end of a word), where 'middle' means any position in the word so long as the first and last characters are not involved. The lower case characters v and c in search strings are wildcards indicating any vowel or consonant, respectively. The replacement strings replace only the upper e characters in the corresponding search strings. Thus S CLv KL states that CL is replaced by KL if the letters CL start a word and are followed immediately by a vowel. The substitution instructions are obeyed in the order shown in Table 2. When the location is in the middle of the word and the search string appears in more than one middle position, then it is replaced at each occurrence. Two sets of experiments were carried out. The results listed under M1 in Tables 3 and 4 used the correction methods as described in Section 3, while those listed under M2 involved applying the substitutions in Table 2 to the query modern-form and to each of the old-forms in the master dictionary.

4.4 Measurement of Performance

The effectiveness of retrieval was evaluated by means of the recall at a number of fixed cutoff points, though only those for cutoff-20 are reported here, where the recall of a search for a given modern-form is defined to be the percentage of the appropriate old-forms that are retrieved. If a modern-form has a set of X appropriate old-forms and if a set of Y appropriate old-forms has been retrieved, then the recall is defined to be:

$$\frac{Y}{X} \times 100$$

Each modern-form in the pairs dictionary was used in turn as the query, and the results averaged over the entire set of query modern-forms. Table 3 shows the results for each method using a cutoff of the 20 most-similar old-forms, while Table 4 illustrates the effect of variations in the values of the editcost functions for insertion, deletion and substitution.

5 Results And Discussion

An inspection of Table 3 shows that both of the n-gram methods can give high recall, reaching 95% and 89% for digrams and trigrams respectively. The superior recall of the digram searches is achieved at the cost of an increase of about 20% in the overall execution time, when compared with the trigram searches.

The skeleton key was found to outperform the omission key in all of the SPEEDCOP experiments, the best results being obtained when the skeleton key was used with the phonetic-substitutions list. However, even this result, of 76% recall, is substantially inferior to the recall for most of the the n-gram searches, despite the fact that the skeleton key has similar memory requirements and that its processing time is about 50% greater.

The experiments with the Wagner-Fischer algorithm generally gave very impressive results, with a maximum recall of 96%, which is slightly higher than that obtained with digram matching. Table 4 shows the effect of varying the values for the three cost functions when the editcost measure is used; the variations in recall are small but, interestingly, the simplest weights seem to give the best performance. More disparate sets of weights were found to give substantially inferior results to those listed in the table. In common with the LCS and digram experiments, the editcost searches are little affected by the use of phonetic substitutions, whereas their use in our previous studies proved to be extremely beneficial [18]. Unfortunately, the dynamic-programming approach is very time-consuming, since the processing of the Hartlib test data using the Wagner-Fischer algorithm took about 30 times as long as using digram matching; the matching of a single query modern-form against the master dictionary using this algorithm took at least 30 CPU seconds on IBM 3083 equipment. The best-known lower bounds on the execution time of dynamic programming [20] are such that some type of pre-processing or of parallel hardware would be required if these algorithms were to be used in an interactive environment.

The results obtained here with the digram-matching and dynamic-programming methods are comparable with the best of those obtained in our previous experiments [18]. We hence believe that spelling-correction methods provide an effective way of carrying out high-recall searches for historical word forms in 17th-century English text. However, much work remains in optimizing these techniques; account must be taken of computer time and memory requirements, as well as any pre-processing needed, and work continues in this area. In addition, three further test collections, drawn from titles in the Eighteenth Century Short Title Catalogue [4], and the 16th and 17th-century titles from the catalogue of the library of Canterbury Cathedral [22] are currently being created. These will act as checks on the results that we have obtained with the Hartlib data. We are also about to implement the most appropriate method(s) in a front-end system that will allow a searcher to select oldforms that appear to correspond to a query that has been submitted in modern English.

The results presented here and elsewhere [17,18] demonstrate that it is possible to obtain high recall, but the precision of the searches is generally low: there are only one or two appropriate old-forms for most of the modern-forms in the pairs dictionary (the maximum number of old-forms is five) and the retrieval of the 20 most-similar old-forms must inevitably result in low precision. Accordingly, it will be for the searcher to specify which of the displayed old-forms should be used to query the database.

Acknowledgement. This work has been funded by a grant from the British Library Research and Development Department. We thank Michael Leslie for providing the Hartlib data and Heather Rogers for the preparation of the pairs and master dictionaries.

References

[1] Angell, R.C., Freund, G.E. and Willett, P. (1983). *Automatic spelling correction using a trigram similarity measure.* Information Processing and Management, 19, 255-261.

[2] Bechtel, W. and Abrahamsen, A. (1991). *Connectionism and the mind: an introduction to parallel processing in networks.* Oxford, Basil Blackwell.

[3] Burgess, A. (1975). *Language made plain.* London, Fontana Paperbacks.

[4] Crump, M. and Harris, M. (eds.) (1983). *Searching the eighteenth century.* London, British Library.

[5] Damerau, F.J. (1964). *A technique for computer detection and correction of spelling errors.* Communications of the ACM, 7, 171-176.

[6] Elman, J.L. (1990). *Finding structure in time.* Cognitive Science, 14, 179-211.

[7] Ford, N. (1989). *From information to knowledge-management: the role of rule-induction and neural net machine learning techniques in knowledge generation.* Journal of Information Science, 15, 299-304.

[8] Gadd, T.N. (1990). *PHONIX: the algorithm.* Program, 24, 363-366.

[9] Jagota, A. and Hung, Y-.S. (1990). *A neural lexicon in a Hopfield-style network.* In IJCNN-90: International Joint Conference on Neural Netu)orks, vol. 2, Applications Track, 607-610.

[10] Jordan, M.I. (1986). *An introduction to linear algebra in parallel distributed processing.* In Rumelhart, D.E. and McLelland, D.E. (eds.). Parallel distributed processing: explorations in the microstructure of cognition. Vol. 1: Foundations. Cambridge, MIT Press, 365-422.

[11] Jordan, M.I. (1986). *Attractor dynamics and parallelism in a connectionist sequential machine.* In Proceedings of the Eighth Annual Conference of the Cognitive Science Society. Hillsdale, NJ. Lawrence Erlbaum, 10-17.

[12] Kruskal, J.B. (1983). *Macromolecular sequences.* In Sankoff, D. and Kruskal, J.B. (eds.). Time warps, string edits, and macromolecules: the theory and practice of sequence comparison. Reading, Mass., Addison-Wesley Publishing Co., 45-53.

[13] Leslie, M. (1990). *The Hartlib Papers Project: text retrieval in large datasets.* Literary and Linguistie Computing, 5, 58-69.

[14] Pollock, J.J. (1980). *SPEEDCOP: Task A.l - Quantification.* Chemical Abstracts Service Internal Report.

[15] Pollock, J.J. (1981). *SPEEDCOP: Task B.2 - Automatic correction of misspellings.* Chemical Abstracts Service Internal Report.

[16] Pollock, J.J. and Zamora, A. (1984). *Automatic spelling correction in scientific and scholarly text.* Communications of the ACM, 27, 358-368.

[17] Robertson, A.M. and Willett, P. (1991). *Digram and trigram matching for the identification of word variants in historical text databases.* In McEnery, T. (ed.) *Proeeedings of the British Computer Soeiety 13th Research Colloquium on Information Retrieval. Lancaster*, British Computer Society, 12-21.

[18] Rogers, H.J. and Willett, P. (1991). *Searching for historical word forms in text databases using spelling-correction methods: reverse error and phonetic coding methods.* Journal of Doeumentation, 47, 333-353.

[19] Rumelhart, D.E. and McLelland, J.L. (1986). *Parallel distributed processing: explorations in the microstructure of cognition.* Vol. 1: Foundations. Cambridge, MIT Press.

[20] Sedgewick, R. (1988). *Algorithms.* Reading, MA., Addison-Wesley Publishing Co.

[21] Servan-Schreiber, D., Cleeremans, A. and McLelland, J.L. (1988). *Encoding seyuential structure in simple recurrent networks.* Pittsburgh, PA. Carnegie-Mellon University, Technical Report CMU-CS-88- 183 .

[22] Shaw, D. (1991). *MARC catalogues of early-printed books at the University of Kent.* Program, 25, 339-347.

[23] Vallins, G.H. (1965). *Spelling.* London, Andre Deutsch.

[24] Wagner, R.A. and Fischer, M.J. (1974). *The string-to-string correction problem.* Journal of the ACM, 21, 168-173.

Modern-Form	Old-Form(s)
ABBREVIATIONS	BREVIATES
ACCOUNT	ACCOMPT, ACCOUMPTE, ACCOUNTE
AFFAIRS	AFAYRES, AFFAYES, AFFAYRES
ARITHMETIC	AERITHMATICKE
BREASTWORK	BRESTWOORKE
CANVAS	CANUAISE
DISOLVE	DOSSOLUE
FRIEND	FFRINDE, FREIND, FREND, FRINDE
FUEL	FEWELL
HOWSOEVER	HOWE SOEUER
JUSTLY	IUSTELY, IUSTLIE
LIKELIHOOD	LIKELYHODE, LIKELYHOODE, LYKELYHOOD
MANUFACTURE	MANIFACTURIE
MEEKNESS	MEKNES
NEIGHBOUR	NEYGHBOR
PROFIT	PROFFITT
RECRUIT	RECREUT, RECRUITE
REVERENCING	REUERENCINGE
SABBATH	SABOTH
THYME	TIME
UNHAPPINESS	VNHAPINES
VALUE	VALEWE
WHERE	WARE
YEW	EUGH
YIELD	YELDE

Table 1: Modern-forms and their equivalent old-forms.

Location	Substitution	Location	Substitution
S	Vc → U	ME	IGHT → IT
S	IN → EN	ME	YGHT → IT
S	IM → EM	ME	GHT → GH
S	Yc → I	ME	LOUGH → LOW
S	J → I	ME	OUGH → OF
M	DG → G	SME	vUv → V
ME	CE → SE	ME	RUv → RV
ME	CK → K	ME	LUv → LV
M	vQv → KW	ME	DUv → DV
M	vJv → Y	M	J → I
M	OWG → OUG	E	ETH → S
ME	GTH → GHT	ME	MPT → MT

Table 2: Phonetic substitutions list.

Correction Method	$M1$	$M2$
Digram Matching	94.5	95.0
Trigram Matching	88.8	74.5
SPEEDCOP Skeleton	67.6	76.2
SPEEDCOP Omission	57.8	68.4
Wagner-Fischer LCS	95.4	95.8

Table 3: Comparative recall at a cutoff of the 20 most-similar matches. $M1$ employed no pre-processing, while $M2$ applied phonetic substitutions to both the modern-forms and old-forms.

Cost Functions	M1	M2
1/1/1	96.4	96.3
1/1/2	94.2	95.0
1/2/1	88.7	89.4
1/2/2	87.4	89.1
2/1/1	94.2	94.1
2/1/2	92.1	93.2
2/2/1	88.7	89.3

Table 4: Effect of parameter values on the recall of the Wagner-Fischer algorithm when the editcost distance is used. The three weights listed in each row of the column of the table are the cost functions for insertion, deletion and substitution, respectively, as defined in Section 3.3.

Hypermedia Links and Information Retrieval

Zhuoxun Li, Hugh Davis and Wendy Hall,
The Department of Electronics and Computer Science,
The University of Southampton,
U.K.

Abstract

Link creation in most existing hypertext / hypermedia products is a time consuming task. Microcosm is an open hypermedia system, in which various dynamic techniques have been used to attempt to ease the task of linking large bodies of information. This paper introduces the Microcosm model, and focuses on a technique for using computational power for dynamically creating links, known as retrieval links. The algorithm used for creating retrieval links is described and some preliminary experiments to assess the value of this facility are discussed.

1 Introduction

Hypertext / hypermedia systems have many potential applications in the field of information retrieval, since they provide new, and potentially very powerful, interfaces to information systems. The impact of hypertext / hypermedia on information retrieval is likely to be greatest on the development of multimedia information systems. This paper describes work being undertaken at the University of Southampton to integrate the two processes of hypermedia link following and information retrieval in a novel way.

Most hypermedia information systems depend upon specifically anchored links that have been manually created to allow the user to navigate through the information. However it is doubtful whether this method of linking information will scale up successfully to large information systems. Microcosm is an open hypermedia system that has been developed with the intention of dealing with large amounts of multimedia material [Fountain90], and permits the manual creation of dynamically anchored links which may be followed from any point in the system. It is also possible to request that the system computes dynamic links to offer to the user. Both of these facilities reduce the amount of manual effort that is involved in creating links, but at the possible cost of reducing the quality of information available in the destination of the link. The implementation and integration of these computed links, known as retrieval links, is the primary topic of this paper.

2 The Microcosm Model

Microcosm is an open hypermedia System. Within Microcosm it is possible to browse through large bodies of multimedia information by following links from one place to another. It is also possible for the user to add links and further information to the system. In this respect Microcosm provides all the services that would be expected in any hypermedia system. However, Microcosm adds many significant features to this basic model, which place it at a higher level than most currently available hypermedia systems, and make it a particularly suitable environment for integrating data and processes. In order to understand the facilities that Microcosm provides it is necessary to examine the underlying model.

Microcosm consists of a number of autonomous processes which communicate with each other by a message passing system. No information about links is held in the document data files in the form of mark-up. All data files remain in the native format of the application that created them. Instead, all link information is held in link databases, which hold details of the source anchor (if there is one), the destination anchor and any other attributes such as the link description. This model has the advantage that it is possible for processes to examine the complete link database as a separate item, and also it is possible to make link anchors in documents that are held on read only media such as CD-ROM and video disk.

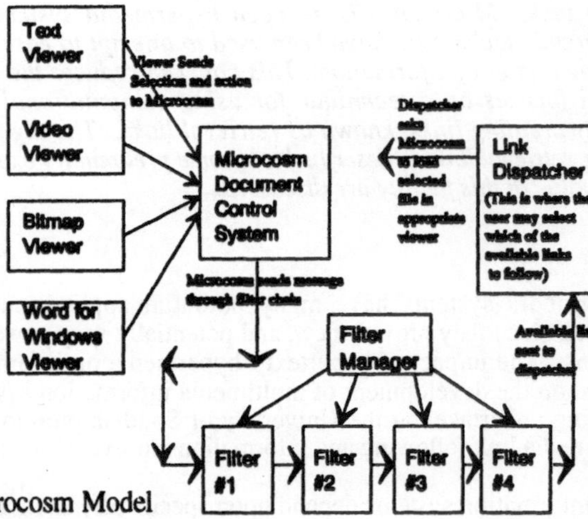

Figure 1: The Microcosm Model

Microcosm allows a number of different actions to be taken on any selected item of interest, so consequently use of the system involves more than simply clicking on buttons to follow links. In Microcosm the user selects the item of interest (e.g. a piece of text) and then chooses an action to take. We may see this as selecting an object then sending it a message. A button in Microcosm is simply a binding of a specific selection and a particular action. A particular feature of Microcosm is the ability to generalise source anchors. In most hypertext systems the source anchor for any link is fixed at a particular point in the text. In Microcosm it is possible for the author to specify three levels of generality of link sources.

1) The generic link. The user will be able to follow the link after selecting the given anchor at any point in any document.
2) The local link. The user will be able to follow the link after selecting the given anchor at any point in the current document.
3) The specific link. The user will be able to follow the link only after selecting the anchor at a specific location in the current document. Specific links may be made into buttons.

Generic links are of considerable benefit to the author in that a new document may be created and immediately have access to all the generic links that have been defined for the system.

The basic Microcosm processes are viewers and filters.

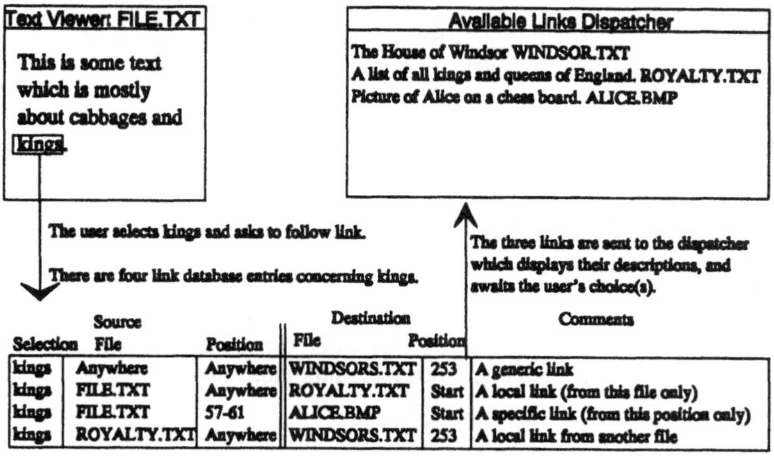

Figure 2: Following Links

2.1 Viewers

Viewers are programs which allow the user to view a document in its native format. Included with Microcosm are viewers for ten formats including various forms of text, bitmaps, video and audio.

The task of the viewer is to allow the user to peruse the document, to make selections and to choose actions. Typical actions are follow link, make link and complete link (where links may be to processes as well as to documents). The actions themselves are not effected by the viewer. The viewer is responsible for binding the information into a message, which is sent on to the filter chain where it will look for one or more processes that can satisfy this request. Any Windows application might be used as a viewer, with the proviso that it is possible to select objects, and at the least copy them to the clipboard. Microcosm is capable of taking actions upon objects on the clipboard. In cases (such as Word for Windows and Superbase) where the application has some level of programmability, it is sometimes possible to add a menu to the application so that the application is a viewer in its own right.

A major strength of Microcosm is its ability to integrate other applications. In fact Microcosm may be seen as an umbrella environment, allowing the user to make links from documents in one application package to documents in another application package.

2.2 Filters

Filters are processes which are responsible for receiving messages, taking any appropriate actions, and then handing the message on to the next filter in the chain. The actions that filters take will be of the nature of changing the message, or adding or removing messages. The order that the filters appear in the chain is under user control, and may be dynamically re-ordered and filters may be installed and removed. Some of the filters that are provided with Microcosm include:

Link Databases

Link Databases hold all the information referring to links. More than one database may be installed at a time. It possible to have a concept of public and private databases.

Show Links

When a user selects a chunk of text and uses the Show Links action this filter will organise the display of all available links, including those links which are not buttons, such as generic links.

Compute Links

Sometimes no links have been defined for a particular subject. On these occasions it is desirable to offer the user some further assistance. Microcosm has a facility that allows a user to batch a set of text files and to index these documents. Once this indexing has been done a block of text may be selected and the action, compute link, may be chosen. The system will very rapidly return a number of other documents within the system that have a similar vocabulary to the selected block, in the order of best match. This facility is analysed in greater detail in Section 3.

Navigational Filters

There is a history mechanism that keeps a list of all documents that have been visited, and allows the user to return to a chosen point, and a Mimic filter which allows the user to follow a tour through a set of documents pre-defined by the author.

A further aid to navigation is the book mark mechanism.

2.3 Implementations

Currently Microcosm is implemented on Windows 3.x, and will require at least a 286 machine to run but is best on a 386 machine with at least 4 Mega Bytes of memory. A Beta test version of most of this software is available. Versions of Microcosm are under development for Apple Macintosh computers and for Unix machines running X-Windows.

3 Classification of Links

Most hypertext / hypermedia systems only support links that allow the user to traverse the link from a specific source anchor point in a document to a specific destination. In designing Microcosm we have created three distinct kinds of links. The different classifications of links allow for different levels of access to the information in the system.

Some Terminology:

A *static link* is a link for which both the source and the destination of the link have been well defined before it is used. The attributes of the static links are physically stored in the hypertext system. They may either be embedded in the information units (documents) or be stored separately.

A *dynamic link* is a link for which the source and/or the destination of the link have not been defined until the link is followed. The source and/or the destination of a dynamic link
is decided according to some rules at the time that the link is followed.

Computed links are created by the system according to some predefined rules. Computed links may be either static links or dynamic links, depending on when the link creation is completed.

From the point of view of link creation, there are manually created links and computed links. From the point of view of following links, there are static links and dynamic links. A static link may be created either manually or by computing, whereas a dynamic link can not be created manually.

In the above terminology, most hypertext systems support manually created static links; the link attribute information is usually stored within the information unit or document in the form of hidden mark-up. However, by separating the link attributes from the documents we achieve certain advantages.

The ability to implement Generic links. These are manually created, dynamic links, in that the source anchor is not fixed.

The system remains open in the sense that the documents remain unchanged by Microcosm, and may be viewed, edited and processed by other applications.

It is possible to batch process all the information in the link database.

Link databases may be passed between users.

Clearly manually created static links (e.g. buttons) give the most specific access to information, since the author of the link has clearly defined the link between two specific pieces of information. This is why we call such links specific links within Microcosm. However such links also require a considerable amount of manual effort to create a suitable network through the information units.

Where specific links are not available, we have generic links. These allow us to follow a link from any point at which a given item, such as a word or phrase, occurs, to a specific destination. Clearly the quality of such information may be lower, as the author can only create the destination, and users may find ways of following such links from inappropriate sources. However, the manual effort is decreased as the author need only create the destination of the link once, and then the link will be available from any document.

Where no specific or generic links are available, we have retrieval-links. These are computed links which are dynamically created. Such links require no intervention from the author, but the quality of the information found by following such links may be lower than manually created links.

The remainder of this section is devoted to explaining how retrieval-links have been implemented within Microcosm.

3.1 Requirements of the Retrieval Process

In designing retrieval-links, one needs to consider how to integrate information retrieval into the hypertext environment and to convert the retrieval processes into dynamic links. One needs also to consider the proper design of information retrieval processes so that the advantages of hypertext systems and information retrieval can both be attained.

1. Automatic indexing.
Automatic indexing is a process that uses machine power to produce document identifiers which would be used to match with the identifier obtained from queries. Since one of our purposes of designing retrieval-links is to use machine power to replace some manual work, the ability to automatically index is essential.

2. Fast retrieval speed.
Because hypertext systems work interactively, it is not feasible to keep users waiting for a long time in order to follow a retrieval-link. Generally, a "follow link" operation should give a response as soon as possible. Research has shown that

"the difference between one system with a response of several seconds and another with subsecond response is so great as to make them seem qualitatively different." [Akscyn88]

3. Ease of use.
Users of a hypertext system may have various backgrounds. To avoid the necessity of learning extra skills before using a retrieval-link, a retrieval mechanism should be designed to be easy to use. In other words, the retrieval operations should be similar to the operations of following an ordinary link. This requires that the information retrieval queries should be expressed in natural language so that users can directly select part of a document as the source of a retrieval-link.

4. User controlled results.
The environments provided by hypertext / multimedia systems are suitable for browsing quite a large number of documents efficiently. This means that users are more involved in the retrieval process, and are able to assist in judging the usefulness of the retrieved documents. This user involvement also means that the retrieval process may have higher recall and a relative lower precision.

In the Microcosm implementation, the retrieved documents are ranked before being presented to users. The ranking is based on the similarity between the text in the query and the textual content of each document. The number of retrieved documents is controlled by a set of rules to avoid too many documents being offered to the user.

Here, the most important things to be considered, when designing an information retrieval mechanism for a hypertext system, are the speed of retrieval and the ability to automatically index. Conklin [Conklin87] pointed out that the most distinguishing characteristic of hypertext system is its machine support links, and another essential characteristic is the speed with which the system responds to link referencing.

3.2 Retrieval-links Design

The index information about documents is stored in an inverted file. The inverted file currently used is based on the single term frequency obtained from each document. Each term has a group of weights to mark the importance of the term in representing the documents in a collection. We believe that this information can reasonably represent the content of documents

Single term weightings in an inverted file can be extracted from documents by automatic indexing processing, can be stored in a simple data structure and then can be accessed quickly for retrieval calculation.

The following steps are used to form such an inverted file.

(1) Separate the words from the documents.
(2) Eliminate stop words by consulting a stop words list.
(3) Reduce words variants to a single form which is called the stem.
(4) Count the stem frequency for all remaining stems in each document and create weighted values for each stem in each document.

It is easy to see that all words remained after removing the stop words are included in the inverted file. This obviously can increase recall of retrieval, and as addressed previously, this is what we need.

3.2.1 Stop Words

The stop words are those that are frequently used in textual documents but have no real meaning for retrieval. These words appear in almost all the documents, but they are not suitable to represent the contents of documents. We prepared our own stop words list that contains about 300 words. Experiments showed that removing these words from documents could reduce the document's length by 30 to 60 percent. Obviously, the more stop words contained in stop words list, the less the size of inverted file.

3.2.2 Stemming Algorithm

A stemming algorithm is used to reduce the variation in word forms. There are two advantages to using a stemming algorithm. First, stemming makes various words that share same stem look the same. This can improve the recall of a retrieval, since stemming increases the chance of matching. Second, stemming reduces the length of words used to characterise each document so the space used to store these stems is reduced as well.

After studying the possible choices, we chose the stemming algorithm designed be Lovins [Lovins68].

This stemming algorithm is based on the longest-match. To stem a word means to remove the ending from the word. In order to do so, an ending list is used. Comparing endings of a word with the endings list, if more than one ending provides a match, then the ending which is longest should be removed. According to Lovins, to remove the longest ending is better than to remove several short endings one by

To cope with the spelling exceptions, two steps are used in stemming a word. First, the longest ending will be removed from a word, and then, the rest part of the word will be processed by another routine called the recording procedure. This will modify some of the remaining part according to 34 prefixed rules [Lovins68].

3.2.3 Weighting Documents' Stems

It is the weighted values of stems that is stored in the inverted file to represent the content of the documents. A weighted values is produced according to the frequency of occurrence of a stem in a document. To avoid the length of a document affect the weighting, a stem frequency would be divided by the document length.

To save storge space used by the inverted file, a weighted values is stored by just one byte. This means there could be a maximum of 256 different weighted values. In other words, any weight value would finally be mapped to one of 256 values. We used a logarithmic function to achieve this mapping, rather than a linear function. This has the effect of giving much greater significance to the difference between a stem occurring once or twice, than to the difference between a stem occurring 99 or 100 times. If a query stem occurs twice in a document, the document is probably twice as significant as a document in which the stem only occurs once, whereas there is little difference in significance between documents containing 99 and 100 occurrences, which will both be heavily weighted anyway.

3.2.4 Query Stem Weighting

Research has shown that showed that weighted query stems can lead to more effective retrieval than unweighted query stems. Jones [Jones72] gave a weighting method called inverse document frequency. The idea was that the importance of a stem in retrieval was based on how this stem can distinguish one document from another. If a stem was shared by most of the documents in a collection, then it was less useful in distinguishing the documents. If a stem was only used by a few documents, then it was very useful in distinguishing these documents from others.

Let's suppose there are K stems in a query, then if the inverse document frequency method was used, the weight for stem i should be:

$$w_i = log(N/N_i)$$

where N is the total number of documents in the collection and the Nj is the number of documents that shared the stem i. This weighting method, by favouring stems shared by less documents, emphasises the function of stems as devices to distinguish documents from the collection.

In the retrieval procedure designed for retrieval-links, the weight of the query stem i was defined as:

$$w_i = N/N_i$$

instead. This change gave more emphasis to stems shared by less documents and simplified the similarity calculation. Since documents would be indexed by all the stems appearing in each document, it is important to stress the effect of the important stems.

3.2.5 Similarity Function

The match between a query and documents is based on the weighted values associated with the document stems and the query stems. The similarity function we used was defined as:

$$S\ (q,d_j) = \sum_{i=1}^{k} ?w_i \times stem_{ij}$$

where q stands for a given query that contains *k* stems, *dj* stands for document *j* , *Wi* is weight for query stem *i*, stem *ij* is weighted value of stem *i* in document *j*.

The similarity between the query and all documents needs to be computed in order to rank the documents according to their similarity to the query. Since in the inverted file all stem *ij* are stored continuously for a given stem *i*, the process of calculating all *S(q,di)* using the above formula is very fast.

3.2.6 Results Control

For each query, similarities between the query and all the documents in the collection is calculated. If none of the query stems were used in document *i*, then *S(q,di)* = 0, which means that the document *i* is unlikely relevant to the query. That does not means when *S(q,di) > 0*, document *i* is relevant to the query. As the similarity function we used does not produce normalised similarity values, there is no fixed threshold that can be used to decide whether a document is relevant to a query. So, the following rules are designed to produce a dynamic threshold.

(1) Calculate the average value of the similarities of all documents. Use the average value as a sub-threshold; only the documents whose similarity values are above the average value would be passed to next step.

(2) To avoid too many documents becoming destinations of a retrieval link, another subthreshold whose value is defined as M is used to control the maximum number of destinations. Considering a document collection containing a large number of documents may have more relevant documents to a query than a small document collection, another sub-threshold whose value is defined as percentage P is used to control the maximum number of destinations of a retrieval-link.

(3) Rank the documents according to their similarity values in decreasing order. Then the *max(M,P)* documents that have bigger than average similarity values are chosen as the destinations of the retrieval-link.

At present M=S and P=10%. For a collection that has 35 documents, a maximum of 5 destinations would be permitted. For a collection that has 100 documents, a maximum of 10 documents could become destinations.

In the above procedure, step one has the ability to control the relative quality of the retrieval results, step two is mainly used to avoid the relevant documents being buried in too many other documents.

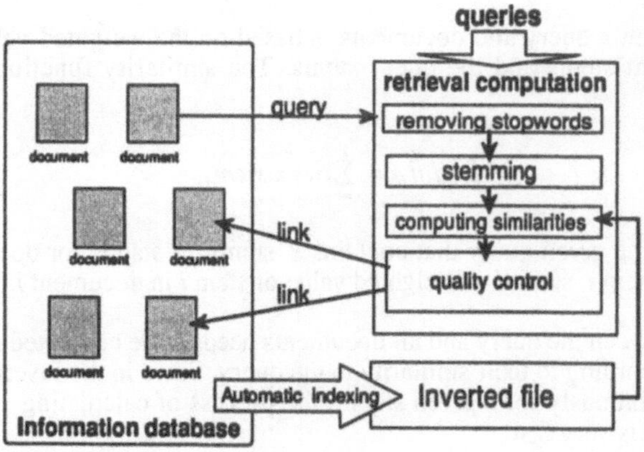

Figure 3: Retrieval Links

3.3 Experimental Results

To evaluate the design and performance of retrieval-links, experiments were carried out in retrieval effectiveness, response time and the time needed to create the inverted file.

To examine the performance of retrieval links, 20 departmental CSTRs (Computer Science Technical Reports) were used as a collection of documents.

Ranking of expected document	number of documents that satisfied the ranking	percentage
1	17	85%
2	2	10%
3	0	0%
4	1	5%

Figure 4: Experimental results: using document titles as the sources of retrieval-links.

As designed, the destinations of retrieval links are a group of documents. We expect that the destinations of retrieval-links are relevant to the source of the retrieval-links.

In one experiment, the *titles* of the 20 CSTRs were used as sources of the retrieval-links. In this case, we would expect that the destinations of retrieval-links would contain the document (expected-document) whose title was used as the source of the retrieval-links. Since the destinations of retrieval-links are ranked according their similarities to the source, we also expect that the expected-document will rank above all the other documents. The table above gives the experimental results.

In the this table, we can see that in most cases (85%), the expected-documents were ranked top of the destinations of retrieval links. Notice that there were no special weights for titles, authors names, and abstracts of documents in the inverted file, so a title received no more weight than a sentence in the document. In another experiment with 100 RFC network protocol documents, 92% of the expected documents were ranked first. In a further experiment, some selected keywords were used as the source of retrieval-links and the results were also satisfactory. The decision to chose all stems from documents as keywords was made based on a similar consideration. Such results shows that the indexing procedures and similarity function calculations used by the retrieval mechanism produce satisfactory results, and further work will be conducted to verify these results using the CACM collection.

The response time of retrieval-links was tested for a document collection containing 176 documents. Experiments showed that when several words were used as the source of a link, there was no significant delay to follow a retrieval-link. For a query with about one hundred words, it needs a couple of seconds to produces the destinations of retrieval-links.

The retrieval mechanism is based on the inverted file which contains extracted information about each document. Since the retrieval process needs to access weighted values of a stem on all documents, while inverted file creation process can only process the documents one by one, a data structure for the inverted file must be chosen that either ensures a quick retrieval process or makes the creation of the inverted file simple. To ensure fast retrieval response, the data structure of the inverted file is optimised in the form that can be quickly accessed by the retrieval process. This makes inverted file creation hard work. By carefully designing the creation process, we can now create inverted files in reasonable time. For instance, to index 176 documents (total size over 2MB) takes about 15 minutes.

4 Conclusions and Further Work

Microcosm has been in use for around two years. The facility to create generic links has been welcomed by authors, but early studies indicate that users need greater prompting to investigate the possible existence of such links. Retrieval links have only been added to the system within the last few months. Once users discover this facility they tend to make considerable use of it. [Davis92]

There are a number of possible further improvements that we are currently investigating.

> It would be possible to allow authors a tool to use retrieval links to suggest links that might be followed, then to choose which links would made into static links by including them into the link database.

One of the link attributes, stored in the link database is a short textual description of the data that will be found by following the link. We are investigating the possibility of using this information for either enhancing the current computed links accuracy, or for offering some level of computed links in an information set that has not been pre-indexed.

Retrieval links currently offer destinations that are whole documents. We are investigating the possibility of enhancing the system to automatically offer destinations within the document when such a link is followed.

We are investigating the use of a synonym filter, that would increase the probability that a search for a given word in an index would be successful.

We are attempting to extend the index to include certain word pairs (phrases). It seems likely that where a phrase occurs in a query and a document there is a higher probability that this is a useful match than in the case where the words appear separately in the document. The current system is unable to distinguish between these two cases.

It is our belief that a computed links facility, enhanced as described above would make an extremely accurate and useful facility for both authors and users, and will enable hypermedia systems to make the transition into dealing with large information systems.

References

[Akscyn88] Robert M. Akscyn, Donald L. McCracken, and Elise A. Yoder. KMS: *A distributed hypermedia system for managing knowledge in organisations.* Communications of the ACM, 31:820-835, July 1988.

[Conklin87] J. Conklin. *Hypertext: an introduction and survey.* IEEE trans. computer, 1987.

[Dsvis92] Hugh Davis, Wendy Hall, Gerard Hutchings, David Rush and Rob Wilkins. *Hypermedia and the Teaching of Computer Science: Evaluating an Open System.* in David Bateman and Tim Hopkins (eds). *The Proceedings of the Conference on Developments in the Teaching of Computer Science.* The University of Kent. 1992.

[Fountain90] Andrew M. Fountain and Wendy Hall and Ian Heath and Hugh C. Davis. *MICROCOSM: An Open Modelfor Hypermedia With Dynamic Linking* in A.Rizk and N.Streitz and J. Andre (eds). *Hypertext: Concepts, Systems and Applications. The Proceedings of The European Conference on Hypertext,* INRIA, France, November 1990. Cambridge University Press 1990.

[Hammond88] Hammond, N.V and Allinson, L.J. *Travels around a learning support environment: rambling, orienteering or touring*? In Soloway, E, Frye, D and Sheppard, S.B. (eds), CHI '88 Conference Proceedings: Human Factors in Computer Systems, ACM Press: New York, 269-273.1988

[Jones72] Karen Sparck Jones. *A statistical interpretation of term specificity and its application in retrieval.* Journal of Documentation, 28: 21,1972

[Lovins68] Julie Beth Lovins. *Development of a stemming algorithm.* Mechanical Translation and Computational Linguistics, 4:22-31, 1968.

Natural Language For Database Retrieval- A Practical Perspective

J.Sidhu
Department Of Manufacturing Engineering,
Nottingham Polytechnic,
Burton St,
Nottingham,
NG1 4BU.

Abstract

An application is highlighted that introduced natural language to an organisation to replace a structured query language. Users were introduced to natural language while a parallel group of users was introduced to a structured query language. The exposure to natural language and the structured query language in parallel was done not as a strict scientific study. It was done as a means of introducing a natural language interrogation tool to the company. This does not detract from its usefulness because so little work has been done on natural language evaluation in a business environment (Jarke, Turner, Stohr, Vassiliou, White Michielson 1985, Krause 1979). This application involved users using natural language to solve real world problems as opposed to controlled laboratory experiments (Reisner 1977, Welty and Stemple 1981). The users of the natural language and the structured query language worked in the same open plan office environment. The new users of the natural language system were initially happy with it, but over a period of months began to migrate and preferred the structured query language tool.

1 Introduction

Previous research shows that it is very difficult to reproduce the way humans behave naturally in a laboratory environment (Ellis 1984). Much work into the way users interact with computers was conducted in this 'false' environment and has been criticised (Smithson 1989 and Ellis 1984)

"It is frankly infeasible to reproduce, in a laboratory, the information seeking behaviour of a 'real' user who is motivated by the desire to resolve a 'real' problem."
Ellis (1984)

It has also been suggested that evaluation subjects should be drawn from the target populations, i.e. industrial users not academic students (Whittaker & Stenton 1988). In a business environment an individual has a different motivation to finding answers to 'real world' problems than in a laboratory study. Advantages of this business based evaluation approach include :-

(i) checking to see whether the specification has been achieved i.e. 'can it deliver what it said it could',

(ii) giving an indication of the direction of the technical staff, i.e. the degree of customisation and the time and effort expended. A study has shown that the degree of customisation required to set-up a particular natural language interface can be prohibitive (Sidhu 91),

(iii) suggesting improvements from real world users,

(iv) providing realistic queries to real world problems in a business environment where information may be needed immediately from ad hoc database enquiries.

These points are discussed further by Weischedel (1986).

This paper will highlight users of a natural language interrogation system and a structured query language in a business environment. It will focus on users who have hands on experience of solving real world commercial problems (this is further discussed by Sidhu 1991).

The ability to communicate between a human and a machine has involved the user adapting to the mode of communication of a computer. Natural language interrogation moves the computer such that it appears to adapt to human communication in the form of a 'limited plain English'.

The company involved had 12 production systems with small amounts of data, 5-10,000 records. The natural language system was obtained to transfer information into different departments, for writing reports and ad-hoc querying. The natural language system was chosen for its suitability as a querying tool because it was felt it was appropriate and adaptable to the company's system needs.

The company originally used a technical ICL querying system but this presented problems for non technical people (see also Jarke, Turner, Stohr, Vassiliou, White, and Michielsen 1985). Then an IBM mainframe system was obtained utilising DBII, this was seen as a positive progression. Query Master Formulation (QMF) was then utilised. This is a structured querying access language used as a formatting tool for laying out data after retrieval. It was while this was being used that the decision was taken to utilise a natural language interrogation system.

The reasons for obtaining a natural language interrogation system were linked to :-

(i) expanding the user base for casual and non technical users, allowing interaction by users of varying levels of experience. This is discussed by Hendrix (1982).

(ii) the ability to use the natural language interrogation system as an executive information system.

An advantage of natural language is that non technical users needing information quickly can use it as a business tool for effective information retrieval (Birkhead 1989). Claims concerning natural language products include their ability to :-

(i) provide reasonably good access to specific databases,

(ii) answer direct questions e.g (what is Smith's salary),

(iii) do basic report generation.

Hendrix (1982).

Various problems were encountered when the natural language interrogation system was installed, these included :-

(i) very tedious problems were encountered when setting the system up with respect to system parameters and options,

(ii) the system being 'very fussy', it was very difficult to set up in their general environment. Tailoring the system such that it was able to suit their specific operating system, database names and conventions. The system was much more difficult to install than general 'shrink-wrap' products where the application is inserted copied across and then run.

(iii) the natural language interrogation system clashed with QMF and other systems especially when accessing certain files.

(iv) security was a drawback, the natural language interrogation system was an 'all or nothing' security system that did not fit in with the needs of the company.

(v) the system was not precise. The answer generated may vary slightly from the expected answer. In other words the system could accept a query and interpret it differently to the way the user intended.

(vi) the errors in (iii) were too serious to justify use in certain applications , e.g if a query on customers debt is input and erroneous data arises this could potentially be very damaging, however, this tended only to occur in complex queries.

A study based on application developers, senior managers and users of natural language interrogation systems is discussed by Sidhu (1991).

2 Training

The natural language interrogation system was introduced to approximately 80 users who worked in the same office environment as users who were introduced to QMF. The natural language training was in the form of a half day, one to one, one to two or one to three supervised tutorial session. The users were then encouraged to use the natural language system. A follow up visit to assess progress was undertaken a few weeks and then months later.

A structured query language already existed in the company and the introduction of a natural language interrogation system did not increase the information available but made information access easier.

3 Results

Initially the QMF users were cautious of having to learn a structured query language, unlike the users learning the natural language system. The natural language system took a shorter time to learn, and was easy initially for both experienced and casual users. More time was required to learn the QMF system. It was also difficult to learn initially, and experienced users progressed quicker than casual users. The experienced users learned QMF by reinforcing concepts by regular interaction which would have aided the learning process. While casual QMF users may have suffered from a compounding learning problem. Initially users had a more favourable view of the natural language interrogation system than the QMF system.

As the users became experienced they began to favour QMF. QMF users became experienced and began to learn short cuts to information access, using efficient QMF code they were able to strip off information from the database. Thus, having learned the system they were able to optimise their QMF queries, and as a result increased QMF functionality. They felt reasonable happy with the QMF system as a mode of information access. The natural language users though initially happy with their mode of information access did not with experience gain in functionality by learning short cuts. As users of the natural language interrogation system became more experienced they complained that interaction became tedious.

The initial novelty of natural language interrogation began to wear off leaving the user to input a query as a limited plain English query. As they became experienced the natural language interrogation users began to gain confidence in the systems. Users soon began to increase the complexity of their queries and as a result to notice the systems' limitations. They also felt that the flexibility of natural language led users to lose sight of the restrictions of the limited English domain in which it operated. Users began to ask questions outside the domain of the database which were rejected leading them to be frustrated. They felt it was very good initially but then found themselves having to put in a 3-4 line verbose English query. Their QMF counterparts were able to query much quicker once knowledge of how to use QMF was gained.

With natural language, questions had to be carefully phrased and as a result were sometimes verbose, and some questions were not answered at all. Questions can not be answered that are outside the limited English subset and outside the knowledge domain. Knowing these boundaries may well have been a problem for the natural language users. Users in the same environment noticed the limitations of the natural language interrogation system compared to the QMF system.

When a sample query is input in 'plain English' it can be a simple task requiring little training. A simple query with QMF is not very hard to do but does require a certain amount of experience of the system through technical training. A complex query in English to an experienced natural language interrogation system user may take a few lines of verbose English. An experienced QMF user is able to produce efficient code and fire off the query with less character input than the natural language user.

The experienced users of natural language wanted something a little more cryptic, something they could revert to once they began to push the system to its' limitations. Users began to feel the natural language system was verbose and had input restrictions, as a result felt they were not fully satisfied with the performance and functionality. As users became more experienced they felt the QMF was the more efficient mode of information access.

One senior manager became aware of experienced users of the natural language interrogation system who began to ask QMF colleagues how to formulate their queries into QMF because they felt it to be more efficient.

It was noted that natural language interrogation users were migrating over to the QMF language in preference to the natural language interrogation system. This was not expected as evidence indicates that natural language interrogation is an easy to use technology (Morik 1984 and Hendrix 1982). This applies particularly to applications involving users with a range of experience from casual to experienced users (Hendrix 1982, and Copestake and Jones 1990).

The company then decided that this trend away from natural language and the difficulties experienced on installing and inconsistencies of use in certain applications could not justify continued maintenance and support. Thus the natural language interrogation system was not heavily used and eventually run down over a time. The structured query language (QMF) was then adopted as the main query tool.

This progression from novices to experienced users is illustrated in figure 1. and figure 2.

This industrial insight showed that for frequent users of a querying system, natural language querying systems may not be the long term answer. In the case of regular interaction with QMF, users were able to learn how to interact effectively and did not suffer from the problems of a lack of reinforcement. QMF users began to progress the learning curve to use QMF more efficiently and effectively. The natural language users meanwhile, became frustrated with the limitations, e.g having to type in verbose limited English queries. With casual natural language users natural language may well have been a good tool for information access. This showed that for frequent users, natural language may not be better compared to SQL's. If the natural language users were infrequent users

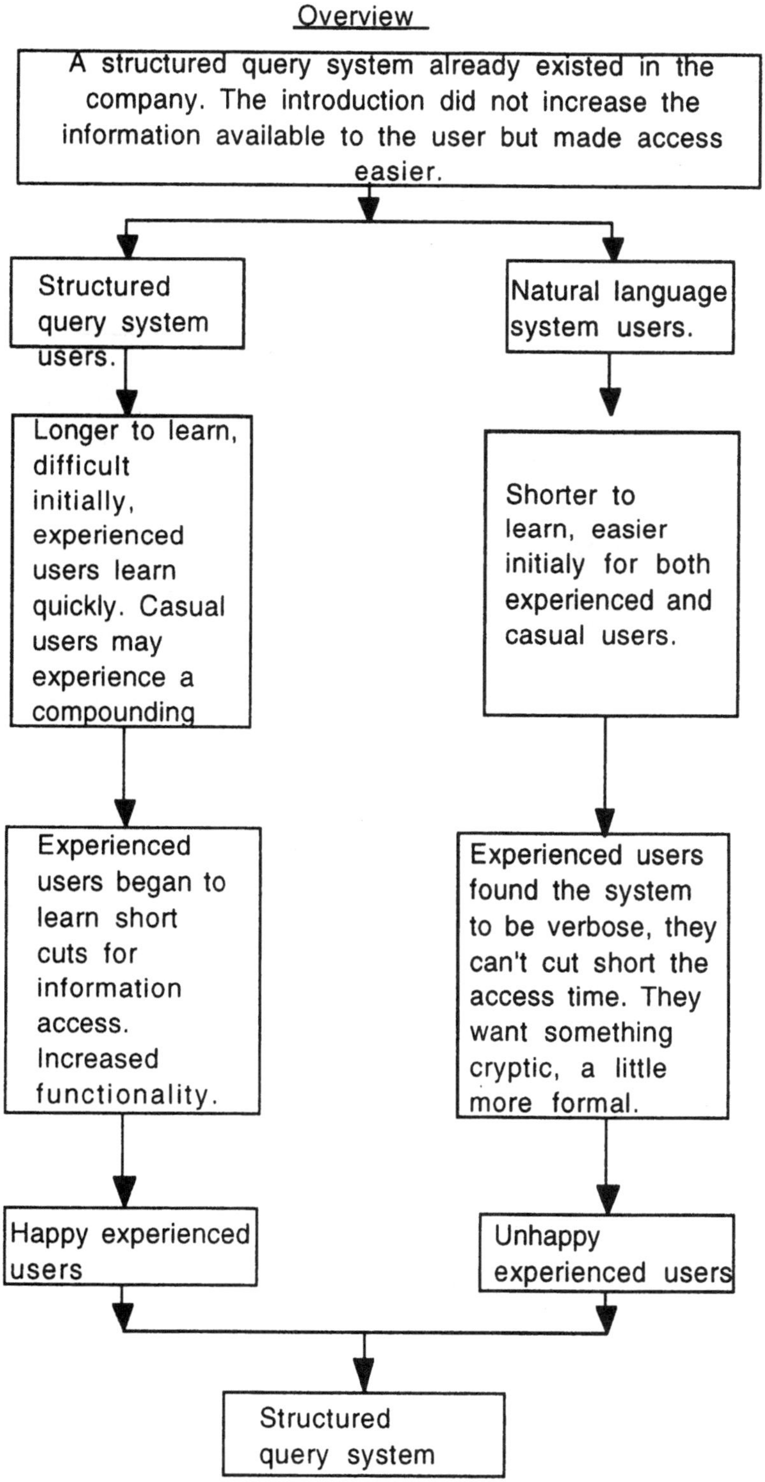
Overview
A structured query system already existed in the company. The introduction did not increase the information available to the user but made access easier.
Structured query system users.
Natural language system users.
Longer to learn, difficult initially, experienced users learn quickly. Casual users may experience a compounding
Shorter to learn, easier initialy for both experienced and casual users.
Experienced users began to learn short cuts for information access. Increased functionality.
Experienced users found the system to be verbose, they can't cut short the access time. They want something cryptic, a little more formal.
Happy experienced users
Unhappy experienced users
Structured query system

Figure One

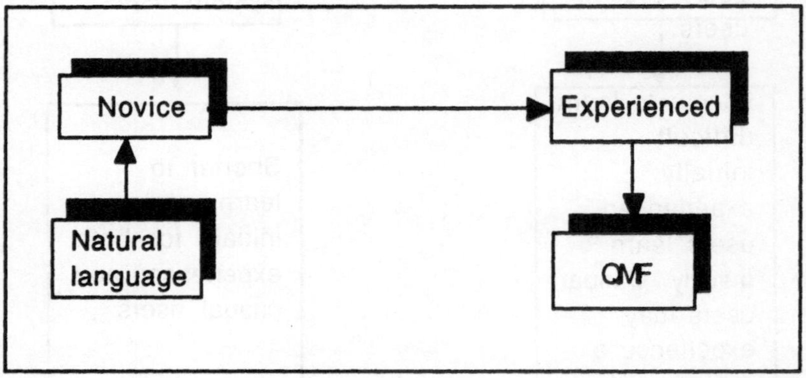

Figure Two

then the results might not have been the same. They would not have had regular reinforcement which aides learning and may not have had the confidence to extend the system such that regular interaction led to frustration. This investigation verified conclusions drawn by Shneiderman (1981). Here the main beneficiaries of natural language systems were users who have semantic knowledge of a database, but don't have much syntactic knowledge.

4 Natural Language Evaluation

Other natural language evaluation work has been done by Jarke, J, Turner, J. A, Stohr, E. A, Vassiliou, Y, White, N. H, and Michielsen, K. (1985). They investigated natural language versus SQL for database access using ad-hoc enquiries. The research was intended to reflect the regular and infrequent use of an application system that might be typical of novices or specialist professional users. Their results indicated :-

(i) SQL users performed almost twice as well compared to natural language system users in terms of task performance i.e. how many queries were answered correctly,

(ii) SQL used 40% more time, on the average number of queries,

(iii) subjects were approximately twice as likely to complete a query in SQL than in natural language,

(iv) in a test of eight subjects, all preferred SQL because it was consistent, reasons for query failure in natural language were not apparent. SQL constructs were difficult and error prone for complex queries and were often easier to formulate in natural language.

They found that SQL out performed natural language with essentially correct task completion by more than 2:1. Natural language users used approximately 50% more queries per task than did SQL subjects. When reviewing the effort expended for input SQL averaged about three times the length of natural language queries:

" Even if the 50% greater number of queries is taken into account, natural language system appear more concise than SQL"

This confirmed previous work by Vassiliou, Y, Jarke, J, Stohr, E. A, Turner, J. A, and White, N. H. (1983). Work done by Small and Wheldon (1983) led to the conclusion that there is no evidence that natural language is better than SQL for database information access. Work by Burton, Steward and Davenport (1989) indicated infrequent computer users are unlikely to be able to develop and maintain the level of expertise required to interact with a system via SQL. Further work shows that using natural language for querying a database is technically feasible and practically useful and that natural language is better for non standard ad-hoc queries (Harris 1977, Krause 1979, and Lehman , Ott and Zoeppritz 1978).

The results of the company study are in agreement with work done by Kowalski(1986). They go on to say that natural language front ends force the user to be very verbose and force the user to use long winded queries in English. This opposed to short concise queries of structured query languages.

Work by Paxton and Turner (1984) indicates the different needs expert and novice users have :

(i) novices want computer messages in English,

(ii) experienced users want coded messages.

This confirmed the results of the company study. They go on to say that users should be offered messages in English and coded forms to cater for both novice and experienced users,

(iii) give English versions only if required,

(iv) allow novice users to switch to coded messages when they progress to an experienced user, see figure two.

Velardi (1988) discusses an application of natural language in which the progression of users from casual to experienced was associated with a change in attitude. The users on becoming experienced felt the natural language system was no longer ergonomically sound, too much typing was involved. In the long run this problem could be solved by future developments e.g speech technology, voice recognition and parallel processing.

Work done by Rich (1984) indicates that some studies show users like to start with pure English queries and move to cryptic and telegraphic systems as they become familiar with the systems. Thus experienced regular users of natural language prefer to progress to a concise mode of access. The company study verified this. Small and Wheldon (1983) highlight a comparison of natural language and SQL. They found that natural language users were not reliably more accurate using English than SQL. They were reliably faster using SQL suggesting that the SQL is easier to use. Hendrix (1982) concluded that natural language was unsuitable for some applications because it provides flexibility at a cost of verbosity.

Natural language interrogation systems have been used effectively for over ten years. The technology is still relatively new and it has been predicted the demand will rise by a significant amount over the next five years. Engellieson and McBryde (1991).

There is still however room for improvement in commercial natural language systems. Developers need to produce systems that give greater functionality and support to the naive user (Copestake and Sparck Jones 1990). Developers need to move the interface nearer to the users thus enabling an expansion of the user base and to widen the access community.

The successful application of natural language technology as a querying tool should be targeted to an environment where :-

(i) there is a complicated database within a limited domain,

(ii) the access community needs to be increased,

(iii) users are naive and will be expected to use the system regularly over the period of time but at infrequent intervals during this time period,

(iv) when learning an SQL is impractical due to an unwillingness on the part of the user, or where cost is limiting.

These factors can help natural language systems to be utilised to their full potential.

4.1 Limitations of Natural Language Processing

The main problem of Natural Language Processing (NLP) is that current parsing systems and processing techniques are not able to sufficiently accept an input, and convert them into an appropriate structure, enabling the correct meaning to be determined.

The basic problem of ambiguity is to convert an input into an unambiguous internal representation language through parsing and NLP techniques. This will only be convincingly overcome when a computer is able to hold large amounts of information about the real world knowledge. But some sentences are in fact ambiguous. For example:

"I saw a man on a hill with a gun."

has three meanings.

There are two linked problems, the recognition of ambiguity and the subsequent resolution. Systems should not just "pick a meaning" arbitrarily.

Natural language processing as a tool is not equipped to handle unrestricted communication between the user and the computer. McEnery, Oakes and Reid (1990) discuss how menu systems can be more attractive than natural language interfaces. They discuss as a limitation of natural language interfaces how the logic of natural language can be erroneously interpreted in database retrieval systems. How natural language interface interpretations incorrectly attempt to mirror formal logic. They discuss how :

"attributes of logical connectives in natural language render it a problematic medium of interaction, especially for a user naive to the constraints of formal logic."
McEnery, Oakes and Reid (1990)

They go on to make the point that attributes of logical connectives in natural language are problematic. They also make the point:

"that no deterministic set of rules can be generated to bridge this problem, and any putative solution could only be deemed heuristic."
McEnery, Oakes and Reid (1990)

Copestake and Sparck-Jones (1990) discuss that in a limited domain menu systems may offer the best interface.

5 Conclusion

In this company the users were initially inexperienced but progressed on to become experienced and used the system frequently. The company felt that QMF was the better option once experience was gained using the language in their particular application.

Natural language allowed access in an easy and timely way for casual users but for experienced users natural language was not the best solution. Natural language was so easy to use initially that this advantage was cancelled out when the users became more experienced and wanted a more cryptic querying tool.

Natural language technology is most effective in an environment where the users are casual and infrequent users. Where the domain is well constrained and these constraints are well known to the users.

Bibliography

Birkhead, E. The Natural. DEC Professional, Vol 8, Part 9, (1989).

Burton, A., Steward, A., and Davenport, C. Natural Language & Pattern Matching Problems. British Computer Society Information Retrieval Specialist Group. 11th Information Retrieval Research Colloquium, (1989).

Copestake, A., and Sparck-Jones, K. Natural Language Interfaces To Databases, The Knowledge Engineering Review, No 5, part 4, (1990).

Ellis, D., Theory and explanation in information retrieval systems, Journal of Documentation, Vol 26 no 1, (1984).

Engellieson, B., and McBryde. R. Natural Languages Markets: Commercial Strategies, Ovum Ltd., ISBN 0903969610, (1991)

Harris, L. R. User oriented Data Base Query with the ROBOT Natural Language Query System. International Journal of Man-Machine Studies, Vol 9, (1977).

Hendrix, G. G. Natural Language Interface. American Journal Of Computational Linguistics. Vol 8, Part 2, (1982).

Jarke, J., Turner, J. A., Stohr, E. A., Vassiliou, Y., White, N. H., and Michielsen, K. A Field Evaluation Of Natural Language For Data Retrieval. IEEE Transactions On Software Engineering, Vol. SE-11, No. 1, January, (1985).

Kowalski, R, and Kriwaczek, F. Artificial Intelligence Masters, Video by Addison Wesley, VL/AL-3, (1986).

Krause, J. Preliminary Results of a User Study with the User Speciality Languages System, and Consequences for the Architecture of Natural Language Interfaces. IBM Heidelberg Scientific Center TR 79.04.003, Heidelberg, Germany, (1979).

Lehman, H., Ott, N., and Zoeppritz, M. User Experiments with Natural Language for Data Base Access. Proceedings of the 7th International Conference on Computational Linguistics, Bergen, Norway, (1978).

McEnery, A, M., Oakes M, P., and Reid, D, C. Pantheon : Rapid Prototyping of Natural Language Interfaces To Large Databases. Proceedings of British Computer Society Twelfth Information Retrieval Research Conference. (1990)

Morik, K. Customers' Requirements for Natural Language Systems: Results of an Enquiry. International Journal of Man Machine Studies, Vol 21, (1984).

Paxton, A. E., and Turner, E. J. The Application Of Human Factors To The Needs Of The Novice Computer User. International Journal of Man-Machine Studies. Vol 20, (1984).

Petrick, S. R. Natural Language Database Query Systems. Technical Report RC 10508 IBM Thomas J Watson Research Laboratory Yorktown Heights, (1984).

Rich , E. Natural Language Interfaces. Computer, September, (1984).

Shneiderman, B. A Note On Human Factors Issues Of Natural Language Interaction Information Systems, Vol 6, no 2, (1981).

Sidhu, J. Use of Natural Language in Industry, Dept. Manufacturing Engineering Nottingham Polytechnic Internal Report, (1991).

Small, D. W., and Wheldon., L, J. An Experimental Comparison Of Natural and Structured Query Languages. Human Factors Vol 25, no 3, (1983).

Smithson, S. The Evaluation Of Information Retrieval Systems: A Case Study Approach. Prospects For Information Retrieval Informatics. Vol 10, (1989).

Vassiliou, Y., Jarke, J., Stohr, E. A., Turner, J. A., and White, N. H. Natural Language For Database Queries: A Laboratory Study. MIS Quarterly, December (1983).

Velardi, P. Entity Relationship Approach To The User. Proc Of The Seventh International Conference. Rome November (1988).

Weischedel, R M. Issues and Red Herrings In Evaluating Natural Language Interfaces. Empirical Foundations of Information and Software Science IV; Empirical Methods of Evaluation of Manmade Interfaces, Proceedings of the Fourth Symposium. Bolt Beranek and Newman Laboratories, Massachusetts, USA. (1986).

Welty., C and Stemple., D. W. Human Factors comparison of a procedural and non procedural query language. ACM Transaction Of Database Systems, Vol 6, no 4 (1981).

Whittaker., S. and Stenton, P. User studies and the design of Natural Language Systems. Proceedings of the European ACL, Manchester, (1990).

Author Index

Published in 1990–92

AI and Cognitive Science '89, Dublin City University, Eire, 14–15 September 1989
A. F. Smeaton and G. McDermott (Eds.)

Specification and Verification of Concurrent Systems, University of Stirling, Scotland, 6–8 July 1988
C. Rattray (Ed.)

Semantics for Concurrency, Proceedings of the International BCS-FACS Workshop, Sponsored by Logic for IT (S.E.R.C.), University of Leicester, UK, 23–25 July 1990
M. Z. Kwiatkowska, M. W. Shields and R. M. Thomas (Eds.)

Functional Programming, Glasgow 1989
Proceedings of the 1989 Glasgow Workshop, Fraserburgh, Scotland, 21–23 August 1989
K. Davis and J. Hughes (Eds.)

Persistent Object Systems, Proceedings of the Third International Workshop, Newcastle, Australia, 10–13 January 1989
J. Rosenberg and D. Koch (Eds.)

Z User Workshop, Oxford 1989, Proceedings of the Fourth Annual Z User Meeting, Oxford, 15 December 1989
J. E. Nicholls (Ed.)

Formal Methods for Trustworthy Computer Systems (FM89), Halifax, Canada, 23–27 July 1989
Dan Craigen (Editor) and Karen Summerskill (Assistant Editor)

Security and Persistence, Proceedings of the International Workshop on Computer Architecture to Support Security and Persistence of Information, Bremen, West Germany, 8–11 May 1990
John Rosenberg and J. Leslie Keedy (Eds.)

Women Into Computing: Selected Papers 1988–1990
Gillian Lovegrove and Barbara Segal (Eds.)

3rd Refinement Workshop (organised by BCS-FACS, and sponsored by IBM UK Laboratories, Hursley Park and the Programming Research Group, University of Oxford), Hursley Park, 9–11 January 1990
Carroll Morgan and J. C. P. Woodcock (Eds.)

Designing Correct Circuits, Workshop jointly organised by the Universities of Oxford and Glasgow, Oxford, 26–28 September 1990
Geraint Jones and Mary Sheeran (Eds.)

Functional Programming, Glasgow 1990
Proceedings of the 1990 Glasgow Workshop on Functional Programming, Ullapool, Scotland, 13–15 August 1990
Simon L. Peyton Jones, Graham Hutton and Carsten Kehler Holst (Eds.)

4th Refinement Workshop, Proceedings of the 4th Refinement Workshop, organised by BCS-FACS, Cambridge, 9–11 January 1991
Joseph M. Morris and Roger C. Shaw (Eds.)

AI and Cognitive Science '90, University of Ulster at Jordanstown, 20–21 September 1990
Michael F. McTear and Norman Creaney (Eds.)

Software Re-use, Utrecht 1989, Proceedings of the Software Re-use Workshop, Utrecht, The Netherlands, 23–24 November 1989
Liesbeth Dusink and Patrick Hall (Eds.)

Z User Workshop, 1990, Proceedings of the Fifth Annual Z User Meeting, Oxford, 17–18 December 1990
J.E. Nicholls (Ed.)

IV Higher Order Workshop, Banff 1990
Proceedings of the IV Higher Order Workshop, Banff, Alberta, Canada, 10–14 September 1990
Graham Birtwistle (Ed.)

ALPUK91, Proceedings of the 3rd UK Annual Conference on Logic Programming, Edinburgh, 10–12 April 1991
Geraint A.Wiggins, Chris Mellish and Tim Duncan (Eds.)

Specifications of Database Systems
International Workshop on Specifications of Database Systems, Glasgow, 3–5 July 1991
David J. Harper and Moira C. Norrie (Eds.)

7th UK Computer and Telecommunications Performance Engineering Workshop
Edinburgh, 22–23 July 1991
J. Hillston, P.J.B. King and R.J. Pooley (Eds.)